FUN WITH THE FAMILY
Hawaii

Praise for the *Fun with the Family* series

"Enables parents to turn family travel into an exploration."
—Alexandra Kennedy, Editor, *Family Fun*

"Bound to lead you and your kids to fun-filled days,
those times that help compose the
memories of childhood."
—Dorothy Jordon, *Family Travel Times*

Help Us Keep This Guide Up to Date

Every effort has been made by the author and editors to make this guide as accurate and useful as possible. However, many changes can occur after a guide is published—establishments close, phone numbers change, hiking trails are rerouted, facilities come under new management, etc.

We would love to hear from you concerning your experiences with this guide and how you feel it could be improved and be kept up to date. While we may not be able to respond to all comments and suggestions, we'll take them to heart, and we'll make certain to share them with the author. Please send your comments and suggestions to the following address:

The Globe Pequot Press
Reader Response/Editorial Department
P.O. Box 480
Guilford, CT 06437

Or you may e-mail us at: editorial@GlobePequot.com

Thanks for your input, and happy travels!

FUN WITH THE FAMILY SERIES

FUN WITH THE FAMILY

Hawaii

Hundreds OF Ideas FOR Day Trips WITH THE Kids

SEVENTH EDITION

Julie Applebaum-DeMello

gpp®

travel

Guilford, Connecticut

The prices, rates, and hours listed in this guidebook were confirmed at press time. We recommend, however, that you call establishments to obtain current information before traveling.

To buy books in quantity for corporate use or incentives, call **(800) 962-0973** or e-mail **premiums@GlobePequot.com.**

Text design by Nancy Freeborn and Linda Loiewski
Maps by Rusty Nelson © Morris Book Publishing, LLC
Spot photography throughout © Photodisc and © RubberBall Productions

ISSN 1541-8944
ISBN 978-0-7627-4859-4

Printed in the United States of America
10 9 8 7 6 5 4 3 2 1

Dedicated to my sweet Mahealani and Kelii,
may all their travels be filled with Aloha,
and may they learn to love and appreciate the journey.

Hawaii:
The Big
Island

Maui

Molokai

Lanai

Oahu

Kauai

Contents

Introduction

Hawaii is a playground for young and old with activities, attractions, and historic sites galore. Everybody can find something to enjoy, and many activities are **free**, relatively cheap, or once-in-a-lifetime thrills that are worth the money. The ocean is the ideal playground. You can swim, snorkel, scuba, surf, fish, sail, canoe, kayak, sailboard, bodysurf, parasail, cruise, or stroll along the shore picking up shells and exploring tide pools.

Several shops on every island rent water-sports equipment including surfboards, boogieboards, sailboards, and snorkeling and scuba gear. Additionally, many hotels, resorts, and condominiums offer rentals and lessons from the central activities desk.

Snorkeling is a very easy activity available to anyone who knows how to swim. In less than an hour, you can become acquainted with the basics and be able to master the equipment. If your hotel doesn't offer **free** snorkeling equipment, shop around before you rent. Often dive or water-sport shops offer less-expensive alternatives than the larger hotels. A mask, snorkel, and fins usually cost $15 a day. By all means, consider using a disposable underwater camera, about $15, which helps capture the aquatic images permanently.

If you or your children want to try surfing, be aware that it takes many years to become an expert. Lessons are readily available, however, and with a little coordination you'll be good enough to stand up and ride gentle waves. (And it makes for some great photo opportunities.)

Windsurfing, also called sailboarding, is a little easier than surfing because you depend on the wind instead of the waves. Sailboards are much larger, more stable, and easier to stand on than ordinary surfboards. The sail that propels you across the water is mounted on the board. Rental sailboards are usually more expensive than surfboards. Lessons are available on all major islands.

Boogieboarding is definitely a sport that water-safe kids—those who can swim without assistance—will be able to master within a few minutes. The boards are made of heavy-duty foam and are about 3 feet long. Many boogieboarders also wear fins to help propel them toward a wave, but for beginners it's not necessary. Boards are for sale everywhere, from drugstores and supermarkets to surf shops. You can also rent them at the same places you rent snorkeling equipment.

Just as there are many water-sport rental shops scattered throughout the islands, there are also many companies that offer guided tours to the best spots in Hawaii's ocean playground.

Generally, these tours are worthwhile, usually led by guides knowledgeable about the local marine life and Hawaiian history. There are many to choose from, and each chapter of this book reveals a small sampling. Many guided tours, hikes, and cruises can be booked online prior to your arrival—often at significant discounts. So if you're the type who likes to preplan vacations, Web sites are included throughout this book to help guide your process.

Every island also offers land-based fun, such as tennis, golf, horseback riding, bicycling, hiking, backpacking, hunting, and freshwater fishing. There are also several land-based tours available, ranging from air-conditioned buses to passenger vans. These are a good way to get a general overview of the island but often lack the opportunity for in-depth exploring. The premise of this book is that you're more likely to discover the real nuances of each island on your own . . . equipped with this guidebook, a good map, and a sense of adventure.

Island **Safety**

The ocean beckons around every curve in the road, but please use caution before letting kids swim just anywhere. Hawaii has basically two seasons—summer and winter. In the summer the north-facing beaches are usually calm, almost lakelike, and are safe for swimming, while the south shores often feature heavier surf and dangerous currents. The situation switches, and the differences magnify, in winter when the islands' north shores get pummeled by some of the biggest waves in the world and the undertow is sometimes strong enough to pluck unsuspecting spectators right from the beach. Pay attention to the posted flags and signs before entering the water. Also, it's a good idea to ask the lifeguard about the current conditions.

If you venture to a small or deserted beach where lifeguards are absent, study the water before entering. Note the frequency and size of the waves. You can often judge the strength of the currents by watching how fast the sand is sucked into the water.

In some places, such as Hanauma Bay, Oahu, the fish are so tame they'll eat right from your hand, but in other places some creatures of the deep add an element of danger. Parents should always arrive at the beach equipped with a bottle of meat tenderizer. Certain weather patterns bring pests known as Portuguese man-of-war, whose sting is sharp and painful, although usually not life threatening. Meat tenderizer rubbed into the wound helps ease the pain.

Also, realize Hawaii is close to the equator, and the ultraviolet rays beat down with full force here. Constant application of strong sunscreen is a necessity (otherwise a bad sunburn could ruin your vacation on the first day). Even on cloudy days the potential of sunburn remains serious because ultraviolet rays burn through the cloud cover.

For that reason you also will notice the book does not include every restaurant or hotel/resort property. The restaurants mentioned are by no means inclusive of all the greats but are ones that have been personally taste-tested. Accommodations range from simple bed-and-breakfast inns and tent camps to five-star luxury resorts, with a variety of options and prices. To mention and review them all is enough material for another book, but a few of the more famous are included. Most of the larger properties offer children's programs that let the parents have a day off. The *keiki* (child) activities usually include a variety of outdoor fun, lunch, arts and crafts, and a souvenir T-shirt. Additionally, most of the larger properties offer babysitting services in which the caregiver will come to your hotel room.

The islands are full of kid-magnet attractions such as video arcades, movie theaters, and miniature-golf courses; however, as these are similar to ones in your hometown, they were omitted from this book.

The book does focus on Hawaii-specific recipes for fun. Many of the ingredients include visits to museums, where Hawaii's natural and cultural histories are explained and displayed. Many kids would prefer to be building sand castles or "hanging ten" (local surfer's lingo) on a wave, but Mother Nature may call for another activity. It rains often in Hawaii (although the weather remains warm), and it's a good idea to have a choice of indoor activities.

Island History

Hawaii's history is fascinating. You can learn about the Polynesian culture that thrived in these islands before Capt. James Cook arrived and exposed Hawaii to the rest of the world. The ancient Hawaiians lived a religious life, with separate gods and goddesses for everything from fishing and fertility to volcanoes. Not only are examples of this culture evident in museums, but remains such as *heiau* (religious temples) and petroglyphs (images or inscriptions carved on rocks) still exist on all islands.

Each island used to be led by one high chief, *ali'i,* until Kamehameha the Great united them in approximately 1795. Kamehameha was the first of eight monarchs who ruled these islands until 1893, when the traditional Hawaiian government was overthrown.

As you drive throughout the islands, you'll notice that most places of historical importance are so noted by the presence of a Hawaiian warrior atop a pole. These "warrior-signs" were placed by the Hawaii Visitors Bureau to identify everything from scenic overlooks to ancient *heiau.*

Hawaiian gods and goddesses live on, with a strong movement among modern Hawaiians to revive culture through the ancient practice of hula (dance) and through local legends and customs. In the Maui chapter, for example, you'll learn about the demigod Maui, who performed great feats of athleticism to slow down the sun so his mother could dry her *kapa* cloth. In the Big Island chapter you'll meet Pele, the goddess of volcanoes, who has been angrily spewing lava since 1983.

Environmental and Cultural Respect

Whether you're traipsing through the ruins of an ancient temple or hiking on a mountain trail, remember that Hawaii's environment is extremely fragile. In fact, 98 percent of all plants and animals included on the federal endangered species list are endemic to Hawaii. Please remain on well-worn paths; a single misstep could damage a root or flower that is a food source for an endangered bird. Hawaii's beauty is in a precarious state, and environmentally conscious visitors can help preserve it for the next generation.

Throughout the book a large variety of churches are mentioned as attractions and places to visit. This is not done with any religious significance or disrespect, but rather to emphasize the historical importance of the missionary era. Congregational missionaries, preachers, doctors, and teachers sailed here from New England in 1820. Determined to rid the native Polynesians of their "heathen" lifestyles, they built church after church, trying to save the local souls. They brought "white man's civilization" to these remote islands and forever changed the native culture. Many of the churches they built still stand, a testament to the hardiness and persistence of their founders, who traveled thousands of treacherous miles at sea to complete their mission.

Getting Around the Islands

People who have never been to Hawaii often mistakenly associate Oahu with the entire state. That's like eating only the fudge frosting on top of a cupcake. Sure, it's tasty and can be wonderfully satisfying all by itself. But when combined with the whole cupcake, the frosting is so much more enhanced. Yes, Oahu, known as the "gathering place," is wonderful. Yes, families can enjoy an action-packed vacation solely on Oahu. But a visit to all the islands truly gives you the "whole cupcake" experience. Every island offers its own sense of identity and mystique, complete with an abundance of adventures for families of all ages.

On Oahu this guidebook will take you through Waikiki and a scenic Circle Island Tour that includes Pearl Harbor and the big-wave country of the North Shore. On Maui, the Valley Isle, you'll travel everywhere, from great whale-watching and snorkeling sites to the top of Mount Haleakala and to the edge of the island at Hana. On the Big Island your family shouldn't miss a trip to the country's only active volcano, acres of tropical rain forests, and lush coffee plantations. On Kauai the beauty of the majestic Na Pali Coast will linger in your memory long after you've returned home. On Lanai you can visit two of the state's most luxurious resorts, ride horses through virtually untouched country, and explore the mysterious Garden of the Gods. And it will seem as if time has passed by the people of Molokai, the Friendly Isle, where small-town charms await visitors and miles of unspoiled coastline beg for exploration.

A few travel particulars: Hawaii law requires that children three years old and under be strapped into a car seat, and children ages four through seven must be in a car seat or booster seat. You can either bring your own and check it with your baggage on the plane or you can reserve one when you make a reservation with a car rental agency. If you chose the latter, expect a minimal added charge, computed daily. Also, when making

Baby Gear Rentals

In case you don't want to lug mounds of baby gear, two companies rent everything from high chairs and strollers to cribs and swings. If you're staying on the Big Island, you can choose from Aloha Baby Rental, which offers rentals by phone, online, or on site; North Kona Shopping Center, 75-5629 Kuakini Highway, Kailua-Kona, (808) 326-1700, (808) 989-3269; www.aloha-babyrental.net (they also deliver to your hotel/condo and to the airport); or Baby's Away, which offers rentals only by phone or online; (808) 987-9236, (800) 996-9030; www.babysaway.com. Baby's Away also covers Oahu (808) 685-4299, (800) 496-6386 and Maui (808) 875-9030, (800) 942-9030.

reservations with any hotel, car agency, or airline, be sure to ask about family specials. Many hotels offer a "kids stay **free**" program in which keiki share their parents' rooms, sleeping on portable beds. Similarly, many restaurants offer **free** or discounted meals for kiddies (it pays to shop around). Don't forget to ask about accruing bonus miles on any frequent-flier accounts you maintain. Most car agencies and the larger, national resort properties can apply your total bill to a variety of airlines.

The following key applies to the attractions, accommodations, and restaurants listed throughout this guidebook:

Rates for Lodging
$	up to $100
$$	$101 to $250
$$$	$251 to $300
$$$$	more than $301

Rates for Restaurants
$	up to $8
$$	$9 to $15
$$$	$16 to $25
$$$$	more than $25

Rates for Attractions
$	up to $5 per person
$$	$6 to $10 per person
$$$	$11 to $20 per person
$$$$	more than $20 per person

Please don't let high hotel prices discourage you from planning a trip to Hawaii. The majority of hotels offer discounts and packages that include airfare, rental car, and accommodations. It's best to check with a travel agent for seasonal deals.

Family-Oriented Web Sites

These days, many travelers plan their entire trip via information gleaned from one of the major travel Web sites. However, we've found a few that focus less on the commercial aspects of booking your trip, but pack a whollop of useful information.

- www.familytravelforum.com. The Family Travel Forum is dedicated to the ideals, promotion, and support of travel with children, providing its members with unbiased information.
- www.thefamilytravelfiles.com. Includes an abundance of information and articles, as well as resources with direct links to hotels, resorts, and activities.
- www.familytravelnetwork.com. Great access to all aspects of traveling with kids.

For More Information

Hawaii Visitors and Convention Bureau, 2270 Kalalaua Avenue, Suite 801, Honolulu, HI 96815; (800) GO-HAWAII (800) 464–2924; www.gohawaii.com.

The area code for the whole state is 808. Calls originating in and destined for the same island are considered local, and calls from one island to another are long distance, requiring you to first dial the numeral 1.

Attractions Key

The following is a key to the icons found throughout the text.

SWIMMING	FOOD
BOATING / BOAT TOUR	LODGING
HISTORIC SITE	CAMPING
HIKING / WALKING	MUSEUMS
FISHING	PERFORMING ARTS
BIKING	SPORTS/ATHLETIC
AMUSEMENT PARK	PICNICKING
HORSEBACK RIDING	PLAYGROUND
SKIING/WINTER SPORTS	SHOPPING
PARK	PLANTS/GARDENS/NATURE TRAILS
ANIMAL VIEWING	FARMS

Oahu

O ahu is by far the most populated island in the Hawaiian chain. More than 875,000 of the state's 1.2 million residents live here. Honolulu is home to the state capitol, the financial district, medical centers, and universities. It's also home to Diamond Head Crater, Punchbowl Cemetery, Pearl Harbor, and Waikiki Beach.

First-time visitors expecting Waikiki and Honolulu to be an idyllic, tranquil island paradise had better be prepared for a city that also has a frenetic pace and an accelerated pulse. Honolulu has evolved into a multicultural, cosmopolitan city, with a little bit of the laid-back, "local-style" feel remaining, especially in our treatment of others. Enriching museums, cultural events, historic sites, a top-notch symphony, opera, and theaters compete for attention with sporting events, backcountry hikes and camps, botanical gardens, and a world-class zoo and aquarium. Humpback whales arrive each November and stay

Julie's
TopPicks for Family Fun on Oahu

1. Hiking Diamond Head

2. Visiting Iolani Palace, the United States' only royal residence

3. "Hanging ten" with Hawaiian Fire Surf School

4. Hiking through the Makiki-Manoa Trails

5. Exploring the Pacific's unique flora and fauna at Hawaii Nature Center

6. Snorkeling or SNUBA diving (a cross between scuba diving and snorkeling) at Hanauma Bay

7. Riding an outrigger canoe at Waikiki

8. Watching the marine creatures at Sea Life Park

9. Climbing to the top of the windswept Pali Lookout

10. Strolling through Bishop Museum

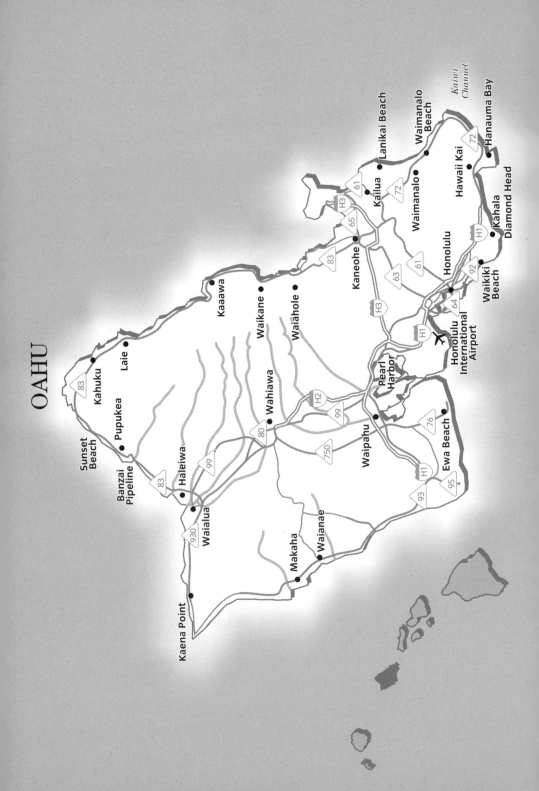

OAHU

Kaiwi Channel

Hanauma Bay

Diamond Head

Kahala

Waikiki Beach

Honolulu

Hawaii Kai

Waimanalo Beach

Waimanalo

Lanikai Beach

Kailua

Honolulu International Airport

Pearl Harbor

Kaneohe

Waiahole

Waikane

Kaaawa

Laie

Kahuku

Sunset Beach

Pupukea

Banzai Pipeline

Haleiwa

Waialua

Wahiawa

Waipahu

Ewa Beach

Makaha

Waianae

Kaena Point

72

72

1

92

64

61

63

H3

61

65

H3

83

H1

H2

99

80

99

750

76

1

95

93

930

83

83

until April or May, breaching, spouting, mating, and calving. In winter you can catch college football at the Aloha Stadium in Honolulu. Among all these activities you'll perceive the spirit of "aloha" that embraces neighbors and newcomers alike.

As many people unfamiliar with the islands mistakenly associate Oahu with all of Hawaii, just as many mistake Honolulu and Waikiki for all of Oahu. The entire island encompasses 608 square miles and 112 miles of coastline, and Waikiki is a crowded, concrete-laden, 2-mile stretch of hotels fronting a sandy beach. The remaining land is filled with homes, offices, farms, a few remaining acres of pineapple and sugar cane, lush mountain ranges, and dry flatlands.

After landing at Honolulu International Airport, most visitors head directly for Waikiki, where the majority of hotel properties are situated. But there is a smattering of great resorts and bed-and-breakfast inns throughout the island.

For purposes of easy orientation, this chapter begins in Waikiki and then expands to circle the entire island for a complete guide to Oahu's family adventures. After Waikiki you'll be guided to adventures in the surrounding communities of Downtown, Chinatown, Nuuanu, Punchbowl, Makiki, and Manoa. Then you'll head toward Leeward Oahu, the dry side of the island, and travel through Aiea, Pearl Harbor, Waipahu, Ewa Beach, Waianae, Makaha, and Kaena Point.

Back in Waikiki you'll drive around the island in what's appropriately referred to by locals as a Circle Island Tour. This goes from the southeastern area (Kahala, Hawaii Kai, Waimanalo) to the Windward Side (Kailua, Kaneohe, Kualoa, Kaaawa, Kahuku) to the North Shore (Waimea, Sunset, Haleiwa) and back to Waikiki via the central plains of Wahiawa.

To begin with, Oahu is magnificently accessible via a public transportation system known as TheBus (808) 848-5555 or (808) 848-1500; www.thebus.org, on which a full Circle Island Tour costs just $2 for adults, $1 for students through high school age. A four-day unlimited pass costs $20. Please have exact change. Although you're not permitted to bring suitcases on board, you can ride TheBus to every adventure listed in this chapter. Pick up a schedule at the main office, 811 Middle Street, or at any satellite city hall, or from the Web site. Oahu's public transportation is considered better than that of any of the other main Hawaiian Islands. If you're considering not renting a car, Oahu would be the only island where you wouldn't really miss it. Additionally, many hotels offer **free** shuttles to and from the airport.

Rental cars are readily available from a variety of companies, and a little research can garner some great deals. With kids it's good to have your own set of wheels for easy access to pit stops and places to burn off restless energy. If you require a car seat, check the rates to rent one from the car rental agency. You can rent other kiddie equipment, such as strollers and cribs, from some of the hotels or from Baby's Away (808) 222-6041, (800) 496-6386; www.babysaway.com.

Waikiki

Waikiki Beach may be the most famous stretch of sand in the world. It's been the backdrop for many a Hollywood movie, and hundreds of celebrities, politicians, and foreign dignitaries have been photographed while enjoying its splendors. And for good reason. The weather is usually warm and sunny, the ocean calm and inviting. Developers must have known what they were doing as, one after another, huge hotel towers were built to house the millions of visitors who come every year for a taste of Waikiki's magic.

The ocean here offers an ideal outlet for almost any type of recreation you can imagine, whether it's simply bobbing around on a raft to soak up the sun, diving below the surface in a submarine, or barreling down a wave in a six-person outrigger canoe. Several beachside stands offer everything from surfing lessons to luau tickets.

Don't let the multitude of hotels overwhelm you. As crowded as it is, Waikiki's status as the ultimate playground in paradise remains well deserved. Kids flock to the ocean here for hours at a time, singles rock and roll at the surplus of nightclubs, and couples stroll the golden sands by moonlight, marveling at the steely blue Pacific. Waikiki has something for everyone. If your budget allows, splurge for an ocean-view room—the sunsets, picturesque Diamond Head, and the crystal-blue water will linger in your memory long after you've returned home.

For kids who've seen surfboards only in the movies, it's a good idea to invest in some lessons. Waikiki offers ideal gentle waters for first-timers. The beachboys in Waikiki are experienced watermen and can have almost anyone standing up after a few basic hints. Expect to pay about $50 an hour for a group lesson and $80 to $100 an hour for a private lesson.

Boogieboarding is a little tamer and a lot easier to learn. Again, Waikiki's gentle waters make it an ideal location for the inexperienced. While surfboards are about 6 feet long and weigh about twelve pounds, boogieboards are about 3 feet long and weigh about one pound. Both can be rented from beachside stands. There's no need to take a lesson to ride the waves, and even if your kids don't manage to "rip through the tubes," they'll still have a good time floating along the shoreline.

The beach stands also offer outrigger canoe rides, in which six people and one beachboy, all armed with paddles, take to the sea. The leader turns the boat around, and presto, the waves glide the canoe to shore. The sport of canoeing has been immensely popular since the days when Hawaiians first settled on these lands. It's great fun and easy to learn.

For more information about beachside services and rates, check the big rack of standing surfboards at Kuhio Beach, the eastern tip of Waikiki. Additionally, if your hotel does not have an activities desk, contact the Outrigger Waikiki on the Beach, 2335 Kalakaua Avenue; (808) 923-0711. You needn't be a guest to book activities here. Also, several beach stands are situated directly on the beach.

If you or your kids are a bit squeamish about underwater life, you can get great views of life below the ocean surface without even getting wet. Consider underwater cruises

Waikiki's Family-Friendly **Resort Hotels**

Kids are loved and welcomed with the ohana spirit at many Waikiki hotels. Most hotels feature an activities desk or a concierge who can help organize any activity to suit your fancy. Many, such as the **Hyatt Regency Waikiki** (800)-233-1234, offer children's programs. At the Hyatt guests receive a free brochure, "Children's Guide to Fun Under the Sun," which doubles as a coloring book and lists kid-friendly things to see and do within walking distance of the hotel. Another booklet, "101 Wonderful Things to Do on Oahu," is free for all guests. Camp Hyatt, the hotel's family program, offers special amenities, services, and activities, including scavenger hunts, hotel tours, and video games for children ages three to twelve.

The Rainbow Express Young Explorer's Club is available for guests ages five to twelve at the **Hilton Hawaiian Village** (808) 949-4321. Activities include one-on-one encounters with sea creatures in the Touch-n-Feel pool at the Waikiki Aquarium. Kids love tickling a sea cucumber and holding a hermit crab. The children's program is offered year-round, seven days a week. Full- and half-day programs are available.

These programs are just a few examples of the many benefits awarded to families traveling with children. For more information it's best to consult a travel agent.

aboard submarines. They are offered daily and transport you to a colorful world of pristine reefs alive with yellow angelfish, spiny puffers, striped parrotfish, stingrays, turtles, and sometimes even sharks.

Beware, however, as bad weather can affect the schedule. Rough surface conditions don't necessarily affect a submarine but can make for an unpleasant shuttle ride out to the vessel. So call ahead if the wind is whipping up whitecaps or if breakers look unusually big.

Atlantis Submarines (children over 3 feet tall)

Reservations, (808) 356-1800; www.atlantissubmarines.com. Prices vary, depending on which ride you choose. The Premium Submarine Tour ($$$$) is the most popular underwater adventure, but shorter and less expensive trips are available.

The submarines operate year-round. The total tour (Premium) lasts about an hour and a half, with about forty-five minutes spent underwater. The ride out to the sub is on a surface boat and takes about fifteen minutes. The nice thing about Atlantis is that its pier is right in Waikiki, at the Hilton Hawaiian Village. They also offer complimentary shuttle transportation from select Waikiki locations.

Waikiki Historic Trail (all ages)

Guided walking tours of Waikiki are offered by appointment, for a fee. Information: (808) 441-1404; www.waikikihistorictrail.com. Tours begin at Royal Hawaiian Shopping Center Stage, oceanside of Kalakaua at Seaside Avenue. Fee determined by group size.

The Waikiki Historic Trail takes you behind the modern facade of concrete buildings to the region's glorious past, when Hawaii's kings and queens frequented these beaches, where the waters were known for special healing powers. The Waikiki of yesteryear was a patchwork of native fish farms and wetlands crops, not to mention the site where surfing was introduced to the world by legendary waterman Duke Kahanamoku. The Queen's Tour features historians sharing stories of Waikiki's compelling history, including the Wizard Stones of Kapaemahu, the statues of Duke and Princess Kaiulani, and other historic sites along the trail. If you'd like to walk the tour on your own for **free**, you can download the map from the Web site. Surfboard markers along the way display stories and pictures of Waikiki's history.

Waikiki Trolley (all ages)

Information, (808) 591-2561; www.waikikitrolley.com. The trolley runs from 8:30 a.m. to 8:30 p.m. (certain routes). All-day and four-day passes are available. $$$–$$$$

The open-air Waikiki Trolley is a great way to get a complete overview of the town. The trolley travels to many nooks and crannies of the city, including many of its historic sites. Passengers can get on and off an unlimited number of times. You can make a day of it, exploring, stopping for lunch, and hitting the road again. Tickets are available online, at the DFS Galleria Waikiki, Ala Moana Center (ocean side), and the Hilton Hawaiian Village. Or you can simply board at any one of the stops, and the conductor will sell you a ticket.

Damien Museum (all ages)

130 Ohua Avenue, at the far end of Waikiki on the grounds of St. Augustus Church; (808) 923-2690; www.hawaiiweb.com/html/damien_museum_and_archives.html. Open 9:00 a.m. to 3:00 p.m., Monday through Friday, 9:00 a.m. to noon, Saturday; closed on Sunday. free. The museum is about 3 blocks from the zoo, between Kalakaua and Kuhio Avenues.

Father Damien came from Europe to care for the people who were afflicted with Hansen's disease (leprosy) and exiled to the isolated Kalaupapa Peninsula on Molokai. He helped build homes, churches, and hospitals for hundreds of ill people and eventually died of the disease himself. The museum offers a glimpse into Hawaii's past and a look into the life of this selfless person who helped so many. A twenty-minute video tells the history of Kalaupapa settlement.

Hawaii Trivia

Hawaii's official state marine mammal is the humpback whale.

Battery Randolph Army Museum (all ages)

At the far end of Waikiki, at the corner of Kalia and Saratoga Roads on Fort DeRussey Military Base; (808) 955-9552; www.hiarmymuseumsoc.org. Open every day except Monday from 10:00 a.m. to 4:15 p.m. Admission is free but a donation is appreciated. The museum validates parking for two hours.

Just east of the Hilton Hawaiian Village Hotel, the Battery Randolph Army Museum will give you a glimpse of the military's importance in the islands. Kids are allowed to play on a real tank and examine the structure of a cannon.

Military history is recorded here as far back as Kamehameha I (1753–1819). Exhibits include rifles, swords, and illuminating old photographs of popular sites, such as Waikiki and Diamond Head. The museum features a tribute to soldiers from Hawaii who fought in World War II, Korea, and Vietnam.

Ala Moana Beach County Park (all ages)

At the western end of Waikiki, across the street from the Ala Moana Shopping Center. Amenities include snack bars, a picnic area, restrooms, telephones, and lifeguards.

This popular hangout for locals offers visitors recreational fun just outside of Waikiki. You'll see lots of people here surfing, swimming, picnicking, jogging, and in-line skating. In the middle of the park is Magic Island, a manufactured structure that juts out from the coastline, providing a calm inside bay for young children.

The view from here looks back toward Waikiki and is nothing short of stupendous, especially during sunset. If you happen by on a Friday evening, you'll be treated not only to a spectacular sunset, but also a colorful panorama of sails as boats race back to the harbor, a long-standing local tradition. The park isn't a good place to be at night, however, so it's best to leave the vicinity when the sun sets.

Ward Warehouse and Ward Centre Shopping Centers (all ages)

1050 Ala Moana Boulevard; (808) 596-8885; www.victoriaward.com.

Ward Warehouse and Ward Centre Shopping Centers are adjacent to each other, encompassing four city blocks with one-of-a-kind shops and big-value retailers, twenty-three restaurants, and even a farmers' market. You'll find an entertainment center featuring a sixteen-screen megaplex and a midway of interactive high-tech attractions. Hawaii's crafts renaissance is in full flower at the various stores here. You'll see carved wooden bowls (the locals call them calabashes), feather leis, capes, and quilts. Check out the fishhook pendants at the Native Books and Beautiful Things showroom. Carved of bone, wood, or fossilized ivory, the fishhook shape has survived since antiquity.

Kapiolani Park (all ages)

At the far eastern end of Waikiki, across from Kuhio Beach and the Honolulu Zoo.

Kapiolani Park is a great place to go for some old-fashioned, Frisbee-flinging fun. The park encompasses 140 acres and was built in the 1800s. It's named after Queen Kapiolani, King David Kalakaua's wife.

Surfing Lessons

- You can learn how to surf through the **Hans Hedemann Surf School,** located at various hotels on the island (808-924-7778; www.hhsurf.com). Two-hour private lessons cost $150. Discounts available for semiprivate and group lessons. They offer complimentary transportation to and from Waikiki hotels.

- One of the newest surf schools on Oahu is **Hawaiian Fire Surf School** (808-737-3473 or 888-955-7873; www.hawaiianfire.com). The school is the dream of three Honolulu city firefighters who love surfing, love the Hawaiian culture, and love sharing their knowledge with visitors. Parents should feel very safe entrusting their kids to this group: Because they are firefighters, they are all certified in numerous life-saving techniques, including CPR and open-water rescue.

  Students are picked up at their hotel at 7:00 a.m. or 9:30 a.m. and return at 11:30 a.m. and 2:00 p.m., respectively. The surfing instruction takes place at a secluded, sandy beach with ideal "learning" waves. Prices are $99 for a group lesson; $179 for an adult private lesson; and $129 for a children's private lesson (ages twelve and under).

- **Hawaiian Watersports** (808-262-5483; www.hawaiianwatersports.com) teaches kiteboarding, windsurfing, bodyboarding, and kayaking at various Oahu locations. A two-hour, four-person group lesson costs $95 per person. A two-hour individual lesson costs $175. Online discounts are available. They specialize in surf breaks close to Diamond Head, away from the crowds, and wave riding is guaranteed!

- **Waikiki Beach Services** (808-352-2882; www.waikiki beachservices.com) is the formal organization that grew from the original Ambassadors of Aloha—the Waikiki Beachboys. You can find them at **Outrigger Waikiki,** (2335 Kalakaua Avenue; 808-542-0608 or 808-306-5789) and **Outrigger Reef on the Beach** (2169 Kalia Road; 808-352-2882 or 808-306-5789). Group lessons are $40 per person, and private lessons are $75 per person—lessons run about one and a half hours.

Locals flock here daily for soccer, rugby, Frisbee, picnics, kite flying, softball games, and volleyball. In addition to a spacious grassy area, features of the park include jogging trails, bicycle paths, gymnastics equipment, and tennis courts. The Royal Hawaiian Band performs for **free** every Sunday from 2:00 to 4:00 p.m. at the bandstand. The bandstand also hosts other **free** outdoor concerts, publicized in the local newspapers. At the far end of the park, Waikiki Shell hosts several outdoor events, with an amphitheater designed for optimum acoustics.

Honolulu Zoo (all ages)

151 Kapahulu Avenue, Honolulu; (808) 971-7171; www.honoluluzoo.org. Open daily 9:00 a.m. to 4:30 p.m. $–$$, children 5 and younger free when accompanied by an adult.

Families can get in touch with their "wild side" at the Honolulu Zoo, home to more than 1,000 mammals, birds, amphibians, and reptiles. Special features for children include a petting zoo full of barnyard animals and a ladder that lets them climb to the eye level of a giraffe.

The Reptile House is also popular with children, as is the Elephant Encounter, but by far the most impressive feature is the African Savanna. This exhibit lacks the barriers or fences found in most zoos to keep the animals restricted to a certain place. Instead, creatures such as hippos, zebras, rhinos, lions, chimpanzees, baboons, and antelopes wander freely throughout land that's configured to resemble their natural African habitat. You'll feel as if you're walking through a wild jungle!

Just outside the zoo is a huge old banyan tree that's home to thousands of white pigeons. These pigeons are not indigenous to Hawaii but have flourished here and grown to an immense population. Nearby convenience stores (such as the ever-present ABC, Hawaii's version of a Circle K or 7-Eleven) sell birdseed that you can feed to the pigeons. The birds have been feeding off the generosity of visitors for so long that they have become tame enough to eat right from an outstretched hand.

Waikiki Aquarium (all ages)

2777 Kalakaua Avenue, Waikiki, within walking distance of the zoo to the east, across the street from Kapiolani Park; (808) 923-9741; www.waquarium.org. Open 9:00 a.m. to 5:00 p.m. daily, although visitors are no longer admitted after 4:30 p.m. $$, free for children 4 and younger.

For a chance to visit Hawaii's famous underwater world up close, don't miss the newly renovated Waikiki Aquarium. Founded in 1904, the aquarium is the third-oldest public aquarium in the United States. Here you can look nose-to-nose at a reef shark and catch a glimpse of Hawaii's colorful state fish, the humuhumunukunukuapua`a. The kids will love watching the comical expressions exhibited by the Hawaiian monk seals, whose faces are so cute they're almost human.

Besides the monk seals, displays include an underwater Coastal Garden, an Edge of the Reef tank, a Hunters of the Reef tank, a jellyfish exhibit, and a reef machine that simulates the effects of waves and underwater currents.

Sans Souci Beach (all ages)
At the very eastern tip of Waikiki.

Also known as Kaimana Beach, this is a lovely strip of sand that fronts the New Otani Kaimana Beach Hotel. Locals frequent this area to take advantage of Waikiki's balmy weather and tranquil waters without the crowds. This is a great place to take children because it's quiet and uncrowded compared to the more popular Waikiki beaches. This beach and adjacent park have long been our family's number-one pick for spending the day together at the beach. We barbecue at the park, and the adults visit there while the kids play safely in the water. Parking is always easy, too, though it's a few minutes' walk from central Waikiki.

Where to Eat

The following is just a small sampling of what's available. The concierge in your hotel, the local newspapers, and telephone directories have more complete information.

The Golden Dragon. At Hilton Hawaiian Village; (808) 946-5336. Exquisite gourmet Chinese dishes that range from traditional to nouvelle cuisine. Chef Steve Chiang's most famous recipes, including cold ginger chicken and lobster with curry sauce, are worth the visit. $$$

Halekulani Hotel. At 2199 Kalia Road; (808) 923-2311. For a truly elegant meal in traditional resort style, one can always rely on the Halekulani Hotel's Orchids or La Mer. **La Mer** is the premier dining room for the prestigious Halekulani resort. Because the food is incredible, the view magnificent, and the service swift and sure, the award-winning La Mer ranks at the top of the finest restaurants in the islands. $$$$

While La Mer upstairs is a five-star dinner house, **Orchids at Halekulani** has earned four stars and is open for breakfast and lunch as well as dinner. Breakfast or lunch on the veranda is pure delight, while dinner is a gustatory revelation. $$$$

For an atmosphere just a bit less formal, you can't beat the Halekulani's House Without a Key. $$$

Hau Tree Lanai. At New Otani Kaimana Beach Hotel, 2863 Kalakaua Avenue; (808) 921-7066. The atmosphere in this Diamond Head restaurant is like the Hawaii of old. The Hau Tree blends crisp service and outstanding food with its beachside location to guarantee a pleasing experience. Futhermore, it's one of the absolute best places in Waikiki to watch the sunset. $$$

Hy's Steak House. 2440 Kuhio Avenue in the Waikiki Park Heights Hotel; (808) 922-5555. At this restaurant you can dine in either a cozy, library-like dining room or a modern art deco eatery. Steak is the specialty, but the menu includes a wide choice of poultry and fresh fish, as well as a special children's menu. It's a bit off the beaten path, so you're likely to find more residents than visitors here—it's been a local favorite for twenty-five years. $$$$

Makai Market. Located on the lower level of Ala Moana Shopping Center, on Ala Moana Boulevard and Piikoi Street, less than a mile from Waikiki. Imagine a supermarket of restaurants all in one place, and that's what one finds at Makai Market at Ala Moana Center. Twenty-one food shops, offering everything from chocolate-chip cookies to exotic Asian delights, surround a huge central seating area. There are Filipino, Korean, Chinese, Japanese, French, Hawaiian, and American seafood, salads, and sandwiches. Whatever you like, you'll find it here in nearly endless variety. This is a great place to take a break or meet family or friends for a meal between visits to the Ala Moana Shopping Center stores. $

Matteo's. 364 Seaside Avenue in the Marine Surf Hotel; (808) 922-5551. Classic Italian specialties prepared in gourmet style, served in an intimate atmosphere. Consistently one of the island's best restaurants. $$$

Oceanarium Restaurant. 2490 Kalakaua Avenue, Pacific Beach Hotel; (808) 921-6111. Here's a place where the entertainment is as good as the food. The "entertainment" is inside a 280,000-gallon, three-story aquarium, while the dining is just outside the heavy acrylic windows. The best views, however, are from the tables closest to the tank on the lower level, especially at feeding times (for the fish) at 9:00 and 11:30 a.m. and 12:30, 6:30, and 7:30 p.m. daily. Seafood is

the house specialty, of course, but there are beef and chicken dishes, too, and a children's menu. $$$$

Prince Court. 100 Holomoana Street; (808) 944-4494. Situated on the third floor of Waikiki's lush Hawaii Prince Hotel and overlooking the Ala Wai Harbor, this quietly elegant dining establishment features crisp service, excellent buffets, and wonderful interpretations of Hawaii Regional Cuisine. Hakone, on the same floor, offers traditional Japanese dishes. $$$$

In between Waikiki and downtown Honolulu are what locals refer to as the McCully, Makiki, and Kapiolani Districts, mostly places where people live, work, and shop, with little interest for visitors. There are, however, some great restaurants around here.

Alan Wong's. 1857 South King Street, third floor; (808) 949-2526. This is by far my favorite restaurant in all Oahu, but the kids are underwhelmed—best for a night out with your significant other. The menu changes

Luaus

A variety of luau shows performed in Waikiki and throughout the islands offer semiauthentic Hawaiian food and entertainment. Although locals may scoff at the glitzy, tourist-oriented performances, the luaus are good fun, geared for the whole family, and are definitely an experience worth attending.

In Waikiki the longest-running, and currently the only, luau is held at the **Royal Hawaiian Hotel** (808-923-7311; www.royal-hawaiian.com) on Monday and Thursday, 6:00 to 8:30 p.m. The cost is $99.25 for adults, $55.25 for children ages five through twelve; kids younger than five are admitted free.

Two companies offer a worthwhile luau experience far removed from the hustle and bustle of Waikiki. Visitors are transported in air-conditioned buses to the leeward side of the island for a complete Polynesian extravaganza. **Germaine's "Too Good to Miss" Luau** (808-949-6626 or 800-367-5655; www.germainesluau.com) costs $69 for adults, $49 for kids ages six to thirteen, and $59 for kids ages fourteen to twenty. (Closed Mondays.) The **Paradise Cove Luau** (808-842-5911 or 800-775-2683; www.paradisecovehawaii.com) offers three luau packages, ranging in price from $75 to $125 for adults and $55 to $100 for children.

daily, and the *pupus* (appetizers), entrees, and desserts feature the latest and greatest in Hawaii Regional Cuisine. His most famous pupus include hoisin BBQ baby back ribs and shredded Kalua pig wrapped in taro pancake on poi vinaigrette with Lomi tomato relish. Chef Alan Wong has earned more accolades and awards than any other local chef; don't miss a chance to experience his cuisine. Open for dinner only; reservations needed. $$$$

Auntie Pasto's. 1099 South Beretania Street, at the corner of Pensacola; (808) 523- 8855. If you love good Italian food at the kind of prices you pay in Italy, not New York, you'll love this storefront bistro. Serving a wide array of pasta dishes, from a top-of-the-line lasagna to a creamy pesto, Auntie Pasto's feels like eating at a friend's house. Reservations are not accepted, so get here early if you don't want to wait in line. There is a second location in the Kunia Shopping Center, 94-663 Kupuohi Street, Waipahu; (808) 680-0005. $$

Chiang-Mai. 2239 South King Street; (808) 941-1151. Specializing in Northern Thai cuisine, Chiang-Mai's menu offers a variety of curries, salads, soups, and noodles. There's also a large vegetarian selection to choose from. The food is fresh and tasty, and the special Thai sticky rice is done to perfection. Be sure to regulate the "hotness level" if you don't care for ultra-spicy food; mild versions of all dishes are available. $$

Grace's Inns. 98–280 Moanalua Road, Aiea; (808) 484-2028; 1296 South Beretania Street; (808) 592-2202; and 2919 Kapiolani Boulevard; (808) 732-0041. A minichain of "local-style" fast-food shops. Plate lunches are standard fare with such delicacies as chicken katsu, sweet-and-sour pork, and chili with rice, as well as hamburgers and hot dogs. Not gourmet, but filling and inexpensive. $

I Love Country Cafe. 451 Piikoi Street, (808) 596-8108; and Mililani Town Center, 95–1249 Meheula Parkway, (808) 625-5555. There's always a crowd at this small plate-lunch place, and after one meal, you'll understand why. The menu is quite diverse, ranging from low-fat, low-cal, boneless, skinless grilled chicken breast with papaya salsa to cholesterol-laden Philly cheese steak. There are plenty of vegetarian selections and tasty fruit smoothies. This is a favorite local lunch spot, so either arrive early or expect a wait. $$

Mekong Thai. 1295 South Beretania Street; (808) 591-8841; and 1726 South King Street; (808) 941-6212. In two locations, this family-run restaurant features outstanding Thai food in a low-key, friendly atmosphere. Try the spring rolls appetizer and the satay for a main dish. Be sure to have a spice tolerance—Thai food is not for the weak. (You can request mild seasonings.) $

Just beyond Waikiki are two shopping centers, Ward Warehouse (1050 Ala Moana Boulevard) and Ward Centre (1200 Ala Moana Boulevard), both of which offer a great variety of eateries.

The Chowder House. In Ward Warehouse; (808) 596-7944. Simmering bowls of either red, Manhattan-style chowder or creamy, Boston-style chowder are served. Chowder House has a nice variety of other seafood dishes, with luncheon specials and a children's menu. $$

Compadres. At Ward Centre; (808) 591-8307. From the interesting, reasonably priced Mexican menu, try the smoke-oven specialties: baby back ribs or pollo borracho (drunken chicken), a whole bird smoked, marinated in white wine, and then grilled. $$

Kincaid's Fish, Chop & Steak House. In Ward Warehouse; (808) 591-2005. This excellent eatery has always-interesting daily seafood specials. Open for lunch and dinner, Kincaid's has a wide variety of standard dishes on the menu, including entrees just for kids. $$$–$$$$

Mocha Java Cafe. At Ward Centre; (808) 591-9022. This delightful coffee bar in the

Free Waikiki **Entertainment**

There's a slew of **free** entertainment throughout Waikiki as well as dinner shows that offer everything from hula dancers and Hawaiian food to Elvis impersonators and magic shows. Freebies can be found at the following locations:

- A nightly torchlighting ceremony, Molehu I Waikiki, is held Saturday and Sunday at **Kuhio Beach Park,** the far eastern end of Waikiki, 6:15 to 7:00 p.m.
- The **Royal Hawaiian Shopping Center** features **free** weekday entertainment. On Thursday at 9:30 a.m., Poakalani hosts quilting demonstrations and sells quilting kits. On Tuesday and Thursday from 4:15 to 5:15 p.m., there are hula lessons with Halau Hula O Maiki. There are also ukulele lessons and **free** Hawaiian shows during the week. Check www.shopwaikiki.com for more information.
- Several of the Waikiki resorts, and many restaurants, offer **free** Hawaiian entertainment at least once a week. You can get the schedules in advance from the respective Web sites.

Ward Centre pavilion features a wide selection of gourmet coffees and pastries. The menu also features delicious vegetarian and vegan gourmet food, omelets, and breakfast served all day. Creative crepe specialties, soups, and salads. Our family favorite: macadamia nut banana pancakes. Stop in for an espresso milk shake after a busy afternoon window-shopping the boutiques. $

Where to Stay

There are hundreds of hotels, condos, and resorts in the Waikiki area. What follows is a small sampling, all of which have been tested time and again by our family and won approval, from both Mom and Dad, as well as the kids. A more comprehensive list may be found at www.visit-oahu.com.

Diamond Head Beach Hotel. 2947 Kalakaua Avenue; (808) 922-1928; www.dbhotel.com. At the quiet end of Waikiki, across from Kapiolani Park. After high season (December through March), room rates drop to $168, with steeper discounts in slower periods. $$–$$$$

Halekulani. 2199 Kalia Road; (800) 367-2343 or (808) 923-2311; www.halekulani.com. The 456-room luxury property offers plush rooms with lanais and views of Diamond Head even from the bathtubs. The House Without a Key, the hotel's informal outdoor cafe, is the favorite place for sunset mai tais and hula under a one hundred–year-old kiawe tree, close to the swimming pool with an orchid mosaic on the bottom. $$$–$$$$

Hilton Hawaiian Village. 2005 Kalia Road; (808) 949-4321; www.hiltonhawaiianvillage.com. On the beach, with a great kids' program. $$–$$$$

Hyatt Regency Waikiki. 2424 Kalakaua Avenue; (808) 923-1234. Across the street from the beach; nice activities for kids. $$–$$$$

New Otani Kaimana Beach Hotel. 2863 Kalakaua Avenue; (800) 356-8264; www.kaimana.com. The 125 rooms, in pastels and tropical decor, are on the third to ninth floors of an atrium-style building and have balconies and small refrigerators; some have kitchenettes. The New Otani is on the beach, near

Kapiolani Park and the Waikiki Aquarium, and its restaurant, Hau Tree Lanai, is practically on the sand. At the Diamond Head end of Waikiki. $$–$$$$

Outrigger Hotels and Resorts, seven locations in Waikiki; Outrigger Waikiki on the beach, (808) 923-0711; Outrigger Reef on the Beach, (808) 923-3111; Ala Moana Hotel, (808) 955-4811; Wyland Waikiki, (808) 954-4000; Outrigger Waikiki Shore, (808) 923-3871; Outrigger Luana Waikiki, (808) 955-6000; and Outrigger Regency on Beachwalk, (808) 922-3871; www.outrigger.com. Some properties feature complete kitchens, which make for more affordable meals, and they often offer discount packages for families. $$–$$$$

The Royal Grove Hotel. 151 Uluniu Avenue; (808) 923-7691; www.royalgrove hotel.com. This budget hotel is 2 blocks from Waikiki Beach; rooms are clean and the staff friendly. Rooms have a kitchenette and TV. $–$$

Westin Moana Surfrider Hotel. 2365 Kalakaua Avenue; (808) 922-3111; www .moanasurfrider.com. Beachfront; good kids' program. $$–$$$$

Waikiki Beach Marriott Resort. 2552 Kalakaua Avenue; (808) 922-6611; www.mar riottwaikiki.com. Offers generous discounts for kids. $$$–$$$$

Family Vacation Rentals

If you would prefer to stay in a vacation home rental, rather than a hotel or resort, Oahu has a plethora of styles and prices available. Ranging from beachfront cottages to mountaintop mansions, the possibilities are too many to mention. The best resource is the Oahu Visitors Bureau (www.visit-oahu.com).

Downtown Honolulu

Downtown Honolulu is the financial and commercial heartbeat of the city, but it's also home to several historic structures representative of Hawaii's multicultural roots. Within its boundaries are the only royal palace in the United States, a 162-year-old church built from coral blocks, and a living museum dedicated to preserving life as it was during the missionary era.

Juxtaposed among these old relics are sparkling new high-rises, the state capitol, Chinatown, and the Aloha Tower Marketplace. Downtown is a wonderful place to stroll and people-watch. While lawyers, bankers, and politicians hustle to their next appointment, merchants in Asian herb shops sell such unusual products as snake tails and bat eyes. With its art galleries, flower shops, and coffee kiosks, combined with its Asian flavor, business sense, and history, downtown Honolulu is a potpourri of the old and the new.

Iolani Palace (ages 5 and up)

Corner of King and Richards Streets; for recorded information call (808) 538-1471; to make reservations call (808) 522-0832; www.iolanipalace.org. Guided forty-five-minute tours by well-trained docents given Tuesday through Saturday 9:00 a.m. to 11:15 a.m.; reservations recommended. Other self-guided tours are available in the afternoons until 4:30 p.m. Children younger than 5 are not admitted (there are too many priceless antiquities to risk exposing to energetic toddlers). $–$$$

Iolani Palace was built in 1882 during the reign of King David Kalakaua and is among the most significant historical structures in all Hawaii. It's the only royal palace in the United States and is designated a National Historical Site, representative of an era when kings and queens rode regal horse-drawn carriages. There were royal celebrations that lasted for days during Kalakaua's reign.

It was important to King Kalakaua that Hawaii be equal to Europe in its manifestations of majesty, and he designed the building to resemble Queen Victoria's royal residence in England. It was the first place west of the Mississippi to have running water, electricity, and phone service.

Sadly, the palace is also the site of the Revolution of 1893, when a select group of local businessmen, officially known in history books as the Committee of Safety, overthrew Hawaii's monarchy and deposed its ruler, Queen Liliuokalani, sister of the then-deceased Kalakaua.

Royal Hawaiian Band (all ages)

Iolani Palace grounds. Most Fridays from noon to 1:00 p.m. Weather permitting, you can check the schedule at www.co.honolulu.hi.us/rhb/.

It's a good idea to plan your Iolani Palace tour for a Friday morning. After the tour you can enjoy a picnic on the lawn and listen to the **free** concert given by the Royal Hawaiian Band. The band has a long tradition of sharing Hawaii's music with the world. The popular "Aloha `Oe," with lyrics by Queen Liliuokalani and music by Bandmaster Henry Berger, was first introduced to the American public by the Royal Hawaiian Band in San Francisco in 1883.

Kawaiahao Church (all ages)

At the corner of South King and Punchbowl Streets; (808) 522-1333. Open Monday through Saturday 9:00 a.m. to 3:00 p.m. Sunday services at 9:00 a.m. free.

Situated kitty-corner from Iolani Palace is Kawaiahao Church. Honolulu's oldest church was constructed from 1836 to 1842 under the supervision of its missionary minister, Hiram Bingham. More than 14,000 coral blocks were taken from offshore reefs to build the structure, and its 162-year-old weather-beaten facade remains a hearty testimony to the craftsmanship. During the monarchy's heyday, the church functioned as the royal chapel, where kings, queens, princes, and princesses came to pray. It was also the site of royal weddings, funerals, and inaugurations.

Oahu Hotels and **Children's Programs**

- **Hilton Hawaiian Village.** 2005 Kalia Road; (808) 949-4321; www.hiltonha waiianvillage.com. $$–$$$$. Hilton Hawaiian Village's year-round children's program, Rainbow Express, is offered daily for keiki ages five to twelve. Once children register and receive their "Rainbow Express Passport," they can experience educational and recreational activities, all with a Hawaiian focus. Activities include arts, crafts, nature walks, wildlife feedings, fishing, and visits to Bishop Museum, Waikiki Aquarium, and Honolulu Zoo.
- **Hyatt Regency Waikiki Hotel.** 2424 Kalakaua Avenue; (808) 233-1234; www.waikiki.hyatt.com. $$$–$$$$. Camp Hyatt offers a variety of activities to keep your keiki busy while having loads of fun. Games include a selection of Hawaiian board games and crafts, which teach some of the basics of the Hawaiian language and culture in a fun and easy way. Camp Hyatt also includes a DVD library with a wide selection of Disney and other children's features as well as Nintendo games. The Camp Hyatt Library contains classic books children love to read. A Hawaiian children's book collection has also been added. In addition to coloring books, crayons, colored paper, glue, scissors, and markers, Hawaiian craft projects treat campers to a slice of Hawaiian culture.
- **J. W. Marriott Ihilani Resort & Spa.** 92–1001 Olani Street; (800) 679-0079; www.ihilani.com. $$$$. Celebrate the vibrant wonder of youth with the Keiki Beachcomber Club. The program hosts supervised international activities for guests between four and twelve years old. Activities include treasure hunts, hula dancing, crafting leis, karaoke, sports, and crafts. Children will engage in diverse activities while making friends with other children from around the world.
- **Kahala Hotel and Resort.** 5000 Kahala Avenue; (808) 738-8911; www .kahalaresort.com $$$$. The Keiki Club at the Kahala Hotel and Resort takes advantage of the area's natural wonders and Hawaii's unique customs to provide an educational and entertaining program for kids ages five to twelve. Full-day or half-day program options are available and include activities such as dancing hula, weaving palm fronds, playing traditional island games, swimming with dolphins, collecting sea shells, and more.
- **Outrigger Hotels & Resorts.** Various locations throughout Oahu; (808) 923-0711; www.outrigger.com. $$–$$$$. Outrigger Hotels & Resorts' Island Explorer program is designed to get kids and their parents out discovering Hawaii's unique natural environment. Kids and their parents will learn nature skills, such as how to conduct ecologically safe explorations, identify myriad

nature's gifts that wash up along the shoreline, prepare for a hike, and recognize the many friendly critters that make their home in Hawaiian rain forests. Upon arrival, kids will receive an Island Explorer Kit that includes a backpack, sunglasses, pen, binoculars, and Reef Adventure Guide.

- **ResortQuest Hawaii** (formerly Aston Hotels & Resorts). Various locations throughout Oahu; (877) 997-6667; www.resortquesthawaii.com. $$–$$$. The new ResortQuest Kids program, "Stay, Play, & Eat Free," offers children ages twelve and under **free** activities, meals, and merchandise (when accompanied by a paying adult) to popular family attractions, restaurants, and Hawaii retailers. All families with children twelve and under will receive an identification card for each child at check-in. Participating vendors include Sea Life Park, Hawaiian Waters Adventure Park, Dixie Grill, Hilo Hattie, and more.
- **Starwood Hotels.** Various locations throughout Oahu; (808) 931-8232; www.starwoodhawaii.com. $$–$$$$. With the Keiki Aloha program, children between the ages of five and twelve can spend part of their vacation doing fun, educational, and cultural activities. The extremely popular program offers off-property excursions year-round. At the Royal Hawaiian, Sheraton Waikiki, Westin Moana Surfrider, and Sheraton Princess Kaiulani, children can experience a wide range of activities such as lei making, catamaran sailing, and surfing in the morning. The excursions will take keiki to such places as the Honolulu Zoo, Waikiki Aquarium, and Bishop Museum. The evening program includes activities such as crab hunting, a hotel scavenger hunt, Honu (turtle) cookie decorating, and cultural games.
- **Turtle Bay Resort.** 57-091 Kamehameha Highway, Kahuku; (808) 293-6000; www.turtlebayresort.com. $$–$$$$. The Keiki Turtle Club at the Turtle Bay Resort offers Hawaiiana projects, arts and crafts, and outdoor activities for kids between five and 12 years of age. Some of the activities include building gigantic, exploding volcanoes out of sand, lei making and hula lessons, exploring the tide pools for underwater creatures, and a night at the beach, complete with a campfire and s'mores. Full- and half-day programs are available on Monday, Wednesday, and Friday, and an evening program is available on Saturday.
- **Waikiki Beach Marriott Resort and Spa.** 2552 Kalakaua Avenue; (808) 922-6611; www.marriottwaikiki.com. $$–$$$$. The Keiki Klub children's program at Waikiki Beach Marriott Resort is seasonal and offers a variety of activities such as creating a smoking, lava-filled volcano; painting a Hawaiian tapa cloth; playing an authentic Hawaiian game called "Ulu maika," and dancing hula.

Aliiolani Hale (all ages)
Directly across King Street from Iolani Palace. free.

Aliiolani Hale is the state judiciary building. Kamehameha V, a predecessor of King Kalakaua, originally directed its construction in 1872 as a royal palace. Kamehameha V died before the structure was completed, and it was later redesigned as a court building because Kalakaua had alternative palace plans.

After the monarchy was overthrown in 1893, all eyes in Honolulu were focused on the steps of Aliiolani Hale. It was here that the first proclamation was read by the members of the Committee of Safety. The proclamation stated that the sovereign nation of Hawaii no longer existed and the land would be controlled by a provisional government. Thus Hawaii began its journey to statehood, which ended with its designation as the fiftieth state in August 1959.

The bronze statue in front of Aliiolani Hale is a tribute to King Kamehameha the Great, who was the first Hawaiian monarch to consolidate all of the islands under one rule. This was no small feat, because each island was under the domain of a different chief or king. Kamehameha and his warriors endured a series of bloody battles and finally triumphed. The result was an organized society with a defined caste system of chiefs and commoners that flourished until the monarchy was overthrown.

As an everlasting tribute, June 11 is King Kamehameha Day, a state holiday in Hawaii, and on this day the statue is draped with hundreds of floral leis bursting with a rainbow of color—quite a fragrant spectacle.

Mission Houses Museum (ages 4 and up)
553 South King Street; (808) 531-0481; www.missionhouses.org. Open Tuesday through Saturday 10:00 a.m. to 4:00 p.m. Hourlong guided tours of the visitor center, Frame House, and Printing Office are offered Tuesday through Saturday at 11:00 a.m. and 2:45 p.m. $$, free for ages 5 and under.

This is a living museum designed to show visitors the importance of the missionary era in Hawaii. The missionaries arrived in 1820 from the eastern coast of the United States with a goal to convert the "heathen" natives to the ways of their Christian god. Their success and the resulting impact on Hawaiian society were tremendous. European-style clothing became commonplace, Christian marriages were performed, and the hula, a rhythmic form of communication, was pretty much discontinued. Missionaries believed the ancient dance to be vulgar and distasteful, and it remained mostly absent from the culture until King Kalakaua assumed control in 1874 and reinstated the hula.

At the Mission Houses Museum, guides and hosts are dressed in period clothing. These actors make believe they are the missionaries who made that long pilgrimage overseas years ago. They welcome questions about their journey, their lifestyle, their religious motives, and, most interestingly, their interactions with the native Hawaiians.

The museum grounds encompass two main houses, a printing-house annex, a library, and a gift shop. Each building is restored and furnished to its former architectural and decorative design.

Honolulu Academy of Arts (all ages)

900 South Beretania Street, across from Thomas Square; (808) 532-8700; www.honolulu academy.org. Tuesday through Saturday 10:00 a.m. to 4:30 p.m., Sunday 1:00 to 5:00 p.m., closed Monday. Guided tours are conducted Tuesday through Saturday at 10:15 a.m., 11:30 a.m., and 1:30 p.m. and Sunday at 1:15 p.m. $–$$; children ages 12 and younger admitted free. First Wednesday and third Sunday of every month are free.

Although the entire family may not be interested in visiting an art academy, there truly is something for everyone at the Honolulu Academy of Arts. This institution boasts an international collection of works by respected artists set among a maze of indoor/outdoor hallways. The kids will be able to occupy themselves in the many picturesque courtyards. There is a restaurant and gift shop on the grounds.

Kakaako Waterfront Park (all ages)

At the oceanside end of Coral Street, off Ala Moana Boulevard.

Kakaako Waterfront Park is a new park situated smack in the middle of an industrial area and offers a nice respite for recreation between Waikiki and downtown. The park features wide paved walkways often filled with in-line skaters and bicyclists. It's a great place for a midday picnic, although the facilities are minimal; you'll have to bring your own supplies.

Hawaii Children's Discovery Center (all ages)

111 Ohe Street; (808) 524-5437; www.discoverycenterhawaii.org. Open Tuesday through Friday 9:00 a.m. to 1:00 p.m.; Saturday and Sunday 10:00 a.m. to 3:00 p.m. No strollers allowed. $$

The center has state-of-the-art participatory learning exhibits that offer new heights of learning and discovery. It's great for kids of all ages. Don't miss the chance to visit this fantastic facility, where you'll feel what it's like to walk on the ocean floor, visit with children in other countries, and learn about the physical properties of bubbles.

Atlantis Adventures' Navatek Cruises (all ages)

Reservations, (808) 973-9800; www.atlantisadventures.com. Boats leave from the Aloha Tower Marketplace. Pier 6, near the intersection of Ala Moana Boulevard and Punchbowl Street. $$$$

The cruises on Navatek vary according to season and type of cruise. The 140-foot high-tech vessel uses a breakthrough design (double-hull) swath technology that virtually eliminates the rocking and rolling from the ocean currents. It's ideal for passengers who are prone to motion sickness.

Oahu Trivia

Electric lights illuminated Iolani Palace four years before electricity reached the White House.

A variety of cruises are available, including seasonal whale-watching luncheon cruises and year-round sunset dinner cruises, many with live entertainment.

The boats travel along the "gold coast" of Kahala, where all the million-dollar mansions are situated. (Atlantis also offers popular submarine tours; see p. 5.)

Aloha Tower Marketplace (all ages)
Waterfront on Ala Moana Boulevard, from Punchbowl to Bishop Streets; (808) 528-5700; www.alohatower.com. Hours vary.

As you travel in an elevator to the top of the tower, note how the high-rises of Honolulu and Waikiki far surpass this tiny structure. When it was built in 1926, it was the tallest structure on the island! Be sure to take the ride to the top. It's **free**, and the panoramic views of the harbor and surrounding cities are spectacular. It's open daily from 9:00 a.m. to 5:00 p.m.

The tower has been restored, and the surrounding marketplace is full of restaurants, recreation venues, and boutique-type shops. Today residents and visitors arrive to dine in the specialty eateries and stroll through the open-air mall. But in the old days, before jet travel carted hundreds of tourists at a time to these fair shores, visitors arrived via steamer ship, and all passengers disembarked at Aloha Tower.

Whenever a ship was due in, it was known as "Boat Day" in town. Locals would greet the incoming visitors in outrigger canoes and on surfboards in the water. It was always a celebration, complete with food, music, and dancing.

Although air travel has rendered the tower's usefulness as an embarkation site relatively unimportant, it is the departure and arrival point for American Hawaii Cruises' *Independence,* which casts off on Saturday evenings.

The tower is a fun place to be on weekend evenings during the *pau hana* (after-work) hour. Free Hawaiian entertainment by well-known local musicians is featured at the open-air Don Ho's Island Grill, weather permitting, usually from 5:00 to 8:00 p.m.

The Maritime Center (all ages)
Adjacent to Aloha Tower Marketplace; (808) 523-6151; www.holoholo.org/maritime. Open 8:30 a.m. to 5:00 p.m. daily, except Christmas Day; $5 parking. $–$$, free for kids younger than 6.

With its isolated location in the middle of the Pacific, Hawaii understandably enjoys a rich maritime heritage. The Maritime Center displays that history in a wonderful interactive setting. The center is actually the site of a former boathouse used by King David Kalakaua in the late 1800s. The facility has been wonderfully restored to house an incredible 2,000 years of Hawaii's oceangoing history.

Exhibits are both indoor and outdoor and include videos, three-dimensional figures, interactive hands-on displays, and a do-it-yourself audio tour with portable cassette players. The tape uses realistic sound effects and voices to present the displays in a fun, educational manner.

You'll see how the first Polynesians arrived and will be able to appreciate the danger and duration of their journey, dependent on wind, weather, celestial navigation skills, and the seaworthiness of their hand-carved canoes. Kids will gravitate to the surfing exhibit, the highlight of which is a film portraying the brave local experts who think nothing of sliding full force down the face of 30-foot waves on Oahu's north shore.

Another popular display focuses on whales. Especially noteworthy is the complete skeleton of a humpback, one of only two on display worldwide. The carcass was discovered on Kahoolawe, an uninhabited Hawaiian island. You'll really get a feel for the whale's immense proportions when standing next to the 750-pound skull.

Falls of Clyde and Hokule`a (all ages)

Adjacent to the Maritime Center, the ship is docked at Pier 7. Open daily 8:30 a.m. to 5:00 p.m. $$

Right next to the Maritime Center, the Falls of Clyde is the only remaining fully rigged, four-masted ship afloat in the world. Now a National Historic Landmark, this ship was part of the Matson Navigation Company and was used as a cargo and passenger liner from 1898 to 1920. Since 1960 the ship has been used as a floating museum.

At the Maritime Center, not only will the *Falls of Clyde* catch your eye, but you'll also be drawn to the *Hokule`a,* an authentic replica of a Polynesian voyaging canoe built in 1976. It recently sailed 6,000 miles to Tahiti and back, manned by a crew that used traditional Polynesian navigational methods. Although some modern materials were used during its construction, the design was kept as traditional as possible, using lots of petroglyphs (ancient rock carvings) and old drawings as the basis.

Where to Eat

Gordon Biersch Brewery Restaurant. At Aloha Tower Complex, 101 Ala Moana Boulevard; (808) 599-4877. Hawaii's first full-fledged brewery offers much more than a tasty selection of beers. From the just-as-tasty menu, kids will love the cheeseburgers and pizzas! $$–$$$

Don Ho's Island Grill. Also at Aloha Tower; (808) 528-0807. This is a waterfront restaurant and bar with live Hawaiian music at night. Enjoy the ambience of "groovy, retro" Waikiki, along with great food, great music; all overlooking Honolulu Harbor. $$-$$$

Several other restaurants in Aloha Tower Marketplace range from casual cafeteria-style to Tex-Mex to steak and seafood.

Dave's Ice Cream. 611 Kapahulu Avenue; (808) 735-2194; www.daveshawaiianicecream .com. Try superb flavors from local ingredients, including guava, pineapple, macadamia nut, coconut, and poha berries. Open noon to 10:30 p.m. $

Ono Hawaiian Foods. 726 Kapahulu Avenue; (808) 737-2275. Serious local eaters stop here for authentic Hawaiian food such as *laulau* (pork or chicken and fish wrapped in spinachlike taro tops and steamed) or roasted *kalua* pig plates with lomi salmon and tomato and onion as a side dish. Open 11:00 a.m. to 7:30 p.m. $$

Teddy's Bigger Burgers. 134 Kapahulu Avenue; (808) 926-3444; also located in Kailua and Hawaii Kai; www.teddysbiggerburgers .com. Pleases children and teenagers with big burgers and old-fashioned, extra-thick milk shakes for unbelievably reasonable prices. Open 10:30 a.m. to 9:00 p.m. $

Where to Stay

With the plethora of choices in nearby Waikiki, there are no downtown accommodations that cater to families.

Chinatown

Hawaii has maintained a rich Chinese heritage since the first laborers arrived in the mid-1800s to work at the sugar plantations. Their passage was a ticket to a form of indentured servitude that typically lasted five years and provided cheap labor for the sugar barons. When their time was up, however, most of them stayed, started businesses, and established the Chinatown that exists today.

In 1900 a major fire burned Chinatown to the ground. But the immigrants painstakingly rebuilt, and some of the old buildings that exist today are not only fine architectural examples of that era, but also a testimony to the determination of its people.

A stroll through Chinatown is likely to be filled with unusual and exotic sights, smells, and tastes—it's a virtual symphony of senses. (It's a good idea to keep a close watch on your children around this area. Although it's basically safe and well policed, some parts are representative of Honolulu's "seedy" side.)

Be sure to check out the recently restored Hawaii Theatre at the corner of Bethel and Puahi Streets. Inside are murals representative of the art deco style popular during the 1920s and 1930s.

For a look at Hawaii's finest lei-makers, and a wonderfully fragrant treat, you won't want to miss the many lei stores situated on Maunakea and Beretania Streets. Prices are very reasonable here, and locals come from all parts of the island to purchase leis for special occasions.

You'll walk by meat markets, where windows display hanging ducks, drying and readying for the next meal. There are acupuncture and herb shops advertising, believe it or not, powdered monkey brain, sure to cure whatever ails you! If that doesn't suit your fancy, there are always signs advertising coiled snake skin and mashed antelope antler.

If you still have an appetite, there's an immense variety of great food priced very inexpensively. The take-out counters next to the Mauna Kea Marketplace, at the corner of Mauna Kea and Hotel Streets, display a feast of ethnic cuisine, from Italian to Vietnamese to Filipino.

Oahu Trivia

Different **heiau**, ancient places of worship, served different purposes; some were for healing, some for refuge from war or crime, and some for quiet meditation.

Chinatown **Walking Tours**

Two organizations offer walking tours that present a good overview of the area for a reasonable price. The **Chinese Chamber of Commerce** sponsors a narrated tour every Tuesday from 9:30 a.m. to noon. The tour begins at the office at 42 North King Street and costs $5; kids younger than twelve are free. For more information call (808) 533-3181 or visit www.chinatownhi.com.

The **Chinatown Historical Society** offers a walking tour that covers the heart of the district. Tours start at 10:00 a.m. and 1:00 p.m. daily. Guides will take you through colorful, exotic shops; historic buildings; and the famous open market. This tour costs $4 for adults; kids twelve and younger pay $3. The tour meets inside Asia Mall at 1250 Maunakea Street. For more information call (808) 521-3045.

Shops at Dole Cannery (all ages)

The cannery is at 650 Iwilei Road; (808) 528-2236; www.dole-cannery.com. Open Monday through Saturday 9:00 a.m. to 5:00 p.m., Sunday 10:00 a.m. to 4:00 p.m.

Heading west out of downtown, you'll soon run into the shops at Dole Cannery, constructed around the canning factory of Hawaii's most famous fruit. The cannery has been converted into a retail center and food court. It's fun to walk around the complex and view the antiquated machinery that's still in place. It's an unofficial museum of Hawaii's pineapple industry.

Foster Botanical Gardens (all ages)

50 North Vineyard Boulevard, at the corner of Vineyard and Nuuanu Streets; (808) 522-7060; www.co.honolulu.hi.us/parks/hbg/fbg.htm. Open 9:00 a.m. to 4:00 p.m. Guided tours are offered Monday through Saturday at 1:00 p.m. $

For a fun family picnic amid stately trees, Foster Botanical Gardens is an ideal locale. The gardens encompass fifteen acres of manicured lawns and are situated on the outskirts of downtown Honolulu. *NOTE:* To keep the kids happy, it's a good idea to bring along some insect repellent.

Where to Eat

Indigo Restaurant. 1121 Nuuanu Avenue; (808) 521-2900; www.indigo-hawaii.com. An elegant upscale hideaway in the heart of downtown Honolulu, Indigo offers Eurasian cuisine: classic European dishes with an Asian twist. The menu features meal-size pizzas with unusual toppings and a variety of fresh fish dishes ranging from salads to pastas. Come prepared to sample new flavors; some of the dishes are served with different dipping sauces on the side. Open for lunch and dinner; reservations recommended. $$$

Sam Choy's Breakfast, Lunch and Crab. 580 North Nimitz Highway; (808) 545-7979; www.samchoy.com. In an industrial area toward the airport, Sam Choy's is the place to find local diner fare: fried poke (fresh tuna) omelet and wok-cooked chicken and saimin (noodle soup topped with crab) for breakfast or lunch. A crab house by night, Sam Choy's serves enormous portions of king crab legs, fresh oysters, and stone crab. $ (breakfast and lunch)–$$ (dinner)

Where to Stay

Nearby Waikiki is the best choice for accommodations that cater to families.

Manoa and Punchbowl Districts

The hills and valleys behind downtown and Waikiki are dotted with small communities called Manoa, Makiki, Nuuanu, and Punchbowl, all of which possess unique characteristics and histories and feature outstanding hiking trails and important cultural sites. Manoa Valley is the site of the University of Hawaii and Punahou School (K–12), the oldest private school west of the Mississippi.

Lyon Arboretum (all ages)

3860 Manoa Road, Manoa; (808) 988-0456; www.hawaii.edu/lyonarboretum/ or www.lyon arboretum.com. Open Monday through Friday 9:00 a.m. to 4:00 p.m. To get there from Waikiki, follow McCully Avenue to Beretania Street, and turn left. Turn right on Punahou Street, which turns into Manoa Road. $–$$

In the back of Manoa Valley, Lyon Arboretum is a fun, but usually wet, adventure. There are many ongoing scientific projects at Lyon, and you'll be impressed with the variety, quality, and abundance of plants here.

Makiki Trails (ages 6 and up)

To get the Makiki/Tantalus Trail from Waikiki, head up McCully Avenue, turn left on Beretania, right on Keeaumoku, then right on Wilder. At the first light, turn left onto Makiki Street. You'll cross Nehoa Street, then go left on Makiki Heights Drive, which eventually winds into Tantalus Drive. You'll soon enter the Makiki Recreation Area and pass Hawaii Nature Center on your right. Eventually a chain in the road will force you to park and walk.

Take a drive to Tantalus and Round Top, an area high in the hills above Makiki that offers breathtaking views of the city and a few good hiking trails. This is a great area for exploring, as the trails receive regular maintenance. There are eleven different trails to take here, but use good judgment; not all of them are suited for young children.

To get to the Manoa Cliff Trailhead, and a great family hike, follow Round Top Drive until you pass Forest Ridge Way. Look for a large turnout that offers parking on both sides of the road. The Moleka Trail is easily navigable and begins on the right. It's only ½ mile long, and the views are outstanding. The trail leads to a bamboo forest and continues on to a wide area with a panoramic view.

The trail to the left leads to Round Top Drive, where it splits into three sections. The Makiki Valley Trail slices across the valley to the right; Ualakaa Trail veers left, goes for about ½ mile, and joins with the Makiki Valley Trail to Puu Ualakaa State Park. The Makiki

Branch Trail goes straight for ½ mile and ends at the bottom of the valley at the Division of Forestry Baseyard.

These trails are very safe and are well maintained by the Division of Forestry and Wildlife. One note of caution: This area is always muddy and mosquito-laden, so dress accordingly and bring some repellent along.

On foot, once you pass the chain, the road narrows and becomes Kanealole Trail. From here a variety of trails cross over and run parallel to Kanealole. You can bring a picnic and spend the whole day up here enjoying the view, or you can do a quick twenty-minute escape to nature, where it's unbelievable that busy Waikiki is less than 10 miles away.

If your family includes young children who are unable to enjoy the hiking trails, by all means you should still drive to the top of Tantalus for a king-sized view of the island.

The Contemporary Museum (all ages)

2411 Makiki Heights Drive, Makiki; (808) 526-0232; www.tcmhi.org. Open 8:30 a.m. to 4:00 p.m. Monday through Thursday and 8:30 a.m. to 6:00 p.m. Friday. Closed weekends and major holidays. $, free for children ages 12 and under. On the third Thursday of each month, admission is free.

The works of six of Hawaii's foremost artists in various media are on display in this 1925 architectural marvel in the Tantalus neighborhood, a gracious, forested residential area with views of Diamond Head. Even nonartistic kids will be captivated by the beautiful setting of the Contemporary Museum. An old estate was converted into a museum, and the exhibits are situated all over the place. The grounds are chock-full of interesting modern sculptures, and visitors may stroll about at their leisure. With the exception of a colorful permanent display of David Hockney works, the exhibits are always changing and reflect different themes in modern art. A great restaurant and wonderfully stocked gift shop are on the premises.

Hawaii Nature Center (all ages)

2131 Makiki Heights Drive, Makiki; (808) 955-0100; www.hawaiinaturecenter.org. Open 8:00 a.m. to 4:00 p.m. $–$$

The Nature Center is a truly wonderful geared-for-kids facility. It provides a hands-on approach that turns learning about Hawaii's unique flora and fauna into a fun experience. Guides lead visitors on trails that feature native plants, flowers, and trees. The trails are geared toward younger children, but everyone is welcome. Participants get a chance to touch, see, feel, and smell nature in its most pristine environment, all under the supervision of resident naturalists. Rain forest walks ($$$$) begin at 11:30 a.m. and 1:30 p.m. Monday through Friday and at 11:00 a.m. and 2:00 p.m. Saturday and Sunday.

Oahu Trivia

Punahou School is the oldest private school west of the Mississippi.

On weekends the Nature Center hosts community programs for families that further explore Hawaii's natural environment through Earth-care projects, nature crafts, and interpretive hikes.

Punchbowl Cemetery (all ages)

Puowaina Drive, Punchbowl, Manoa; (808) 532-3720; www.acresofhonor.com. Open daily 8:00 a.m. to 5:30 p.m. free

A little farther back into the mountains sits the National Memorial Cemetery of the Pacific and the Honolulu Memorial. The area is known as Punchbowl because it's situated in the middle of an extinct volcano and actually resembles the shape of a punch bowl. To get to the National Memorial Cemetery of the Pacific and the Honolulu Memorial from Waikiki, take McCully Street to Beretania Street and turn left. Turn right on Pensacola Street, which eventually curves left and turns into Awaiolimu Street. From there look for Puowaina Drive, which leads to the main gate.

This may be a rather somber site to visit, but after Pearl Harbor, it's the second most attended place in all of Oahu and an important testimony to Hawaii's brave heroes. The cemetery is filled to capacity with 33,143 gravesites, including one for Ellison Onizuka, the Hawaii astronaut who died in the *Challenger* shuttle disaster, and 776 casualties from the December 7, 1941, attack on Pearl Harbor.

The impressive Honolulu Memorial on the northwest wall of the crater was dedicated on May 1, 1966. It honors the sacrifices and achievements of American armed forces in the Pacific during World War II and the Korean conflict, plus those missing from the Vietnam conflict. Park your vehicle behind the memorial and explore the map galleries to see where important battles took place.

From the back of the memorial, walk toward the ocean on the Outer Drive and follow the Memorial Walk up to the overlook area. You'll be rewarded with one of the best views of Honolulu, from Diamond Head in the east all the way west to Ewa Beach.

Where to Eat

Paesano Restaurant. 1752 Woodlawn Drive, Manoa; (808) 988-5923. On the way to Lyon Arboretum, look for Manoa Marketplace off Manoa Road. Try Paesano for lunch or dinner. The menu features a wide selection of pasta, meat, veal, chicken, and seafood. Reservations recommended for dinner. $$–$$$

Willows. 901 Hauston Street, Manoa; (808) 952-9200; www.willowshawaii.com. Best Hawaiian buffet in Oahu. Fantastic atmosphere in the downstairs garden. $$$–$$$$

Where to Stay

Nearby Waikiki is the best choice for family-friendly accommodations.

Nuuanu Valley

Head west of Waikiki on H-1, then detour on the Pali Highway (Route 61).

Lush Nuuanu Valley is home to many religious temples and shrines, representative of the vast variety of ethnic groups that call Oahu home. Route 61, the Pali Highway, continues all the way to Kailua and the windward side of the island, which is included in a later section of this chapter.

Queen Emma Summer Palace (all ages)

2913 Pali Highway; (808) 595-3167; www.daughtersofhawaii.org. Open 9:00 a.m. to 4:00 p.m. daily. $–$$

Volunteers guide visitors through the royal mansion known as the Queen Emma Summer Palace. Queen Emma was married to King Kamehameha IV, and the couple used this beautiful home as a summer retreat. The Daughters of Hawaii have facilitated its meticulous restoration, and many of the family's personal belongings are on display. The architecture and interior decor are reminiscent of Great Britain; Queen Victoria was good friends with King Kamehameha IV.

Pali Lookout (all ages)

Located off the Pali Highway, a few miles beyond the Queen Emma Summer Palace (heading west). The off-ramp to the lookout is well marked from the main road. Open 9:00 a.m. to 4:00 p.m., weather permitting. free.

Hold on to your hats as you climb up the paved walkway to the Pali Lookout. You'll feel as if you're at the windiest spot on the planet! (Although there's no scientific information to prove this and it's probably a bit of an exaggeration, the winds do whip fiercely here.) It's so windy that water from the nearby waterfalls (if it has rained lately) is often carried upward by the winds. The setting offers an unobstructed view of the lush windward side of the island and is nothing short of spectacular. Be sure to bring a jacket or sweater—the winds create quite a chill in the air, making it at least twenty degrees cooler here than it was back in Waikiki.

Some historians claim this is the site of a major battle during King Kamehameha's quest to consolidate all the islands under one rule. Kamehameha won and drove some 16,000 warriors to their deaths over these cliffs. One look down, and you can easily imagine the despair of the losing side.

Judd Loop Trail (ages 6 and up)

To find the trail, exit H-1 West on the Pali Highway (Route 61). You'll pass Queen Emma Summer Palace on your right, then bear right on Nuuanu Pali Drive. The road will fork, but keep bearing right, staying on Nuuanu Pali Drive. Look for a stone bridge over a small stream, after Polihiwa Place. There will be another small bridge marked 1931 that covers a reservoir spillway. Park in the small dirt lot just before the second bridge.

The trail is a little more than 1 mile, and the whole loop will take less than one hour. It's

Oahu Trivia

Oahu boasts more miles of swimming beaches than any other Hawaiian island.

a wonderful forest walk that includes one of Honolulu's most popular isolated swimming holes. It's a good idea to have kids wear tennis shoes, even when swimming, as broken glass may be hidden in the mud. The trail is very easy to follow and passes through groves of banyan and mango trees.

From the parking lot go down to the Nuuanu Stream and cross the stream immediately. (Do not take the trail heading downstream.) A wide trail leads away from the stream, through a bamboo grove. Ignore the side trails along the stream and bear right along the slope. Climb gradually through eucalyptus and Norfolk Island pines. Again, ignore the side trails heading uphill or down to the stream. Enter the Charles S. Judd Memorial Grove of Norfolk Island pines. As the trail descends, bear left into a shallow gully. The turn is marked by a short metal stake. Cross the gully and bear right, parallel to it. Almost immediately you reach the junction with the Nuuanu Trail, which leads off to the left. (The Judd Loop continues straight downhill and back to the starting point.) You can continue on the Nuuanu Trail, which is a little more advanced and is not recommended for young children. The two trails combined cover about 3½ miles. If your kids are young, stick to the Judd Loop.

Maunawili Demonstration Trail (ages 4 and up)

Maunawili Demonstration Trail is one of Oahu's easiest and most accessible trails. Soon after passing the Pali Lookout, you will go through a tunnel. Almost immediately, a sign points to a scenic overlook. Pull off into the parking area and walk back up the highway for about 100 yards, where you'll see a break in the guardrail and a sign for Na`ala Hele, the Hawaiian Trail and Access System.

This trail is great for children because it's relatively flat, with minimal gains and losses in elevation. It offers scenic views as it twists along the windward side of the Koolau Mountain Range. The noisy traffic diminishes, and you find yourself in a beautiful tropical forest.

Hiking all the way to the end will take more than three hours. You can find a nice, scenic, secluded spot for a picnic not too far in. Remember: As with all Hawaiian trails, recent rainfalls make for treacherous footing.

Bishop Museum (all ages)

1525 Bernice Street, Kahili; (808) 847-3511; www.bishopmuseum.org. Open daily 9:00 a.m. to 5:00 p.m. $$$, free for children younger than 4. There is a restaurant and gift shop on the grounds. West from Waikiki on H-1, exit at Likelike Highway and turn right. The second right leads straight to the museum.

A Hawaiian princess, Bernice Pauahi Bishop, founded this four-story, lava-rock museum, the world's greatest repository of cultural and natural artifacts from Hawaii and the

Pacific. Among the displays are royal cloaks crafted from millions of colorful feathers. The difficulty involved in constructing them made them priceless, and only the highest *ali`i* (chiefs) were allowed to don them.

You'll get a firsthand glimpse into the past, in which precontact Hawaii thrived as a Stone Age culture. There are weapons, cooking utensils, and even a replica of a grass hut, or *hale*, that was used for shelter.

A series of fantastic nature exhibits covers the evolutionary adaptations unique to the Pacific Basin. Before humans arrived, the Hawaiian Islands were even more isolated than the Galapagos, which were the primary focus of Charles Darwin's theory on evolution. As a result, species developed here in a completely natural, symbiotic state. For example, rather than forming nests in trees to keep eggs safe, birds were ground nesters because they had no predators.

The cave exhibit is especially fascinating. You can peek into a replica of a newly formed lava tube and learn about the unusual life-forms that exist on the hot, barren lava. The on-site planetarium lets you gaze into the skies above Hawaii and contemplate the vastness of the universe.

Aiea and Waipahu

Keaiwa Heiau State Recreation Area (all ages)

To get here take H-1 west to Route 78 toward Aiea. Exit at Halawa Heights/Stadium, which puts you on Ulune Road. Follow Ulune for a few miles until it dead-ends and turn right on Aiea Heights Drive. Follow Aiea Heights Drive all the way up the long hill, and it will end at the park. Open 7:00 a.m. to 7:45 p.m.

Aiea is pretty much a residential community. But above all the homes, restaurants, and businesses is an important site of Hawaiian history and a fun hike. At first glance this ancient structure will probably look like a bunch of old stones piled together somewhat haphazardly, but don't let its simplicity belie its importance. Ancient Hawaiians used the heiau as a place of worship, a sort of pre-western temple. Different heiau served different purposes; some were for healing, some for refuge from war or crime, and some were for quiet meditation. Keaiwa was a healing place where kahuna (priests) concocted magical potions that cured sickness and disease.

Remnants of the extensive herb garden that once flourished around the stone heiau still exist. Kahuna used every part of these plants—the roots, leaves, bark, and flowers—to mix the concoctions that, when combined with prayer, worked to heal.

As with any significant archaeological site, it's important to tread carefully here, with respect. You may see small rocks wrapped in ti leaves scattered about. These were left by locals as a sign of respect, and visitors are encouraged to convey the same attitude of reverence. This doesn't mean you should feel pressured to find a rock and a ti leaf, but you should encourage your family to properly appreciate this holy spot.

Aiea Loop Trail (all ages)

From the heiau you can follow the park road to the 4½-mile Aiea Loop Trail, which begins here.

This is a fun, easy hike that's suitable for families and takes about three hours. You'll pass through damp forests of eucalyptus trees and come out on one of the ridges of the Koolau mountain range, with scenic, majestic canyons on both sides of you. The views of the mountains and Pearl Harbor below are wonderful, and the feel and smells of the eucalyptus trees are a nice alternative to the sun-soaked, suntan lotion–laden waters of Waikiki, just a few miles away.

Island Seaplane Service (all ages)

85 Lagoon Drive, Honolulu; (808) 836-6273; www.islandseaplane.com. Complimentary shuttle service from Waikiki. $$$$

Kids will love the excitement of departing and landing from the water. Two different flights are run from Keehi Lagoon. The thirty-minute Aloha Flight soars above Honolulu Harbor and Aloha Tower, passing offshore of Waikiki Beach, Diamond Head Crater, Koko Head Crater, Hanauma Bay, Sea Life Park, and the incredible Koolau mountain range. The hourlong Islander Flight extends to Windward Oahu, with such scenics as Kaneohe Bay, Chinaman's Hat, Kahana Bay, and, lastly, the *Arizona* Memorial.

Arizona Memorial at Pearl Harbor (all ages)

From Waikiki take H-1 west, exit at 15A, and follow the signs. The entrance is actually along Route 99, the Kamehameha Highway. The *Arizona* Memorial shuttle bus (808-839-0911) offers round-trip transportation ($$) from several Waikiki hotels. Call (808) 422-2771 for recorded information or (808) 422-0561 to speak to an operator, or go to www.nps.gov /usar. The visitor center is open daily 7:30 a.m. to 5:00 p.m.; closed Thanksgiving, Christmas, and New Year's Day. The shuttle boat runs from 8:00 a.m. to 3:00 p.m. daily (it starts at 7:30 a.m. in the summer). free.

NOTE: Due to increased security levels mandated by the government, no bags are allowed inside the facility. This includes diaper bags and backpacks, as well as strollers with storage compartments. Please do not leave any valuables in your car. An independent vendor operates a bag storage facility in the parking lot.

The *Arizona* Memorial at Pearl Harbor is consistently the most visited, most recognized attraction on Oahu every year. Although Pearl Harbor captured worldwide attention on December 7, 1941, with the surprise attack by Japanese planes that catapulted the United States into World War II, the military controlled the area long before that. In 1887

Oahu Trivia

There were 1.4 million gallons of fuel on the USS *Arizona* when it sank. Today, more than sixty years later, approximately two quarts a day still surface from the ship. Pearl Harbor survivors refer to the oil droplets as "Black Tears."

King Kalakaua signed the Sugar Reciprocity Treaty that provided for profitable, duty-free exportation of sugar in exchange for the U.S. Navy's full control of the harbor.

A visit to Pearl Harbor consists of an onshore museum/display area, a short film, and a boat ride to the memorial. The visitor center emphasizes the area's strategic location and the military's presence in Hawaii since 1887. Today all five services are represented here. Oahu is the headquarters of CINCPAC (Commander in Chief Pacific), which oversees 70 percent of Earth's surface, from California to the east coast of Africa and to both poles.

The museum displays materials from World War II naval history. There are actual letters written by servicemen stationed here to loved ones on the Mainland. The letters paint a poignant picture of young men who lost their lives.

A great system of maps shows the route of the Japanese planes and models of the ships that were damaged. There's even some old wreckage displayed in glass cases.

The film depicts life in the islands before the attack, the military happenings in other parts of the world, and the far-reaching devastation caused by Japan's bombs. It's an emotional and impressive film, made even more meaningful by the elderly veterans who are often there. By the time the movie is over and you're shuttled to the boat, there are more than a few damp handkerchiefs.

The boat takes you to the USS *Arizona* Memorial, where the remains of 1,100 men are entombed forever within the hulk of the once-mighty battleship. The memorial was built in the 1960s, and Elvis Presley staged a benefit concert that helped raise more than $60,000 for the building fund. The structure straddles the sunken ship, and looking out into the water, you can see the *Arizona* sitting on the ocean floor. It is still leaking oil and shows no signs of stopping. The walls of the memorial are decorated with the names of all the soldiers who lost their lives on December 7, 1941.

The facility does become quite crowded; it's best to arrive before 10:00 a.m. for the shortest wait. On average, expect a ninety-minute wait from when you arrive and are given a ticket until your number is called and you're ushered into the theater. During that ninety minutes, however, you can walk around the museum. There are a gift shop, snack bar, and restrooms.

USS *Bowfin* Submarine Museum and Park (ages 4 and up)

Adjacent to the *Arizona* Memorial visitor center; (808) 423-1341; www.bowfin.org. Open 8:00 a.m. to 5:00 p.m. daily (last submarine tour at 4:30 p.m.); closed Thanksgiving, Christmas, and New Year's Day. Children younger than 4 are permitted in the museum but cannot go aboard the ship. $–$$

USS *Bowfin* Submarine Museum and Park is situated so close to Pearl Harbor, it's unfortunately often dwarfed by its famous neighbor. Here you can venture below the deck of the USS *Bowfin,* a fully restored World War II submarine nicknamed "The Pearl Harbor Avenger." Visitors are treated to a glimpse of the tight quarters in which the crew ate, slept, worked, and probably prayed during the rigors of World War II and Korea. The *Bowfin* journeyed on nine successful patrols and was a Naval Reserve training vessel until being decommissioned in 1971.

Next door to the submarine is a museum that chronicles advances in submarine technology from 1776, when the first attempt at building a submersible vehicle was made, to today, when high-technology, nuclear-powered machines patrol the waters.

USS *Missouri* Memorial (all ages)

Adjacent to the *Arizona* Memorial; (808) 973-2494; www.ussmissouri.com. Open 9:00 a.m. to 5:00 p.m. Purchase tickets at the USS *Bowfin* Submarine Museum. A shuttle bus takes you to Ford Island. $$–$$$$

The USS *Missouri* Memorial features guided or self-guided tours of the battleship, which was restored by volunteers and is docked at the 450-acre Ford Island. You can climb between the decks of the "Mighty Mo" and peer into officers' cabins, where shoes are placed neatly beside bunks as if in a time warp.

If you plan to visit all three attractions together (USS *Arizona* Memorial, *Bowfin* Museum, and USS *Missouri* Memorial), you should plan to spend at least a few hours (half a day). Tours of each facility require about ninety minutes, and you'll want time to rest between tours and visit the gift shops.

Hawaii Plantation Village (all ages)

94–695 Waipahu Street; (808) 677-0110; www.hawaiiplantationvillage.org. The village is open Monday through Saturday 10:00 a.m. to 3:00 p.m. Tours are given at the top of every hour, beginning at 10:00 a.m., with the last tour leaving at 2:00 p.m. $–$$

Continuing west on H-1 from Pearl Harbor, you'll soon arrive in the small residential community of Waipahu. Don't miss a visit to the Hawaii Plantation Village, a living museum dedicated to the many immigrants who arrived in Hawaii to labor in the sugar cane fields.

An illuminating guided tour takes visitors through a re-created historic plantation that displays lifestyles during the early nineteenth century. It's a wonderful multicultural experience that comprises eight villages, each representing a different ethnic group. The Plantation Village is a cultural park featuring thirty original and replica buildings—a barber shop, a community *furo* (bath), homes of families from several countries—representing plantation life between 1900 and 1930.

If you visit in September, be sure to attend the annual Plantation Heritage Festival for a great slice of local multiethnic life. There are cultural performances, arts and crafts, and a variety of unusual foods, rides, and games.

Where to Eat

Dixie Grill BBQ and Crab Shack. 99-012 Kamehameha Highway; (808) 485-CRAB. This hot eatery has been packed to capacity since opening—a sign that the food's good. Kids love it here; there's a sandbox, equipped with toys and affectionately known as "Big Ed's Resort," that occupies a corner of the lanai and draws kids like a magnet. $$$

Leeward Coast

This is the dry, desertlike side of the island. In recent years it has become the site of increased development. You'll notice Hawaii's first outlet mall in Waikele.

Beyond Waikele the new resort development is called Ko Olina, home to J. W. Marriott's Ihilani Resort (see sidebar on next page). This area is sure to grow in years to come. The weather is outstandingly sunny, and it offers a calmer, more scenic alternative to Waikiki. And it's only about thirty minutes (during nonpeak traffic hours) from many of the popular sites around the island.

In an effort to steer some of the development away from Honolulu and its traffic hassles, there is a new residential community here called Kapolei. It's one of Hawaii's first attempts at "affordable housing," though one look at the real estate section of the newspaper will lead Mainlanders to consider that term an oxymoron. Nevertheless, attractive prices have lured thousands to the leeward side of the island, and Kapolei will undoubtedly continue to grow and prosper in the future.

Ewa Beach Railway (all ages)

91–1001 Renton Road; (808) 681-5461. Two trips are made every Sunday, at 1:00 and 3:00 p.m. Seating is on a first-come, first-served basis. The narrated ride lasts about ninety minutes. $$

Don't miss a ride on the historic Ewa Beach Railway. Operated by Oahu's Historic Railway Association, the little train travels the same route used by locomotives during sugar's heyday. Tracks were laid here in 1889 to carry sugar from the central plains of the island to ships docked at the harbor. When automobiles and trucks arrived, the trains were rendered obsolete and unfortunately were left to rust and decay. Today they have been painstakingly restored, so you'll feel as if you are one of the plantation workers making the short trek.

Hawaiian Waters Adventure Park (all ages)

400 Farrington Highway in Kapolei, exit 1 off H-1 heading west; (808) 674-9283; www .hawaiianwaters.com. Open 10:30 a.m. to 4:00 p.m. Closed Wednesday in the off season. $$–$$$$

A thirty-five-minute ride from Waikiki, this beautifully landscaped twenty-five-acre tropical water theme park is designed to appeal to all ages and features a unique variety of age-appropriate rides and amenities. It's the perfect place to enjoy safe, secure, and extreme fun under the sun. Experience the many thrilling rides including the "Cliffhanger," a six-story free fall; "The Shaka," a four-story half-pipe; "Typhoon," a four-and-a-half-story storm ride; "Lava Tube," a tube ride simulating the ultimate volcanic eruption; and "Hurricane Bay," a great place to catch waves. "Keiki Kove" is an interactive children's fun pool, full of waterfalls, mini-slides, and animal floaties.

Local **Beaches**

The beach at **Ihilani** is man-made, accessible to nonhotel guests, and one of the prettiest sites on the island. The tranquil setting and warm water are ideal for kids, and the sandy beach will appeal to any sun-worshipping teenager or parent.

When you head out this way, be sure to take a detour on Route 760 to **Ewa Beach Park** or One`ula Beach Park. Both beaches are spacious, sunny, and quite scenic.

Where to Eat

Azul. At Ihilani Resort, 92–1001 Olani Street; (808) 679-0079. Azul is a place for gourmet dinner, with the chef's own special Mediterranean and Pacific Rim cuisine. Appetizers are incredible and entrees are out of this world. $$$

Naupaka Terrace. At Ihilani Resort, 92–1001 Olani Street; (808) 679-0079. Open for breakfast, lunch, and dinner; also offers special Hawaii "fusion" cuisine. The restaurant's open-to-the-sea dining area is Hawaii at its best. $$$$

Where to Stay

J. W. Marriott Ihilani Resort & Spa. 92–1001 Olani Street; (808) 679-0079; www.ihilani.com. A beautiful five-star luxury resort—and an award-winning golf course and spa—with an expansive kids' program. $$–$$$$

Waianae Coast

On H-1 heading west the interstate becomes Route 93, Farrington Highway, which runs north to the tip of the island at Kaena Point.

This is the Waianae Coast, marked by a series of beach parks, mostly maintained by the city or state. Many of the beaches are not good for swimming or for children because of either dangerous currents or rocky shorelines; these beaches, although picturesque, are intentionally not included in this family adventure guide.

Continuing north on Farrington Highway, you'll soon arrive in the little towns of Waianae and Makaha. As the highway curves north, the sparkling blue sea beckons stronger here than almost anywhere else on the island. The different shades of blue, contrasting with the sparkling white sand, framed by lava-rock promontories and the Waianae Mountains, are so pretty that you'll be compelled to pull over and contemplate the view.

After you pass Makaha the road gets a bit rugged. There are plenty of places to pull off and enjoy a picnic. Farrington Highway ends at Kaena Point. This is the only coastal section of the island without paved roads, so it's not possible to drive around the entire island.

It is possible, however, to hike around Kaena Point to Dillingham Field, Mokuleia, and the north shore of Oahu. Of course, if you hiked completely around, you'd have to turn around and hike back because your car would be stuck at the leeward side, so don't worry about making the complete trip. Parts of the journey require a little rock climbing and may be difficult for youngsters, but by all means get out and explore the point.

Swimming is not safe here; strong winds whip the water full of whitecaps. On any given day the largest waves in Hawaii will be at Kaena Point, and the giant tumblers are awe-inspiring to watch.

Hawaiian legend says that Kaena was a departure point for spirits making the journey from Earth to heaven, and numerous heiau are situated here.

Leeward Coast Beaches (all ages)

The first swimmable beachfront is Nanakuli Beach County Park in tiny Nanakuli town. The park features basketball courts, a baseball field, restrooms, and a little playground for kids, in addition to a spacious beach. Lifeguards are here daily, and it's a good idea to consult them about the current safety level. The ocean on this side of the island can be rough and dangerous in winter.

Another little town, Maili, doesn't have much other than a 7-Eleven, a gas station, and a few residential developments. It's just south of Waianae, and the beach here is truly pretty. The park is well maintained, clean, and a great place for family outings. The beach is ideal for snorkeling, swimming, boogieboarding, and surfing. Restrooms are on-site.

Makaha Beach County Park is best known as the site of the Annual Buffalo Big Board Riding Championship. "Buffalo" refers to Richard "Buffalo" Keaulana, one of Hawaii's best-known and top-rated lifeguard/surfers. If you're here during the winter, pull over and witness some of the biggest waves in all Hawaii. (Don't even think of entering the water during the winter, however. Even some of the most experienced swimmers and surfers have had to be rescued from here.) On the other hand, summer visitors will enjoy the calm waters, which are ideal for families.

To find Makaha Beach look for the landmark black rock called Lahi Lahi. There will probably be a smattering of local fishermen congregated around the rock. Behind you looms the Waianae mountain range and Mt. Ka`ala, Oahu's highest peak at 4,020 feet.

Kaneaki Heiau (all ages)

Visit Kaneaki Heiau for a chance to see a replica of the seventeenth-century heiau (temple) built in praise of the Hawaiian god Lono, who represented agricultural harvests and fertility. The heiau has been restored by the Bishop Museum, and visitors here will see grass huts and a spirit tower where kahuna (priests) prayed to the gods.

Southeastern Coast

It is possible to drive around the island if you exclude the aforementioned Leeward Coast. From Waikiki you can go either way, east or west, but for simple geographic preferences—and to go against normal traffic-jam patterns—this guide heads east.

Hiking to the Top of **Diamond Head**

Your first stop heading east should be Hawaii's most famous mountain, Diamond Head. Actually named Mt. Leahi, the crater earned its nickname from some gullible English sailors who mistook glimmering calcite crystals for that precious gem. It's so well known and well depicted in paintings, diaries, and visitor publications, it has become one of the more enduring symbols of Hawaii, along with pineapples, coconut palm trees, and plumeria leis. A visit to Oahu simply would not be complete without being able to tell your friends back home that you climbed to the top of Hawaii's unofficial state monument.

To get here from Waikiki, take Kalakaua Avenue south to Diamond Head Road. Keep driving around the mountain and look for the sign that reads DIA-MOND HEAD CRATER. It's right across the street from the Kapiolani Community College, recognizable for its series of brown buildings opposite Diamond Head.

After turning in you'll pass through a tunnel and emerge at a large parking area surrounded by an even larger grassy field. The area used to be heavily furnished with military equipment when it was a focal lookout point during World War II. There are still some vestiges of war here, such as gun emplacements, and tunnels are built right into the mountain. Today it is home to a Hawaii National Guard depot and the Federal Aviation Administration.

The area is clean and safe, and signs point clearly to the trail. Try to ignore the pesky vendors who have set up stands at the trailhead, selling everything from bikinis to tuna sandwiches to T-shirts that verify the wearer actually climbed Diamond Head. Locals consider these businesses an eyesore at an otherwise beautiful natural setting, and the majority opinion is that such stands should be limited to Waikiki. Nonetheless, the constitution and a business license allow them to sell their products here. The issue is being debated in the courts, but the outcome is anyone's guess. On the plus side, you can stock up on cold water for the hot hike ahead.

The hike is ideal for grandparents, young children, and everyone in between. It's an easy, forty-five-minute trek that offers breathtaking panoramic views of Waikiki, downtown, and the Leeward Coast to the west, and Kahala, Kaimuki, and the eastern shores in the other direction.

The 7/10-mile trail leads from the crater floor to the bunker and lookout at the 760-foot summit. The structure up here was built in 1908 to serve as a U.S. Coast Artillery Observation Station. Although the trail is used frequently and very well maintained, you will definitely develop a hearty thirst. Bring plenty of water, a flashlight, and binoculars, and most important, a camera with enough film. Flashlights are recommended because one section, about 75 yards, is inside the mountain and, therefore, quite dark.

Most of the trail is defined by sturdy guardrails. The only tough part necessitates climbing about a hundred steep cement steps, sure to leave even the most physically fit a little short of breath. The rest is uphill but easy.

While hiking it's intriguing to think that this tufaceous cone is suspected to be more than 350,000 years old. Geologists say it was formed when lava was forced out of a fissure and connected with the ocean in one gigantic explosion of steam and ash. The last eruption here is thought to have been more than 200,000 years ago.

The Clean Air Team, as part of a litter-control project, sponsors free guided hikes from Honolulu Zoo to Diamond Head every Saturday. The group meets at 9:00 a.m. near the main entrance to the zoo, at the corner of Kalakaua and Kapahulu Avenues.

The Circle Island Tour starts at the southeastern side of the island, continues on the windward coast, travels around the bend at Kahuku, through the North Shore, and back to Waikiki via the central plains. It's a beautiful drive that offers an immense variety of sights and adventures. Plan at least a full day to be able to fit in a select choice of activities.

Heading east on H-1 from Waikiki, eventually the highway ends and becomes Route 72, Kalanianaole Highway. You'll first pass through the tony town of Kahala. It's a nice detour to veer off Kalanianaole and head down Kahala Avenue. The multimillion-dollar mansions on both sides of the road are where Hawaii's richest and most famous live. Remember that all beaches in Hawaii are public, so everyone has access to the silky sands that front even the most luxurious homes. Look for the "right of way" signs and enjoy a wonderful, calm stretch of sand ideal for children.

Where to Eat

California Pizza Kitchen. Currently at five locations: Kahala Mall, (808) 737-9446; Ala Moana Shopping Center, (808) 941-7715; Pearlride Center in Aiea; (808) 487-7741; Kailua, 609 Kailua Road; (808) 263-2480; and Waikiki at 2284 Kalakaua Avenue, (808) 924-2000. This fast-growing chain makes pizza like you've never tasted before. Santa Fe Chicken Pizza, for instance, has grilled chicken breast, sauteed onions, and cilantro, topped with fresh tomato salsa, sour cream, and guacamole. Also, there are salads, pastas, and desserts. Takeouts are available. $$

Hale Vietnam. 1140 Twelfth Avenue; (808) 735-7581. While in the funky little town of Kaimuki, don't miss a chance to taste Vietnamese food here. This is a great place to sample popular appetizers: Vietnamese-style summer rolls (same concept as Thai spring rolls but with a different twist) and stuffed chicken wings. There is also a variety of curries and pho (soup). Open for lunch and dinner. $$

Hoku's. At the Kahala Hotel & Resort, 5000 Kahala Avenue; www.kahalaresort.com; (808) 737-8888. Hoku's is the hotel's signature restaurant and presents fine cuisine in an air-conditioned room overlooking the scenic resort. $$$$

N + E of D. Head

Free Dolphin Shows

Even if you're not staying at the **Kahala Hotel & Resort**, it's worthwhile to park and walk around the grounds, filled with a lagoon, waterfalls, and flower gardens, and enjoy the picturesque, safe beach. A pair of dolphins live in the lagoon, and feeding time is a sight to behold. Kids will delight as the dolphins perform amazing antics in expectation of a lunch reward. Feeding times are 11:00 a.m. and 2:00 and 4:00 p.m., and the show is free, although parking costs $6. You can get free parking if you eat at one of the resort's restaurants.

Olive Tree Cafe. 4614 Kilauea Avenue, Kahala; (808) 737-0303. Locals flock to this Greek and Mediterranean restaurant. You order at the counter and sit at a table indoors or out. Try the marinated mussels, hummus, or fresh fish souvlakis in a yogurt-dill sauce. $$

Plumeria Beach House. At the Kahala Mandarin Hotel, 5000 Kahala Avenue; www.kahalaresort.com; (808) 737-8888. This restaurant offers oceanfront dining, fabulous lunch and dinner buffets, and a kiddie menu. $$$$

Where to Stay

Kahala Hotel & Resort. 5000 Kahala Avenue; www.kahalaresort.com; (808) 737-8888. Kahala Avenue ends at the Kahala Hotel & Resort. Formerly the site of the Kahala Hilton, this five-star resort is frequented by movie stars and politicians. The beach here is well protected and very shallow, ideal for children. You can walk about 50 yards out and the water level won't change. $$–$$$

Hawaii Kai

Continuing east on Kalanianaole Highway, you'll pass through the residential communities of Aina Haina, Niu Valley, and Kuliouou before arriving in Hawaii Kai. Previously swampland, this now exclusive area was developed in the late 1960s by Henry Kaiser, a wealthy businessman with a million-dollar dream. Kaiser succeeded, and Hawaii Kai has grown tremendously; it's now home to award-winning restaurants, two shopping centers, a Costco warehouse, and a movie theater.

Hanauma Bay Nature Preserve (all ages)

About ½ mile past Koko Marina Shopping Center on Kalanianaole Highway. In the summer, the park is open 6:00 a.m. to 7:00 p.m. daily except Tuesday. During the winter, the park is open 6:00 a.m. to 6:00 p.m. Call (808) 396-4229 for information and water conditions. $, free for children age 12 and under.

Continuing on Kalanianaole past Maunalua Bay, the road ascends Koko Crater. Hanauma Bay Nature Preserve will be on the right. A visit to Hanauma Bay definitely will be one of your family's Oahu highlights. The natural inlet, surrounded by coral reefs, creates a warm-water safe haven for Hawaii's most colorful exotic fish and has a well-deserved reputation as a world-class snorkeling site.

Snorkeling equipment is available for rent at the visitor center (about $15 a day), so you needn't lug your own down the tiresome hill that leads to the beach. Supplies are limited, so be sure to get there early. Once you've donned the requisite mask, snorkel, and fins, a whole new underwater world unfolds. Coral and more than 1,500 different types of shells sit in a rainbow spectrum of colors, forming a reef that feeds and shelters thousands of multicolored fish.

The water is so clear that even children who don't know how to swim can simply walk along the shoreline and still see multitudes of fish. The aquatic life here is protected by state law, meaning you can look but can't touch, and you most definitely cannot try to bring anything home as a souvenir. As a result, the fish here are so tame and so used to visitors that they will eat right from your hand. Fish pellets are sold on the premises. It's a good idea to bring an underwater camera so Mainland friends and family will really believe you had fish eating from your outstretched palm.

Recently, constant overuse by Oahu's six million–plus annual visitors has begun to affect Hanauma Bay. After so many years of being hand-fed, the fish were beginning to quit nibbling on the reef, upsetting the natural symbiotic relationship. Even worse was the reef's condition, severely compacted and broken from thousands of tromping feet. As a result, the crowds at the beach are now kept to a minimum. When the park gets too full, a friendly police officer is situated at the entrance and will not let any more cars into the park. Also, the bay is closed to the public every Tuesday, allowing park staff and Mother Nature time to repair and replenish.

It's best to arrive early, before 9:00 a.m., to guarantee admittance. Additionally, early-morning hours offer the clearest water, as the sand has yet to be kicked around by hundreds of fins, creating a kind of gray murkiness.

Halona Blowhole (all ages)
A few miles east of Hanauma Bay.

Be sure to stop at the Halona Blowhole, a lava tube through which the ocean shoots forcefully every time a wave comes in. The spray can reach 50 feet high and can even douse the onlookers watching from the cement overhang above. During humpback whale season, from November through April, this is a great spot to scan the horizon for that telltale plume or fluke.

A short scramble down the rocks leads to a picturesque sandy beach, as calm as it is beautiful. You'll probably be the only people there, because not many people know about this secluded sight. The current is forceful just outside the bay and can pull even strong swimmers out to sea, so keep kids close to shore.

Sandy Beach (ages 10 and up)
About two minutes past the blowhole, on Kalanianaole Highway.

Sandy Beach is popular with local boogieboarders and surfers, but it's not recommended as safe swimming for visitors. More broken necks, injured backs, and drownings occur

Ocean Fun at **Maunalua Bay**

People come from all over the island to use the boat harbor along the coast here at Maunalua Bay. On any given day you'll see a dozen craft out in the water, some fishing, some waterskiing, some just cruising.

Commercial vendors have long used the calm waters here to take willing participants on parasailing trips and Jet Ski and Wave Runner rides. Parasailing involves being strapped onto a large parachute and lifted into the air by the boat's forward momentum. You travel about 30 feet above the water and enjoy wonderful views, the wind in your hair, and a daring adventure.

Jet Skis and Wave Runners provide less passive adventures. Jet Skis are like motorized floating motorcycles on which the participant stands or kneels, turning a mechanism on the handlebars to make it go forward. Wave Runners allow the rider to sit and are therefore a bit easier to manage. Rates vary, as do age requirements, so it's best to call for more information. The outlet based in Hawaii Kai at Koko Marina Shopping Center is **Aloha Ocean Sports,** also known as **South Pacific Water Sports** (808) 737-2334. They offer packages that include **free** transportation to and from most Waikiki hotels.

For waterskiing (and banana boat) enthusiasts, the **Hawaii Sports Water Activity Center,** also in Koko Marina Shopping Center, will take all levels of expertise and specializes in beginners. The fee is $59 and includes about twenty minutes on the water combined with on-land instruction and a descriptive video. There is no real age requirement; as long as your kids are water safe, they can learn to ski. For more information call (808) 395-3773.

here than at any other beach in the entire state! Lifeguards here have been known to ask visitors to remain on shore. It is beautiful, however, and it's quite entertaining to watch the local athletes expertly maneuver the big waves.

Makapu`u Beach (ages 10 and up)

A few miles after Sandy Beach, the road winds through a golf course and veers left around a big bend. Directly below is Makapu`u Beach, the best bodysurfing spot in all Hawaii.

Unless you're an expert at bodysurfing, it's best to experience Makapu`u from the sandy shore during winter or spring months. Sandy Beach (above) ranks first in the number of annual injuries, but this ranks a close second. During the summer, however, when the waves and currents are weak, it's quite safe to swim. This beach is also beautiful and great for picnics and parties.

Offshore are two tiny islands that are sanctuaries for seabirds. Manana, the larger one, is known as Rabbit Island because a rancher tried breeding rabbits there in the late 1880s. It worked, and descendants of those original rabbits still hop around there. Locals call Kao-hikaipu, the smaller island, Turtle Island because it looks like a turtle lying in the water.

Sea Life Park and Pacific Whaling Museum (all ages)

Across the highway from Makapu'u Beach at 41202 Kalanianaole Highway; (808) 259-2512 or (866) 393-5158; www.sealifeparkhawaii.com. Open daily 10:30 a.m. to 5:00 p.m. A restaurant and gift shop are on-site. Entrance to the museum is free, but admission is charged to the rest of the park. $$$–$$$$, free for children age 3 and under.

Sea Life Park is a fun-filled, educational marine park that's home to dolphins, sea lions, penguins, and the world's only wholphin (a cross between a whale and dolphin). A new dolphin-trainer program gives you a behind-the-scenes look at this marine park and allows you to meet the star performers. As part of the training, you learn how to touch and feed the dolphins. Enrollment is limited. Call ahead: (808) 259-2512.

One of the more popular exhibits is the 300,000-gallon Hawaiian Reef Tank, filled with colorful creatures from Hawaii's waters, including reef fish, sharks, eels, and turtles. You can walk 3 fathoms down a ramp and go nose-to-nose with more than 2,000 different specimens.

At the open-air Hawaii Ocean Theatre, penguins, sea lions, and dolphins entertain audiences under the patient tutelage of their trainers. The penguins usually steal the show with their comical tricks.

At Whaler's Cove dolphins help tell tales of Old Hawaii in a beautiful lagoon, in which sits a ⅝-size scaled-down replica of the *Essex,* a nineteenth-century whaling ship.

Some of the other attractions include the Penguin Habitat, the Shark Galley, Turtle Lagoon, and the Kolohe (crazy) Kai Sea Lion Show, featuring the park's residents in a variety of comedy routines.

The Pacific Whaling Museum boasts the largest collection of whaling artifacts and memorabilia in the Pacific.

Where to Eat

Assaggio's Ristorante Italiano. 7192 Kalanianaole Highway; (808) 396-0756; Ala Moana Shopping Center, (808) 942-3446. Located in the heart of the Koko Marina Center, Assaggio's offers such picturesque sights, you could sit forever windowside and gaze. Known for its high-quality Italian food, the restaurant offers lunch and dinner menus with a large variety of favorites for the entire family at really affordable prices.$$–$$$.

Cha Cha Cha Salsaria. 377 Keahole Street; (808) 395-7797; www.chachachasalsaria.com. Located in the Hawaii Kai Shopping Center (by Long's and Safeway), Cha Cha Cha offers a casual combination of Mexican and Jamaican tastes. Tortillas are made fresh daily. $

Oahu Trivia

A fluke is the end section of a whale's tail. During mating season the male whales slam their flukes against the ocean surface with a resounding slap that can be heard from several yards away, or as much as 100 yards on a quiet day.

A Memorable **Cove**

As Oahu's landscape changes with more people, traffic, and development, there's a tiny famous pocket of sand that remains unchanged. The world knows this as the beach where Burt Lancaster kissed Deborah Kerr in *From Here to Eternity*, but our family has always called it "Cockroach Bay." No one knows how it got that name—it's not shaped like the unsightly insect, nor is there a higher-than-normal presence of the critters scampering around. Regardless of its name, however, the east Oahu beach is an idyllic respite, a haven of peace bordered by popular, and crowded, Hanauma Bay and Sandy Beach.

To get there you have to hike down a small cliff to the left of the renowned Halona Blowhole. It's about a five-minute walk to the tiny cove, where often-times you'll be the only folks present. The swim-ming is ideal as most of the bay is sheltered, and there are a few tide pools to explore on either side where the lava borders the ocean. The views are expansive; on a clear day you can see Molokai in the distance, and dur-ing whale season you can almost always see a few spouts erupting in the cobalt blue ocean.

As children, we held birthday parties here; in high school it was the site of our football victory parties. Dur-ing holiday vacations from a Mainland college, it was often the first place we visited to capture the feeling that we were really "back home." Now, as adults, we're grateful that this small stretch of valuable coastline has remained undeveloped, as we take our own children there to explore the tide pools and swim in the bay.

Roy's. 6600 Kalanianaole Highway; (808) 396-7697; www.roysrestaurants.com. If seafood is your favorite, a visit to Roy's is absolutely required; Roy's does seafood right! It's truly a fine showcase for Hawaiian Regional Cuisine. Roy's has grown to multiple locations nation-wide, but this Hawaii Kai site is his first—where it all began—and still the best. Go early to get a window seat so you can watch the sunset over Maunalua Bay. $$$–$$$$

Teddy's Bigger Burgers. 7192 Kalani-anaole Highway, Koko Marina Center; (808) 394-9100; www.teddysbiggerburgers.com. $. See entry in the Kapahulu section.

Where to Stay

There are no hotels in Hawaii Kai. Waikiki is a few miles away.

Waimanalo

Route 72 soon leads to the agricultural town of Waimanalo. As soon as you hit the 7-Eleven, you've arrived.

The landscape is dotted with small farms and old homes. Residents are primarily Hawaiian. At one time this was the center of a thriving sugar plantation. When the plantation closed in the 1940s, so did financial security for residents. But the land is rich and fertile, and things have picked up in recent times. Today most of the bananas, papayas, and anthuriums that fill Honolulu's homes and hotels come from Waimanalo.

Waimanalo Beach Park and Sherwood Forest (all ages)

A few miles beyond Makapu`u Beach; the turnoff from Kalanianaole is just after McDonald's Restaurant.

Waimanalo Beach Park is a great place to learn bodysurfing or boogieboarding. The waves are small enough so you won't get hurt but forceful enough to let you maneuver about. There are restrooms, a picnic area, a pay phone, and a lifeguard on duty. This is Oahu's longest stretch of sandy, swimmable coastline—3½ miles long. It's a veritable paradise for beachcombers!

Just beyond Waimanalo Beach Park, look for the turnoff immediately after the McDonald's. The sign for Sherwood Forest is small and difficult to see, but the beach is definitely worth a stop. The surf is calm, inviting, and a great place for the whole family. The waves aren't big enough to surf, and the water is safe year-round for young children.

The only potential hazard here is the frequent appearance of Portuguese man-of-wars. Look around the shoreline for any that have washed up. They look like quarter-size opaque bubbles with long, bluish tails. A sting is really no big deal and feels much like a bee sting, providing you have no serious allergic complications.

If there are no man-of-wars on the sand, then it's a green light to jump in the water. If you do get stung, the quickest remedy is, believe it or not, meat tenderizer. In fact, most local beachgoing moms and dads always bring a bottle of meat tenderizer with them to the beach . . . just in case.

The beach park is open to the public every weekend, from noon on Friday to 6:00 a.m. on Monday, and on every federal and state holiday, from 6:00 a.m. to 6:00 a.m. the following day.

Bellows Beach (all ages)

Right next door to Sherwood's, just a few minutes' drive down the highway. Open to the public on weekends.

At one time this was a U.S. Air Force base. Today it's a retreat for active-duty personnel, complete with cabins, a grocery store, and campgrounds. As with Sherwood's, water is safe year-round for kids of all ages, the only danger being an occasional appearance of Portuguese man-of-wars.

Camping is allowed with a permit from the City and County of Honolulu Parks and Recreation Department, 650 South King Street, Honolulu, HI 96813; www.co.honolulu.hi.us /parks; or call (808) 523-4525.

Windward Side: Kailua and Kaneohe

After Bellows, Kalanianaole Highway rolls through more agricultural/residential areas until arriving at Kailua and the lush, green windward side of the island. Kailua and Kaneohe are residential communities that seem to beat at a slower pace than those neighborhoods closer to Honolulu. There's a U.S. Marine Corps Air Station in Kaneohe, and many military personnel call this area home.

There are no major resorts here and just a few bed-and-breakfast inns. The result is untouristy, uncrowded beaches. Sailboarders crave the constant winds on this side of the island, and on any given sunny day, you'll see at least a few colorful sails jumping over the waves.

To get to Kailua proper, turn right on Kailua Road from Kalanianaole Highway. Kailua Road winds through central downtown, past old-fashioned storefronts, eateries, and sailboard stores. The street dead-ends at Kalaheo Avenue and the beach.

It is possible to get to Kailua directly from Waikiki instead of traveling though Kahala, Hawaii Kai, and Waimanalo. Take H-1 west and exit at Route 61, the Pali Highway. Continue on 61 through Nuuanu, the Pali Lookout (already discussed in an earlier section), and through the tunnel. Eventually, you'll see a sign pointing to Kailua Road and the entrance to town.

Kailua Bay and Kailua Beach County Park outrank all other beaches on the island as the top choice for sailboarders. Not only do the experienced love to come here, but a variety of commercial outlets take first-timers here to learn.

In addition to sailboarders, the water often is chock-full of boats, Jet Skiers, and kayakers, all competing for the right-of-way. All this activity creates congestion that can be hazardous to a casual swimmer. You get the feeling that you've got to be moving pretty fast or get out of the way! If you're there strictly for swimming, it's best to stay in the shallow waters of the lagoon. The park does offer great picnic facilities, showers, restrooms, lifeguards, and a snack bar.

Just beyond Mokapu Peninsula and the military base sits Kaneohe Bay. A host of oceangoing recreational businesses operate from here and offer a different experience from the similar venues at Waikiki.

Continuing on the Circle Island Tour, look for Route 83, the Kahekili Highway, which will take you all the way up the windward coast to the North Shore, where it turns into the Kamehameha Highway. The drive is beautiful, with the majestic wind-carved Koolau Mountains looming on your left and undeveloped expanses of pristine coastline on the right.

Lanikai Beach (all ages)

Just south of Kailua. To get there follow Kalaheo Avenue south to Mokolua Drive, where you'll see posted signs.

Lanikai Beach is the jewel in the crown for windward residents who count their blessings daily that tourists have yet to begin flocking here. It's breathtakingly beautiful: a milelong

Water Sports Rentals, Tours and Lessons

For experienced sailboarders looking to rent a board and sail, or for the inexperienced itching to learn, contact one of the following vendors:

- **Naish Hawaii.** 155A Hamakua Drive; (808) 262-6068; www.naish.com. Robbie Naish is a champion sailboarder, and his company is well known for its custom boards, sails, hardware, accessories, and repairs. The sailboarding and kiteboarding school offers half-day lessons for $40 to $50, depending on the level. Lessons include one and a half hours of teaching and one and a half hours on the water. (Full-day lessons and group lessons are available at slightly different costs.) If you know your stuff and just want equipment rentals, they've got plenty to choose from.

- **Kailua Sailboards and Kayaks.** 130 Kailua Road; (808) 262-2555; www.kailuasailboards.com. Here you can rent a board and try it on your own first. Sailboarders rent for half-day, full-day, and weekly rates. Group lessons are offered for beginners and cost $89 for four hours. During the week the company brings its equipment right to the beach; on weekends the staff will help you with a pushcart or roof rack at no extra charge. Boogieboards and two-person kayaks are also available to rent at $10 and $59, respectively.

- **Tom's Barefoot Tours.** (808) 942-5077. This vendor offers hotel pickup if you didn't drive out here yourself. Your outing will include transportation to and from Waikiki and a four-hour sail complete with a barbecue lunch, offering a dry way to witness the underwater world on a glass-bottomed catamaran. The water is so clear you can easily see what's swimming around beneath you. Cost is $83 for adults. For children ages three to twelve, the rate is $63, **free** for children younger than three.

expanse of soft white sand and shimmering aquamarine ocean. The surf is generally mild, and the beach is completely swimmable year-round.

Haiku Gardens (all ages)

46–336 Haiku Road, Kaneohe; www.haikugardens.com. **free.**

Up in the hills to the left are the Haiku Gardens, so beautiful they have become a favorite place for locals to have outdoor weddings and host special occasions. Anyone is welcome to walk around. In the early 1800s Hawaiian chiefs gave the land to an engineer from England named Baskerville. He took great care to develop this area in a way that would enhance, not detract from, its natural beauty. There is a series of spring-fed lily ponds, a few homes, and acres of flowers, fruits, and ornamental trees. Later a restaurant was built, today the site of Haleiwa Joe's, specializing in seafood.

Valley of the Temples Memorial Park (all ages)

47–200 Kahekili Highway, Kaneohe; (808) 239-8811. Open 8:30 a.m. to 4:30 p.m. $

The next valley over from Haiku Gardens is known as Valley of the Temples, situated in the green hillsides high above the ocean. You can't miss the white Christian cross that's permanently planted up there. Valley of the Temples is a universal-faith cemetery that's so beautiful, it has become a popular visitor attraction.

If it has rained lately, be sure to scan the cliffs surrounding the valley for picturesque, rainbow-hued waterfalls. They're quite common here.

Byodo-In Temple is the main attraction of the Valley of the Temples. It's a replica of Japan's 900-year-old Byodo-In. Hawaii's temple was built in 1968 on the centennial of the first wave of Japanese immigrants to arrive in the islands. Kids will love having the chance to strike a three-ton brass bell; anyone is allowed to strike it after making an offering.

The grounds exude a sense of peace and contentment; gentle streams trickle slowly over well-placed boulders, koi frolic gracefully in a special pond, and birds chirp from distant trees. There is a small gift shop and snack bar.

Hoomaluhia Regional Park (all ages)

In Kaneohe, start at the end of Luluku Road, which starts a little more than 2 miles down Kamehameha Highway from the Pali Highway. It's 1½ miles up Luluku from the highway to the visitor center; (808) 233-7323. The park is open 9:00 a.m. to 4:00 p.m. daily (except on Christmas and New Year's Day), and admission is free. Guided two-hour nature hikes are held at 10:00 a.m. on Saturday and 1:00 p.m. on Sunday.

Hoomaluhia Regional Park is the county's newest and largest botanical garden, a 400-acre park in the hills above Kaneohe. The park is planted with groups of trees and shrubs from tropical regions around the world. It's a peaceful, lush green setting with a stunning *pali* (cliff) backdrop. Hoomaluhia is not a landscaped flower garden but more of a natural preserve. A network of trails winds through the park and up to a thirty-two-acre lake (no swimming allowed). Bring insect repellent and an umbrella! Full-moon hikes, starting at 6:30 p.m., are offered in July and August. Hikers should bring a picnic dinner, flashlights, and covered shoes.

The little visitor center has displays on flora and fauna, Hawaiian ethnobotany, and the history of the park, which was originally built by the U.S. Army Corps of Engineers as flood protection for the valley below.

Oahu Trivia

Built in 1843, Our Lady of Peace in Honolulu is the oldest Catholic cathedral in the United States.

Senator Fong's Plantation and Gardens (all ages)

47–285 Pulama Road at the outskirts of Kaneohe, near Kahaluu; (808) 239-6775; www .fonggarden.com. Guided nature walks take visitors through the five valleys and plateaus and run at 10:30 a.m. and 1:00 p.m. $$

Senator Fong's Plantation and Gardens is the creation of Hiram Fong, Hawaii's state senator from 1959 to 1976. Upon retirement he set out to create his ideal garden. After a lot of hard labor and dedication, his dream was realized in this idyllic spot.

Waiahole, Waikane, and Kaaawa

The next two towns on the Kahekili Highway, Waiahole and Waikane, are rural agricultural areas, where much of Oahu's taro is grown. Taro is a tuber root that Hawaiians grow to make *poi,* a sticky starch that accompanies every meal. (Be sure to sample some if you attend a luau.) The route is well maintained and a pleasure to drive. Inspirational beauty greets you at every turn.

Kualoa Ranch County Regional Park (all ages)

49–560 Kamehameha Highway, Kaaawa; (808) 237-8515; www.kualoa.com. For activities the park is open 9:30 a.m. to 2:00 p.m. The park is open daily 7:00 a.m. to 7:00 p.m., and overnight camping is allowed with a permit. Admission to both park and ranch is free; you pay for whichever activities you choose to participate in. Reservations are required for activities.

Kualoa Ranch County Regional Park is situated against a backdrop of the spectacular Koolau Mountains. A variety of recreational fun is to be had at the ranch—everything from horseback riding to helicopter tours to ocean cruises and Jet Ski rentals.

The beach park is spacious, pristine, and inviting. It's considered by many to be the best on this side of the island. Although the shoreline is rocky, swimming is safe year-round. If you're here at low tide, you can walk on the reef all the way to Chinaman's Hat, the little island sitting offshore. It's so named because it closely resembles the wide-brimmed hats worn by the Chinese laborers to protect themselves from the glaring sun.

If you do trek to the island, be sure to wear some old, but well-soled, tennis shoes. Also, keep a constant watch on your kids. If a big wave were to suddenly hit, it would be very easy to slip off the reef.

This area possesses great historical significance and is included on the National Register of Historic Places. In Old Hawaii all the chiefs sent their royal children to be educated at this site, now considered sacred.

The park across from the ranch contains complete facilities, including restrooms, picnic tables, and lifeguards.

Oahu Trivia

From the powerful, pounding waves of the North Shore to the gentle shore break of Waikiki, there is a perfect beach on Oahu for every family. Water temperatures on Oahu's 139 beaches range from 75 to 80 degrees year-round. Visit www.aloha.com/~lifeguards/ for the official lifeguards' guide to Oahu's popular guarded beaches.

Kahana Bay Beach County Park and Kahana Valley State Park
(all ages)

A few miles north of Kualoa Ranch.

Swimming is a good year-round activity at Kahana Bay Beach County Park, though it's never crowded. There are picnic facilities, restrooms, a small boat launch, and lifeguards here. It's quite picturesque and representative of all the quaint pockets of beach on this side of the island. It's worth getting out of the car and exploring.

Across the highway is Kahana Valley State Park, an idyllic spot for a picnic. It offers restrooms, picnic tables, and a freshwater stream that runs deep into the valley. Locals often kayak up the stream to the isolated area at the base of the cliffs.

Where to Eat

There are no major restaurants on this stretch of road, but a few convenience stores and fast-food joints are scattered along the way.

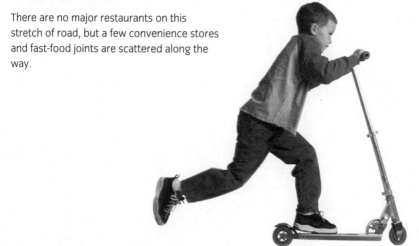

Laie

Continuing on Kahekili Highway.

Brigham Young University, or BYU–Hawaii Campus, is in Laie. Several signs point visitors in the direction of the beautiful Mormon temple.

Polynesian Cultural Center (all ages)

55370 Kamehameha Highway, Laie; (808) 293-3333; www.polynesia.com. Open 12:30 to 6:00 p.m. daily except Sunday. $$$–$$$$, children younger than 5 get in free. A variety of packages are available, including an all-day pass with dinner buffet and evening show (park hours are extended for evening programs). Transportation is also available to and from Waikiki hotels.

Along with Pearl Harbor and Punchbowl, this is among the most-visited sites on the island. The center provides a glimpse into the lifestyles and cultures of the South Pacific Islands.

Here you'll be greeted by islanders representing the seven Polynesian groups: Fiji, Hawaii, New Zealand, Tahiti, Samoa, the Marquesas, and Tonga. Visitors are led through the villages either along waterways in a canoe or on a walking tour. Everyone has the chance to explore the villages, learn the songs and dances, taste the foods, and watch demonstrations of ethnic arts and crafts. A Polynesian extravaganza, complete with hula dancers, fire dancers, and Hawaiian food, is held every night.

A big allure is the IMAX theater, a five-story wraparound movie screen that will make viewers feel as if they're actually paddling a canoe around the sands of Samoa or tromping over trails in the hills of New Zealand.

Kahuku

After passing through Laie, you'll arrive in Kahuku, the last town on this side of the island.

Once a thriving sugar town, Kahuku is now best known for its shrimp farms and fields of aquaculture. You'll see signs advertising fresh (and they do mean fresh) Hawaiian prawns, and there's even a roadside stand with some picnic tables for people who can't wait until they get home.

The Kahuku Mill Shopping Center is on the north end of town. Although it features a few normal mall characteristics, this is no normal place of commerce. It's actually the old sugar mill, cleared of rust and painted in bright colors so it looks like a modern sculpture. If you look carefully, however, you'll be able to see the huge gears and other machinery once used to refine sugar.

Horseback Riding

The guided horseback ride from the **Turtle Bay Resort** takes visitors on a sandy stroll through the complex and into a bit of the natural terrain. Nonguests can participate for a fee, and reservations are required. The forty-five-minute rides are offered daily. Admission for adults is $50. Additional choices include private rides, evening rides, carriage rides, and wagon rides, and for kids too small to ride by themselves, twenty-minute pony rides cost $25. Riders must be at least 4 feet, 6 inches tall. For more information call (808) 293-6000, ext. 25.

Where to Eat

Giovanni's Aloha Shrimp Truck. Next to the sugar mill in Kahuku is a graffiti-covered truck parked on the Kamehameha Highway; (808) 293-1839. Shaded by a tarp, you'll dine on grilled shrimp, shrimp scampi, and hot-and-spicy shrimp. Portions are huge and full of flavor—you won't be disappointed. $$

Where to Stay

Turtle Bay Resort. 57–091 Kamehameha Highway, Kahuku; (808) 293-6000; www.turtle bayresort.com. After the shrimp farms of Kahuku, a large, well-manicured golf course will appear on the right. This is the Turtle Bay Resort, a full-destination property that offers tennis, golf, spa services, horseback trips, and even ATV (three-wheeled all-terrain vehicle) rides on the sand. $$

North Shore

Note that the Kahekili Highway (Route 83) turns into the Kamehameha Highway (Route 99) after the road bends left, or west.

After passing Kahuku and driving around the northern tip of the island, you'll arrive at the fabulous North Shore, a haven for surfers and surf photographers from all over the world. In winter the beaches become the setting where the world's most daring and accomplished surfers ride massive,15-foot waves. When locals say they're going to spend the day in the "country," they're referring to the North Shore, a series of beaches and small towns that radiate relaxed charm and beauty. The water can be very rough here and the currents strong, sometimes even in summer. Kids should be cautioned to stay close to shore.

Sunset Beach is famous worldwide for its huge winter swells, but in the summer it can be as calm as a bathtub. It's appropriately named for its spectacular sunsets, but it's more popular as the site of the World Cup of Surfing. There are no picnic tables or restrooms here, but a lifeguard is on duty.

Directly after Sunset, Ehukai Beach is across the road from the Sunset Beach Elementary School. Ehukai is the site of the famous "Banzai Pipeline," a major attraction for surfers. The pipeline is where the waves break in a round, cylindrical shape, creating a hollow tube. The best surfers are able to disappear inside the tube and emerge a few seconds later on the other side.

Like Sunset Beach, Ehukai is calm and safe during the summer. But in the winter months, do not enter the water under any circumstances.

A large group of tide pools at Pupukea offers an ideal place to see marine life in its natural state. To get there park across the street at the Shell gas station. Look for the long wall that forms a sheltered pool at low tide.

Here safety is an issue only during rough winter swells; when the ocean looks mean and menacing, it's best to stay on dry land. Make sure you wear foot gear and beware of stepping on spiny sea urchins. (They look like porcupines and can poke right through tennis shoes.) It's also a good idea to wear a mask and put your face in the water; you'll be able to see much more.

Continuing on Kamehameha Highway, Waimea Bay is the picturesque beach around the corner from Pupukea. Waimea boasts the biggest rideable surf in the world; wintertime waves can reach 40 feet! During the summer, however, the bay is calm, inviting, and a great place for a family picnic.

Pu`u O Mahuka Heiau State Monument (all ages)

Look for Pupukea Road at the intersection of Kamehameha Highway and Foodland Market. Follow the road up the mountain to beautiful Pu`u O Mahuka Heiau State Monument. At the beginning of the access road, you'll see a sign warning against any farther travel. However, the road is well maintained and safe, and the sign is often ignored.

The heiau occupies about five acres and is marked by a series of stone steps leading to a lower level. It was a luakini temple, different from the healing temple described in Aiea. Human sacrifice was practiced here to honor the war god, Ku. The many stones wrapped in fresh ti leaves are evidence that people still come here to pray.

Waimea Valley Audubon Center (all ages)

59–864 Kamehameha Highway, Haleiwa; (808) 638-7766. Open daily 9:00 a.m. to 5:00 p.m. $$

Located on Oahu's scenic North Shore and formerly known as Waimea Valley Adventure Park, this 1,800-acre site has been transformed from a big-ticket tourist attraction to a true living sanctuary, complete with botanical gardens, wandering peafowl, and a 60-foot waterfall. The new location is thriving; native plants once thought to be extinct are flourishing, as are endangered species of birds. Waimea Valley is home to thirty-six botanical gardens and about 6,000 rare species of plants. In ancient times the valley was a thriving area for taro farmers. Archaeological excavations have uncovered many house foundations and several large heiau. Visitors can enjoy a 3 1/2-mile self-guided nature walk to the 40-foot Waimea Falls.

Haleiwa

The rustic seaside town of Haleiwa sits at the junction of Farrington Highway (Route 930), which continues west along the coast, and Kamehameha Highway (Route 83).

Haleiwa Beach Park is at the entrance to Haleiwa town, a few miles beyond Waimea. The park features a sandy beach, playing field, basketball courts, picnic tables, and restrooms. Jet Ski and sailboarding lessons are available nearby.

Haleiwa's main street is a mixture of funky restaurants, fast-food joints, boutiques featuring handcrafted clothes and jewelry, a few small shopping centers, art galleries, and ramshackle wooden buildings housing surf stores.

You'll see a big crowd in front of Matsumoto's Shave Ice Store, and for good reason. Many locals swear the Matsumoto family makes the best shave ice on the island. (Shave ice is comparable to a snow cone.) The most popular flavor is rainbow, which includes a little bit of everything. For those with a sweet tooth, this is a definite must-visit.

Another "for good reason" crowd will be a little farther down the road at Kua Aina Snack Shop, reputed to have the best burgers this side of Honolulu.

If you pass Haleiwa and continue to head west, Kamehameha Highway changes to Farrington Highway, which ends at Kaena Point. Waialua is adjacent to Haleiwa and is an old but scenic sugar town.

Farther west, Mokuleia is the last nice stretch of beach on this side of the island. It's quite a picturesque site, with picnic facilities, restrooms, lifeguards, and a playground area. The few structures here are part of a camp frequented by local children and church groups during the summer.

Point Natural Area Reserve offers optimal viewing for the albatross, tropical birds, and native vegetation. The point is about 2½ miles from the ends of both the Farrington Highway and Route 930 in Mokuleia. The park is at the most remote point on Oahu, reached by hiking from the western Waianae coast or Mokuleia on the North Shore.

Up in the **Air**

Across the highway from Mokuleia, **Dillingham Airfield** offers a wide variety of airborne tours. Be sure to bring binoculars and a good camera if you choose to flight-see Oahu. The Original Glider Rides offers glider rides that will provide a panoramic view of the North Shore. Flights last about twenty minutes and cost $178 for two people or $100 per person. Flights can be customized to be shorter or longer, so rates vary. Flights are offered daily on a continuing basis, from 10:00 a.m. to 5:30 p.m. There's always a pilot with you to make sure your glider experience includes a return trip.

Flights are available seven days a week, starting at about 10:00 a.m. on a first-come, first-served basis. For more information call (808) 637-0207.

Where to Eat

Café Haleiwa. 66–460 Kamehameha Highway; (808) 637-5516. By far the best breakfast spot in Haleiwa; coveted by surfers, city folks going to the country for the weekend, and locals. It's quick and informal, with generous portions and good values. $$–$$$

Haleiwa Joe's. 66–0011 Kamehameha Highway; www.haleiwajoes.com; (808) 637-8005. This comfy eatery is great for families! It's located next to the Haleiwa bridge, and you'll love the scenic views of the harbor and sunsets. It's a steak-and-seafood-type of place, with both indoor and outdoor seating. There is a kids' menu, too. $$–$$$

Jameson's by the Sea. 62–540 Kamehameha Highway; www.jamesonshawaii.com; (808) 637-6272. Jameson's has become the place to eat, drink, and visit in Haleiwa. It draws crowds and waiting lines even when other nearby restaurants are wide open. The patio atmosphere, with Waialua Bay across the way, adds to the experience. And don't forget to visit the Fudge Factory, which shares space with the restaurant; you won't be able to resist a sample and a take-home supply. $$$–$$$$

Kua Aina. 66–160 Kamehameha Highway; (808) 637-6067. This has been *the* hamburger joint in all of Oahu for as long as my family and I can remember. So many city folks were making the trek out to the "country" for Kua Aina Burgers, they recently expanded to another location in Ward Centre, near downtown—and both sites are packed throughout the day. A must-eat! $$–$$$

Where to Stay

There are no major resorts on this side of the island (the closest one is Turtle Bay, see page 50). Most visitors stay in Waikiki and make day trips out here. However, plenty of vacation rentals are available. For more information visit the Oahu Visitors Bureau Web site: www.visit-oahu.com.

Central Oahu

If you don't detour to Mokuleia and the west side, you'll pass through Haleiwa and the central plains of Oahu on the way back to Waikiki via Route 99.

Dole Pineapple Plantation (all ages)

64–1550 Kamehameha Highway; (808) 621-8408; www.dole-plantation.com. Open daily 9:00 a.m. to 5:00 p.m. $–$$ for tours.

You can't miss the Dole Pineapple Plantation, clearly visible from Route 99. You can taste Dole's field-fresh pineapple slices and juice and the cool Frosty Dole Whip. You'll also get to browse through a collection of unique Hawaiian souvenirs and edibles, including Morrow's nut products and Hawaiian Plantations–brand preserves and condiments. You can buy some fresh-from-the-ground pineapple and walk through the Dole gardens to see the different varieties. The Pineapple Garden Maze ($) covers two acres and is made of 11,400

Hawaii Trivia

The state bird is the nene goose.

Hawaiian plants, including hibiscus, heliconia, joyweed, panax, and plumeria. Along the 3.11-mile path children search for clues at six secret stations to solve the mystery of the maze.

The newest attraction here is the Pineapple Express, a 2-mile, twenty-minute narrated train tour. You'll learn about the history of pineapple and agriculture in Hawaii, hear the fascinating story of James Dole, and see some of the most beautiful scenery on the north shore. Train departs every half-hour between 9:00 a.m. and 5:00 p.m. $–$$

Right next door to the Dole Pineapple Plantation is the Helemano Plantation (www .helemano.org; 808-622-3929), a facility that trains mentally challenged adults. Open to the public daily, the plantation has a bakeshop, two gift shops, a garden, and a restaurant that offers a lunch buffet, salad bar, and sandwich bar.

Look at the intersection of Routes 803 and 80 for Del Monte Pineapple Variety Garden, a small but well-marked and informative roadside garden. Most varieties of pineapple grown worldwide are present and are identified with descriptive signs. There is also a little information about the history of pineapple production in Hawaii. The garden is **free** and well worth the stop.

Wahiawa Botanical Gardens (all ages)
1396 California Avenue; (808) 621-5463. Open daily 9:00 a.m. to 4:00 p.m., except holidays. free.

The gardens encompass twenty-seven acres, with an international collection of exotic trees, ferns, and flowers. Be sure to wear shoes and clothes you don't care about. It's pretty muddy here.

For More Information

Oahu Visitors Bureau. 733 Bishop Street, No. 1520, Honolulu, HI 96813, (808) 524-0722; www.visit-oahu.com.

Maui

Maui, the Valley Isle, is the third most populated and second most visited island. Every year more than two million visitors grace its shores. With 150 miles of coastline, Maui offers several miles of swimmable beaches. Many of these beaches are pristine, shallow, and ideal for children.

The island is named after Maui, a mischievous mythological figure of ancient Hawaii whose antics are recorded in historic chants. One legend says that Maui dragged the Hawaiian Islands out of the ocean with a giant fishhook. Another tale tells of how Maui's mother, Hina, was having a hard time drying out her kapa cloth because the sun moved too quickly across the island. So from the majestic crater of Haleakala, Maui lassoed the sun and forced it to crawl across the sky at a slower pace. Haleakala, known today for its long hours of sunlight and dramatic sunrise views, means "House of the Sun."

Geographically, the island is dominated by Haleakala, the world's largest dormant volcano, and the West Maui Mountains, always picturesque with their ever-present umbrella of lovely green mist.

Julie's TopPicks for Family Fun on Maui

1. Going on a whale-watching trip (in season)

2. Watching the sun rise atop Haleakala

3. Snorkeling at Molokini

4. Driving on the road to Hana and beyond to the Seven Pools

5. Horseback riding on the slopes of Haleakala

6. Visiting the rare animals at Keiki Zoo Maui

7. Riding the Sugar Cane Train in Kaanapali

8. Driving across the northwest tip of the island to Kahakuloa

9. Taking a sailboarding lesson at Kaanapali Beach

10. Exploring the Maui Ocean Center

MAUI

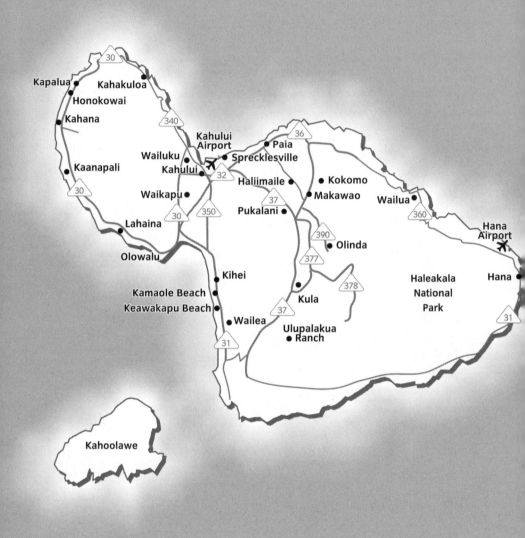

Kapalua · Kahakuloa
Honokowai
Kahana
Kaanapali
Wailuku · Kahului Airport
Kahului
Waikapu
30
350
30
Lahaina
Olowalu
Kihei
Kamaole Beach
Keawakapu Beach
Wailea
31
37
Paia
Sprecklesville
Haliimaile
37
Pukalani
Kokomo
Makawao
Wailua
36
390
Olinda
377
378
Kula
Ulupalakua
Ranch
Hana Airport
Hana
Haleakala National Park
360
31
32
340
30

Kahoolawe

The resorts and condominiums are concentrated in Kaanapali, Kihei, and Lahaina; the rest of the island comprises delightful small towns and nature preserves just begging to be explored.

Beautiful Maui is a sure bet for any vacationer. The lush eastern coast of Hana is replete with isolated waterfalls, fragrant gardens with giant ferns and wild orchids, and old-fashioned Hawaiian charm, while the southern and western coasts of Kaanapali, Lahaina, Kihei, and Wailea offer sunny skies, great snorkeling, and dazzling resorts. In between, dozens of gardens, state parks, and pristine rain forests create a brilliantly colored sparkle over the land.

There is no Circle Island Tour on Maui as there is on Oahu, because the roads do not circumnavigate the entire island. This chapter begins in Lahaina, the most famous city on the island. From there it will cover a circular route as much as possible as it shifts west to Kaanapali and Kapalua and continues over the northwest tip to Kahakuloa and drifts to Kahului. From Kahului we'll head east to Hana and the end of the road at Kipahulu. Then we'll travel the other direction from Lahaina, south along the coast to Kihei and Wailea, to the end of the road at Makena. Inland from Lahaina sits massive Haleakala to the east and Iao Needle Nature Preserve to the west.

Most people fly into Maui's biggest airport in Kahului, although there is a smaller airport in West Maui. Some airlines, including United, Delta, and Hawaiian, fly direct to Kahului from West Coast cities on the Mainland, such as Los Angeles, San Francisco, and Seattle. Otherwise, you'll have to first land at Honolulu International Airport and catch an interisland flight on Hawaiian (800-367-5320; www.hawaiianair.com). Sometimes the connecting flights can be booked as a package deal with your main airfare. If not, expect to spend about $100 to $150 per person. Hawaiian Airlines offers frequent-flier mileage that will be accepted by some major Mainland-based carriers.

Even though many of the island's resorts offer **free** airport pickup, and most of the excursion companies, such as snorkeling and sightseeing tours, offer transportation to and from your hotel as part of the package, it's a good idea to rent a car on Maui. It's easy to navigate around the island, and having your own set of wheels will reward you with miles and miles of beauty to explore.

Whether you're strolling through Lahaina or your own hotel lobby, you'll likely feel overwhelmed with all the tours to choose from: sightseeing, snorkeling, hiking, bicycling, and so on. Tour desks are everywhere and offer extensive choices and venues, ranging from bicycles to catamarans to helicopters. These tours are great because most are led by guides knowledgeable in Maui's flora, fauna, and history, but don't think that packaged tours are a necessity to discover Maui's charms. Armed with this book and a good driving map, you'll be able to devise a do-it-yourself tour that's guaranteed to please.

West Maui: Lahaina

Visitors flock to the historic city of Lahaina, considered by many to be a smaller version of Oahu's Waikiki. There are enough shops, historic sites, restaurants, museums, art galleries, and fun activities to please a variety of discriminating tastes.

Whale-Watching Central

One thing you're sure to notice immediately upon arrival is Maui's fascination with the mighty humpback whale. Of all the islands and all the channels in between, the southwest coast of Maui offers the best chance to see these mighty creatures. The whales seem to favor the warm, protected waters within the boundaries of Kahoolawe, Lanai, Molokai, and Maui. The area of ocean that surrounds Maui has been designated as the Hawaiian Islands Humpback Whale National Marine Sanctuary.

From Kaanapali in the west to Makena in the south, several dozen commercial boat operators offer tours that will guarantee a whale sighting (in season—November through April). It pays to shop around, as some will offer discounts to children and free transportation to and from your hotel. Others offer breakfast and/or lunch and include a snorkeling trip along with the whale watching.

If you opt for a tour that includes a snorkeling excursion and it's during the whale-watching season, be sure to stick your head underwater and listen carefully. One thing that differentiates humpbacks from other whales is their ability to sing. Although no one has yet been able to decipher their songs, it is clear that they communicate. Researchers from the Pacific Whale Foundation in Kihei say the singers are "escort males" that protect the females and their offspring. Intriguingly, all humpback whales sing the same song, over and over again.

Even if you can't hear the song, the whale-watching trip will be an unforgettable experience. You have to keep your eyes on the horizon and look for spouts. As soon as you see a spout, keep looking in that same area for a whale to breach. A breaching whale rises out of the water, arches its enormous body, and splashes back into the Pacific. It's an amazing feeling to witness such an impressive force of nature. When you see a mammal weighing several tons throw its body out of the water and land with a resounding "thump," it's quite awe-inspiring. Full-grown humpback whales can be more than 45 feet long and weigh more than forty tons!

The waters surrounding the Hawaiian Islands are designated a safe haven for these return visitors. Commercial whale-watching tour operators are prohibited from chasing a whale and from moving too close. Nothing, however, prohibits the sometimes curious whales from investigating you! Most boat captains, upon sighting a whale, will simply turn off the engine or take down the sails and drift. Oftentimes, a whale will swim right up to the boat, then turn on its side so it can check out the passengers with its large eye. Once you've stared right into the eye of a whale, you'll never forget the experience. For whale-watching tours families can expect to spend $30 to $99 per person, depending on the season, the length of the tour, and the inclusion of meals. Humpbacks can also be seen along the west and south Maui shoreline. Favorable vantage points along the west shore include Papawai Point, McGregor Point scenic overlook, Launiupoko State Wayside, and Wahikuli State Wayside; on the south shore, Wailea Beach Park. The Pacific Whale Foundation, 300 Maalaea Road #211 (800) 942-5311 or (808) 249-8811; www.pacificwhale .org), supports its research with daily whale-watching cruises beginning in November and running through May.

Not only is modern-day Lahaina a playground for locals and visitors, its colorful history shows it has been a center for fun, frolic, and politics since the early 1800s. By the time King Kamehameha the Great died in 1819, the islands were consolidated under one rule, and the king's successor, Kamehameha II, designated Lahaina as the first capital city. Kamehameha the Great had already commissioned the Brick Palace, Hawaii's first building, in 1801, and ruins from that original structure still remain in Lahaina. Although Kamehameha II later moved the central seat of government to Honolulu, where it remains today, Lahaina continued to be a hot spot of activity.

During the boom of the whaling industry, Lahaina was the world's greatest port, accommodating more than 500 ships at once in its bustling harbor. Whalers were known for their good-time revelry, and a jail was built in 1859 to hold combatants from barroom brawls and vagrants who couldn't handle their liquor.

Then the missionaries came and tried to bring Christianity and order to a society proud of its drunken disorder. Churches and schools were built as followers of Christianity tried to squelch the alleged debauchery and rid the saloons of liquor.

Today Lahaina retains some of that mischievous lifestyle by holding onto its reputation as a "good-time" town. But it's a lot more wholesome and low-key than Waikiki, and residents try hard to keep it that way for 364 days a year. The one day when the rebellious ghosts come alive is Halloween. The whole town celebrates All Hallows' Eve with a daylong party and parade. Everyone in costume is invited to participate, including children, and storekeepers and restaurateurs open their doors to hordes of celebrators. Locals come from throughout the state to join in the fun. It's by far the biggest Halloween party in all Hawaii. If you're on Maui at the end of October, don't miss it.

The rest of the year, Lahaina is frequented by an equal blend of tourists and locals looking for some fun. Friday evenings are known as Art Night. Galleries offer free snacks and drinks, and artists are present to answer questions about their work. It's a fun time, but unless your kids have a strong artistic bent, they may not find it interesting.

Lahaina **Walking Tour**

The best way to visit all the historic sites in Lahaina is with a self-guided, half-day, historic walking tour. The sites are clearly marked on Front Street, the town's main artery. You can pick up a **free** map that highlights the best places at the headquarters for the Lahaina Restoration Foundation, in the Master's Reading Room, on Front and Dickenson Streets; visit www.lahaina restoration.org; or call (808) 661-3262.

Even if you cringe at the thought of shopping for yet another souvenir T-shirt, don't miss a visit to the Crazy Shirts store at 865 Front Street in northern Lahaina. Within the store is a small Whaling Museum full of harpoons, navigational instruments, gaffs, and pieces of engraved scrimshaw. **free** admission; (808) 661-4775. Also check out the Whaler's Locker, (780 Front Street; 808-661-3775), for the popular fishhook pendants.

At the southern end of town, it's impossible to miss the huge 50-foot-high banyan tree. It was planted in 1873 to commemorate the fiftieth anniversary of the first missionary arrival in Lahaina and covers more than two-thirds of an acre with its shade. It's the largest banyan tree in the United States. A flowering of the arts blooms every second and fourth weekend here. Called Art in the Park, it offers affordable paintings, limited edition prints, and a huge variety of crafts from local artisans.

Nearby are the remnants of the Brick Palace and a fort built in the 1830s to prevent cannons fired by angry whalers from destroying a missionary compound. Although today the fort looks like nothing more than a rock pile, it was once 20 feet high. It was built from coral rocks hauled onto shore from the reef.

Don't miss a visit to the Hauola Stone, a historic rock just right of the Brick Palace. You'll notice it right away because it looks like a huge chair. Precontact Hawaiians believed this stone had healing powers and if you sat in it and let the waves wash over you, you would be cured. (*Precontact* is used to refer to the Hawaiian civilization before the arrival of western explorers, such as Capt. James Cook.)

Behind the banyan sits the courthouse, built in 1859. The jail in the basement has been converted into the home of the Lahaina Art Society, where artworks sit behind bars until purchased. The four cannons at the courthouse were salvaged from a sunken Russian barge.

One of Lahaina's most famous landmarks, the Best Western Pioneer Inn, is on the other side of the banyan on Front Street. The inn (808-661-3636; www.pioneerinn-maui .com) was built in 1901 for interisland passengers. Although it has been remodeled, it maintains its old-fashioned charm. Many people think it was built to house the rowdy seamen when whaling was king, but by 1901 the whaling industry was no longer prominent. The inn is decorated as a tribute to Lahaina's former industry, with swinging doors and signs warning against improper behavior.

The Baldwin House Museum (all ages)
696 Front Street; (808) 661-3262. Open daily 10:00 a.m. to 4:00 p.m. $

The museum is one of the first stops on a walking tour of Lahaina. It was home to the Doctor and Reverend Dwight Baldwin, his wife, Charlotte, and their eight children. Baldwin was the first western dentist and doctor in the islands, and his home, built in 1834 and the oldest building in Lahaina, quickly became a local fixture.

The home itself, the household furniture, the aged photographs and artifacts, the displays, and the library present a fascinating picture of life in the the Hawaiian Islands.

The Wo Hing Temple (all ages)
858 Front Street; (808) 661-5553. Open daily 10:00 a.m. to 4:00 p.m. Admission is by donation.

The Wo Hing Temple is another highlight of the historic walking tour. It's at the far north end of town, across the street from the Lahaina Whaling Museum. It has been converted to a museum and is home to a Buddhist shrine and many exhibitions depicting Chinese heritage in Hawaii, especially Lahaina. Also, don't miss a visit to the cookhouse next door, where film clips are played that show Lahaina in 1899 and 1906.

Old Lahaina Luau (all ages)
Held on the beach at 1251 Front Street; (800) 248-5828 or (808) 667-1998; www.oldlahaina luau.com. $$$$.

The food is authentic Hawaiian and delicious. At sunset guests sit at tables or on fiber mats on the ground in front of a grass-mound stage. The program includes intelligent narration and excellent ancient hula.

Various hotels in the Kaanapali/Wailea area also offer Polynesian extravaganzas and, except for a few different dance numbers, are basically equal in terms of value, entertainment, and good food.

Where to Eat

There are dozens of wonderful places to eat in Lahaina, and many of the restaurants offer kiddie menus. What follows is a small sampling and is by no means comprehensive.

Cheeseburger in Paradise. 811 Front Street; (808) 661-4855. Burgers and breezes are the highlight here, though there are salads and fish too. Lunch and dinner only; special kids' menu. Great place for cooling off and relaxing after a hard morning in the T-shirt shops. $

Lahaina Grill. 127 Lahainaluna Road; (808) 667-5117; www.lahainagrill.com. One of the hottest, most popular spots for dinner in Lahaina, and with good reason. Try Chef David Paul's signature dish, tequila shrimp and firecracker rice. A fine wine list accompanies the menu. Be sure to make a reservation since this place is always packed. $$$$

Gerard's. At Plantation Inn, 174 Lahainaluna Road; (808) 661-8939; www.gerardsmaui .com. This gourmet, yet casual, restaurant, founded by a master French chef, offers fresh food and hearty entrees of lamb, pork, veal, poultry, sweetbreads, and salt roast duck. A delicate blend of French ideas with Maui-

Hawaii's First School and First Printing Press

While touring Lahaina, look for the *L* painted on the hills above town. When the missionaries arrived, one of their first projects was to build a school for their own children and the children of natives whom they were able to convert. *Lahainaluna*, completed in 1831, was the first school in all Hawaii. It was a boarding school for children throughout Hawaii and even California.

In 1834 an old Ramage Press was shipped from Honolulu and installed on campus. Students were taught how to set type, operate the press, create copper engravings, and bind books. Textbooks and teaching aids were created and continually improved. The original press printed the first newspaper west of the Rocky Mountains on February 14, 1834. It was a four-page weekly school paper called *Ka Lama Hawaii*. This put Lahaina on the map as a printing capital of the islands. The students also composed a classic tale of ancient Hawaiian life and traditions titled *Mo`olelo Hawaii*. An original 1838 copy is on display at the museum.

It's still an educational institution today, as one of Maui's public high schools, and it still functions as a boarding school. Every year in April the students celebrate the memory of the school's most famous alumnus, David Malo, who wrote *Hawaiian Antiquities* (published in 1898 by the Bishop Museum Press).

grown ingredients produces such enchantments as ahi with bearnaise sauce. Dinner only. $$$$

Kimo's. 845 Front Street; (808) 661-4811; www.kimosmaui.com. Located in the heart of Lahaina, this restaurant gets busy for good reason. The food is wonderful, with the atmosphere provided by a torch-lit balcony overlooking the ocean; there's also a special children's menu. Kimo's is worth a wait. $$$–$$$$

Kobe Steak House & Sushi Bar. 136 Dickenson Street; (808) 667-5555; www .kobemaui.com. A Japanese country inn–style eatery where six to eight guests sit around a large table with a grill in the middle. The chef does his thing right there in front of you, slicing and dicing ("faster than a Vegematic," he claims) in the teppanyaki style of cooking. It's

all stir-fried, and the vegetables and meats are done to perfection. Served with rice and chopsticks (knife and fork optional). The show is as good as the food. Dinner only; special menu for kids. $$$

Longhi's. 888 Front Street; (808) 667-2288; www.longhi-maui.com. One of Lahaina's long-time standards, Longhi's Front Street location is a favorite gathering place for visitors as well as locals. Food is Italian-oriented, though there are plenty of the basics. The menu is provided verbally by the waiter, who may start by asking what you like—salads, sandwiches, pasta, and so on—then expanding on the choices. Also located in Wailea, and at Ala Moana Shopping Center on Oahu. $$$–$$$$

Maui Tacos. A Mexican fast-food restaurant on different parts of the island: Lahaina Square, (808) 661-8883; Napili Plaza, (808)

665-0222; Kamaole Beach Center in Kihei, (808) 879-5005; and Kaahumanu Center in Kahului, (808) 871-7726; www.mauitacos .com; also several locations nationwide. Our kids wanted to eat here every day. Favorite dishes: the Lahaina surf burrito with Jack and cheddar cheese, rice, guacamole, salsa, and charbroiled chicken or steak; and the Hookipa surf burrito of fresh island fish, black beans, salsa, rice, and sour cream. $

Where to Stay

Lahaina Inn. 127 Lahainaluna Road; (808) 661-0577 or (800) 669-3444. This is a wonderfully restored mansion with twelve rooms decorated with antique furniture. $$–$$$

Kaanapali

Heading west from Lahaina on Route 30 on the way to Kaanapali, the first beach worth stopping at is Puamana Beach County Park. The views from here are beautiful, and it's a great spot to enjoy a picnic in the shade.

Continuing on Route 30, look oceanside for Wahikuli State Wayside Park, another ideal picnic spot. Across the street, facilities include restrooms and tennis courts.

Shortly beyond Wahikuli, Route 30 (the Honoapi`ilani Highway) leads west to Kaanapali, an outstanding 4-mile stretch of coastline. Developers sure knew what they were doing when they chose this area for a full-scale resort. The weather is almost always strikingly sunny, and the beaches are among the best on the island. Although the coastline is heavily developed with condos and hotels, you needn't be staying here to enjoy the beach; access is easy and widespread. On the far east end is the Hyatt Regency Maui; from there starts a string of properties ending with the Royal Lahaina Resort. In addition to accommodations, the area includes Whalers Village (description follows), which has a shopping center, restaurants, and world-class golf courses. The beaches are beautiful here and safe year-round. The waters are warm and shallow, ideal for young children.

Kaanapali Beach is a great spot to learn how to sailboard; I learned here myself when I was a child, though we called it windsurfing back then. Lessons can be arranged through any of the hotels' activities desks or from Kaanapali Windsurfing (808-667-1964).

You can ride throughout the area on the **free** Kaanapali Trolley and to Lahaina on the Kaanapali-Lahaina Shuttle. A one-way ride on the shuttle costs $1. It goes from Kaanapali to the Cannery Mall, Hilo Hattie's, the Wharf, and back to Kaanapali.

Black Rock (all ages)
Bordering the Sheraton Maui at the far end of the resort.

Also known as Pu`u Keka`a, this is a large chunk of lava that's part of the restored Sheraton property. Although you'll no doubt see lots of local kids jumping off the rock for a quick thrill, the better action is underwater. Here, snorkelers are treated to schools of brightly

Water **Excursions**

Lahaina Harbor is a busy site, with dozens of boat companies headquartered there. Most of the boats have a ticket booth right on the pier. There is a huge variety of options for ocean tours: snorkeling, whale watching, dinner cruises, sunset cruises, snorkel/whale-watching combos, barbecue lunch cruises, continental breakfast cruises, and so on. All tours will offer snorkeling instruction if needed, and most of the crew members are locals who have a fine appreciation for Maui's waters and are willing to share their marine-biology knowledge. It's best to walk around the harbor and shop for the excursion most suited to your budget and family. The following list is by no means comprehensive; it's a small sampling of companies and tours enjoyed by our family. There are several more options, as evidenced by a short walk around the harbor.

- **Trilogy Excursions** (808-874-5649 or 888-225-6284; www.sailtrilogy.com) cruises to Lanai and serves a breakfast and gourmet lunch on the way. Once on Lanai, you're given a quick tour of Lanai City, then taken to Hulopo`e Bay for snorkeling. Trilogy also goes to Molokini and throughout Kaanapali.

- **Club Lanai** (808-871-1144 or 888-733-9425) also goes to Lanai, where a mini-resort is set up for snorkeling, kayaking, Jet Skiing, cycling, playing volleyball and horseshoes, and even guided wagon tours of the Pineapple Island.

- **Lahaina Divers** (143 Dickenson Street; (808-667-7496 or 800-998-3483; www .lahainadivers.com) offers guided scuba and snorkel dives and rents equipment. Multiple locations on the island.

- **Scuba Shack** (2349 South Kihei Road; (808-879-3483 or 877-213-4488; www .scubashack.com) offers guided tours and a variety of rental equipment, including boogieboards.

For a truly wonderful sensation of flight, try parasailing. You sit in a swing-like harness that's attached on one end to a huge parachute and on the other end to a winch on a boat. As the boat speeds up, the wind catches the parachute and lifts you high in the sky. Not only are the views spectacular, but the fun "weightless" experience is truly one you'll remember long after your vacation ends. (Not wanting to interfere with whale season, parasailing is available from May 16 through December 14 only.) For more information call West Maui Parasail at (808) 661-4060; www.westmauiparasail.com. Kids must weigh more than forty-five pounds to participate.

colored fish frolicking in clear water. (Don't worry, those cliff jumpers can spot snorkelers and are careful about where they land.)

For fabulous scenic vistas you can climb to the top of the rock. There are guardrails and a paved path, so it's safe and easy. Ancient Hawaiians believed this was one of several sites from which the spirits of the dead departed Earth and entered the spiritual world.

Tour of the Stars (ages 6 and up)

At the Hyatt Regency Maui; (808) 661-1234. Three one-hour shows daily, at 8:00, 9:00, and 10:00 p.m. $$$–$$$$

NOTE: Younger kids are allowed to go but may not be so interested.

Kids will love the Tour of the Stars. An in-house astronomy expert leads guests on a tour of the night sky through a deep-space telescope known as Big Blue. The telescope is equipped with a computer that is programmed to identify and locate 1,000 objects, including planets, star clusters, nebulae, and galaxies. This is all done from the hotel rooftop nine stories up.

Whalers Village Mall and Museum (all ages)

The shopping center is located in the heart of Kaanapali. Hours vary for individual shops and restaurants; www.whalersvillage.com. Museum is open daily 9:00 a.m. to 10:00 p.m.; (808) 661-5992. **free**.

Whalers Village Mall and Museum is filled with shops and restaurants and is definitely worth a visit. The **free** display area on the upper level offers an in-depth look at Maui's whaling industry, whaling life, and the brave men who hunted these fearsome mammals. Kids will be fascinated by the real whale skeleton. There is also a reconstructed section of an old whaling ship, accompanied by authentic photographs, drawings, and artifacts from actual ships.

Visitors to the Whalers Village Museum can immerse themselves in the seafaring life of the nineteenth-century whalers via a self-guided audio tour. In the tour a narrator comments on the fascinating hunt for whales as if reading from his own ship's log—complete with sounds of a creaking ship, crashing ocean, and excited shouts of "thar she blows!"

In addition to this tour, the Whalers Village also has a program of daily entertainment and activities. During the evening shoppers may be treated to a keiki ukulele concert, Japanese folk dance, Tahitian dancers, taiko drummers, or an ancient hula kahiko show. Shows are 6:30 and 7:30 nightly. Throughout the week, a Director of Fun leads a daily family program featuring a variety of **free** activities such as sand prints, palm weaving, lei making, and other arts and crafts at the Creation Station. And, for that perfect Kodak moment, shoppers can also become part of a fantasy underwater scene at the Sea Village.

Sugar Cane Train (all ages)

Trains depart Kaanapali at 10:25 and 11:55 a.m. and 1:55, 3:25, and 4:55 p.m. daily. Call (808) 667-6851 or (800) 499-2307; www.sugarcanetrain.com. $$–$$$

Miles and miles of sugar cane still grow in fields across the highway from Kaanapali Resort. Although the sugar industry is no longer the powerful moneymaker it was in the late 1800s, a few scenic, sweet acres remain. The Lahaina, Kaanapali, and Pacific Railroad, today known as the Sugar Cane Train, used to haul the crops from the inland valleys to the coast, where ships waited in the bay, ready to transport the cane to refineries.

The train is a fun excursion and offers a glimpse into a historic way of life that changed Hawaii for generations. The narrow-gauge trains are modeled after steam locomotives that were used in the 1890s and take visitors on the same tracks on which crops were hauled.

There are new options for train lovers aboard the Sugar Cane Train. A new, private, air-conditioned Aloha Coach is available for private parties, weddings, family reunions, and so forth. The weekly Aloha Express family event includes a round-trip train ride, dinner, and special entertainment.

Bicycle Rentals: West Maui Cycles (all ages)

1087 Limahana Place; (808) 661-9005; www.westmauicycles.com. Open Monday through Saturday 9:00 a.m. to 5:00 p.m., and 10:00 a.m. to 4:00 p.m. Sunday.

The Kaanapali Resort area lends itself to exploring via bicycle—you can maneuver between properties and attractions quite easily. To rent a bike and cycle at your own speed, expect to pay about $40 a day, less for multiple-day rentals, for a basic standard mountain bike.

Cultural **Advisors**

Hawaiian culture is undergoing a statewide renaissance, and resorts are taking it upon themselves to educate tourists. Most resorts employ native Hawaiian cultural advisors to help them incorporate local traditions into their programs and oversee celebrations of native Hawaiian arts and events that draw people from all over the island.

The cultural advisor at the Ritz-Carlton Kapalua (One Ritz-Carlton Drive; 808-669-6200) conducts the "Sense of Place" tour every Tuesday and Friday at 10:00 a.m. This free presentation, open to guests and nonguests, begins with the film, "Then There Were None." By the end of the 1800s, disease and displacement had reduced the number of native Hawaiians from 300,000 to 50,000. Europeans and Americans controlled the islands, and Hawaiians became a minority in their own land. At present they can't afford to live on the land their families have inhabited for generations.

The tour continues outside, where you are asked to look across the grounds between the Ritz-Carlton and the beach. The Ritz-Carlton was intended as a beachfront property. During construction, nearly 1,700 graves were discovered beneath these rolling, grassy dunes. Without balking, the company spent several million dollars to redesign and move the hotel. The respect the company showed for this ancient Hawaiian burial ground has been emulated throughout the islands.

Where to Eat

All the resort properties in Kaanapali offer great choices for dining. Here are a few of the many:

Ono Bar & Grill. 2365 Kaanapali Parkway; (808) 667-2525. An all-purpose, do-every-thing, basic eatery, located near the Westin Maui's swimming pool, with permanent umbrellas for shade control over its open-air tables. Ono's has breakfast, lunch, and dinner service; a children's menu; an island breakfast buffet; a Sunday champagne brunch; and a "tapas" style Hawaiian dinner. The buffet is another of those good bargains, but soups, salads, and entrees are better than average too. $$$$

Hula Grill. Whalers Village, 2435 Kaanapali Parkway; (808) 667-6636; www.hulagrill.com. This Hawaiian-style beach house serves sea-food and steak. Light-meal appetizers, salads, sandwiches, and pizza are also available. Try the spicy coconut calamari, grilled chicken sandwich, or pesto pizza with macadamia nuts. $$–$$$$

Leilani's on the Beach. On Kaanapali Beachfront walkway at Whalers Village; (808) 661-4495; www.leilanis.com. Sit as close to the ocean as you can and enjoy the passing parade as you sip tall, cool refreshments or nibble the edibles. Food is reasonably priced standard fare of fish, steaks, chicken, and lamb specialties, with a special kids' menu. Open for lunch and dinner or just beverages from 11:30 a.m. to 11:00 p.m. $$$

Pavillion. 200 Nohea Kai Drive; (808) 661-1234. The all-purpose dining center for the Hyatt Regency Maui Hotel in Kaanapali, this poolside restaurant is open 11:00 a.m. to 5:00 p.m. daily. It offers lunch only, featuring a nice selection of salads, burgers, sand-wiches, and pizzas, but a light-fare menu is available all day, and there's a kids' menu. $$

Rusty Harpoon. At Whalers Village; (808) 661-3123; www.rustyharpoon.com. The view is great, the ambience pleasant, and the food

good. Rusty Harpoon is located at the west end of the Whalers Village shopping mall and projects out toward Kaanapali Beach. Though only a short patch of beach is visible, it's enough to provide a continuous floor show during lunch or dinner. The restaurant is in a huge lanai open to all the breezes, which makes dining doubly pleasant. Children's menu. $$$–$$$$

Son'z Maui at Swan Court. 200 Nohea Kai Drive; (808) 661-1234. Superlatives abound for this five-star dining experience in the Hyatt Regency Maui Resort. Go for breakfast first so you can experience the lagoon-side ambience in bright early daylight. (Son'z Maui is not open for lunch.) Then starve yourself for a day and make a dinner visit to what may be Maui's most elegant restaurant. If you can't do both, then at least make an early evening reservation so you can get a table nearest the lagoon, where you can enjoy the swans floating serenely around the cooling waterfall, the sunset colors, and the incred-ible service. $$$$

Where to Stay

In Kaanapali (and at Kapalua and Wailea as well), most of the hotel/resort properties offer children's programs that will occupy your kids for the better part of a day with a variety of recreational and cultural activities.

ResortQuest Kaanapali Shores. 3445 Honoapi`ilani Highway; (808) 667-2211 or (877) 997-6667; www.resortquesthawaii.com. Offers Camp Kaanapali for children of regis-tered guests, ages five to twelve, 8:00 a.m. to 3:00 p.m., Monday to Friday. Supervised activities include educational nature walks, Hawaiian crafts, storytelling, and hula les-sons. $–$$$$

Kaanapali Beach Club. 104 Kaanapali Shores Place; (808) 661-2000 or (877) 696-6284; www.kaanapali-beach-club.com. Offers Beach Buddies for kids ages five to

Maui Trivia

The east Maui rain forest contains more species of endangered forest birds than anywhere else in the state.

twelve, 8:30 a.m. to noon daily. Activities include lei making, miniature golf, leaf painting, nature walks, bird handling, sand art, coconut designs, T-shirt decorating, and swimming in the one-acre oceanside pool. The program includes a T-shirt on the first day of participation and lunch . $$–$$$

Hyatt Regency Maui Resort & Spa. 200 Nohea Kai Drive; (808) 661-1234; www.maui .hyatt.com. Camp Hyatt Kaanapali available for kids ages five to twelve, 9:00 a.m. to 3:00 p.m. and 6:00 to 10:00 p.m. daily. The greatest adventure your *keiki* (kids) will ever have. Hop aboard a real Sugar Cane Train, build sandcastles, take an undersea submarine adventure, or visit the Maui Ocean Center. Meet native animals face to face on an incredible jungle tour. $$$$

Kaanapali Alii. 50 Nohea Kai Drive; (808) 667-1400; www.classicresorts.com. The Alii Kids Club is for children ages six to twelve. Hours are seasonal; it's best to call ahead to confirm. Registered guests under the age of twelve get **free** membership. Activities include tennis, lei making classes, lauhala weaving, and visits to the Maui Ocean Center. Tennis is also offered daily from 3:00 to 4:00 p.m. $$–$$$

Kaanapali Beach Hotel. 2525 Kaanapali Parkway; (808) 661-0011 or (800) 262-8450; www.kbhmaui.com. Offers daily Aloha Passport for Kids for ages five to twelve. Aloha Passport for Kids is a **free** program of year-round fun for the entire family! All children receive an "Aloha Passport" featuring various "destinations" including shops and restaurants through-out the property, as well as Hawaiian activities such as hula lessons, lauhala weaving, or flower lei making. At each destination, children receive a gift and a stamp in their passport. $$–$$$$

Marriott's Maui Ocean Club. 100 Nohea Kai Drive; (808) 667-1200 or (800) 845-5279; www.marriott.com. Offers Kaanapali Kids for ages five to twelve, 8:00 a.m. to 2:00 p.m. Tuesday, Thursday, and Friday. This year-round program takes kids on exciting outdoor adventures and allows them to experience Hawaiian activities such as learning about Hawaii's marine life, arts and crafts, lei making, hula dancing, and an unforgettable cruise on a glass-bottom submarine boat. $$–$$$

Napili Kai Beach Resort. 5900 Hono-apiilani Road; (808) 669-6271 or (800) 367-5030; www.napilikai.com. Offers Napili Keiki Club for ages six to ten, Monday through Saturday. Activities include Hawaiian games, hula lessons, lei making, parent/child golf putting, and nature/ecology walks. **free** of charge during holiday times; spring break, Thanksgiving, Christmas, and summer (mid-June through August). $$–$$$

Sheraton Maui. 2605 Kaanapali Parkway; (808) 661-0031; www.sheraton-maui .com. Offers Keiki Aloha, for children ages five to twelve, 9:00 a.m. to 3:00 p.m. daily. Half-day and evening programs are also available. This fun-filled program held at Sheraton's sister property, the Westin Maui, combines Hawaiian history and culture with arts, crafts, and games. Build a sandcastle, twist a ti leaf bracelet, learn how to make leis, dance the hula, make tapa prints, mix smoothies, create sand art, and take a wildlife tour. Lunch is included and children receive a souvenir T-shirt on the first day of participation. Children are picked up in the hotel lobby at 8:30 a.m. and returned at 3:15 p.m. $$$$

Westin Maui. 2365 Kaanapali Parkway; (808) 667-2525; www.westinmaui.com.

Keiki Kamp for kids ages five to twelve, 9:00 a.m. to 3:00 p.m. daily. Half-day and evening programs are also available. Hands-on activities include sandcastle building, Hawaiian crafts, water fun, tennis, kite flying, lei making, hula lessons and show, face painting, and friendship-jewelry making. Lunch is included and children receive a souvenir T-shirt on the first day. $$$$

Honokowai, Kahana, and Kapalua

Continuing on Honoapi`ilani Highway beyond Kaanapali, you'll pass through the towns of Kahana and Honokowai, easily noticed by the plethora of apartments and condominiums. This is a great area to stay in if you're traveling on a budget. Although you won't get the variety of amenities offered by such destinations as Kaanapali Resort or Kapalua, farther west, you can find great values, and the beaches remain sunny, beautiful, and, compared to the other resorts, relatively uncrowded.

Honokowai Beach County Park (all ages)
To get to Honokowai Beach County Park in Honokowai, take the Lower Honoapi`ilani Highway, which runs along the coast to the Upper Honoapi`ilani Highway. The beach park is easy to find.

As long as it's not too windy here, the shallow waters are a great place for children to play on an uncrowded beach. There's also an oversized lawn framed by lots of palm trees and dotted with picnic tables.

Ironwood Ranch Horseback Rides (ages 8 and up)
The ranch offers hotel pickup from the Kaanapali and Kapalua resort areas. To participate in rides, children must be at least 8 years old and 4 feet tall and must be accompanied by an adult. For more information call (808) 669-4991, or go to www.ironwoodranch.com. $$$$

The Ironwood Ranch offers tours of this area on horseback. Gentle horses can take beginners for a one-and-a-half-hour ride that costs $90 and includes refreshments. Riders can opt for visiting pineapple fields, mountains, or tropical rain forests, or going on a sunset trip. Rates vary according to the length of the ride. A two-hour sunset ride costs $120 per person.

Road Trip Around the Island's Isolated Western Tip

Continuing on the Lower Honoapi`ilani Highway, the road winds around the whole northwest tip of Maui, eventually turning into Route 33, the Kahekili Highway, and ending up in Wailuku. The road is rugged and the bane of car rental companies, but it is doable, and the sights along the way are extraordinarily beautiful. You'll pass isolated old homes and churches, and new waterfalls will greet you around many of the corners. If it's misty, you'll feel as if you're driving through the clouds to an idyllic spot that time has ignored. You'll pass through a few charming, picturesque towns, the biggest of which is **Kahakuloa**.

Please be cautious along this road; at many spots there's room for only one car, and you have to pull over or back up to let another car pass. If the weather is rainy, it's not a good idea to travel here; mudslides are prevalent. As you come over the tip of Maui, you'll leave the quiet hills and valleys for the next city, Wailuku, mostly a residential community.

Water Sports: A & B Rentals (all ages)

3481 Lower Honoapi`ilani Highway, Kahana; (808) 669-0027. Open daily 9:00 a.m. to 4:00 p.m. $–$$

Here you can rent snorkel gear for $2.50 per day or $8.95 per week, plus a selection of other water toys such as boogieboards, surfboards, beach chairs, bicycles, and umbrellas.

Where to Eat

The Ritz-Carlton Kapalua, located at One Ritz-Carlton Drive, (808) 669-6200, provides several restaurant choices, but these are our two favorites:

Banyan Tree Pool Restaurant. This plantation-style dining room is strategically located right next to the hotel's three-tiered swimming pool so hungry bathers can drop in for a refill (pool open to hotel guests only). Try the white bean soup, a local favorite. Open for lunch and dinner; piano and guitar players entertain in the evening. Kids' menu. $$–$$$$

Beach House. It's a long walk from the beach back up to the main dining rooms, so the Ritz-Carlton thoughtfully provided a convenient oceanfront bistro adjacent to Fleming's Beach. This open-air dining area features high-quality sandwiches, crispy salads, and the ever-present hamburger. Kids' menu. $

The following are some of the other dining options in Kapalua:

The Plantation House. On Plantation Club Drive; (808) 669-6299; www.theplantation house.com. The expansive Plantation Golf

Course's clubhouse has half its top floor devoted to this restaurant, and it's not a waste of space. The food is exceptionally good for golf-course dining, and the ocean views are an unexpected bonus. $$$$

Roy's Kahana Bar & Grill. 4405 Honoapi`ilani Highway, Kahana Gateway; (808) 669-6999; www.roysrestaurants.com. This is the Maui branch of the Hawaii Kai restaurant opened on Oahu by Chef Roy Yamaguchi. The Kahana features an ever-changing array of incredible specials and an equally intriguing fixed menu. The Asian spring rolls are a great starter and mesquite-smoked, Peking-style duck an equally impressive entree. Desserts are simply sumptuous. $$$–$$$$

Where to Stay

Kapalua Bay Resort. One Bay Drive, Kapalua; (800) 527-2582. This resort complex is a few minutes west of Kaanapali and encompasses the Ritz-Carlton Kapalua, Kapalua Villas, which are individual condominium units featuring complete kitchens, and Kapalua Luxury Homes. This full-fledged resort features top-rated golf, tennis, restaurants, and accommodations. If the wind is mild or absent, beaches here can be ranked among the best on the island. However, the pesky, all-too-frequent wind can be annoying and often forces beachgoers to head back east to Kaanapali, Kihei, or Wailea. Despite the wind, the waters are always calm, sheltered by a series of lava promontories that form tranquil bays.

At the newly renovated **Ritz-Carlton**, keiki ages five to twelve can join the Ritz Kids from 9:00 a.m. to 4:00 p.m. daily. Children explore Maui's art, culture, ecology, and nature with activities that are fun and educational with a different theme for each day of the week. Other highlights include a nine-hole putting green and croquet lawn, arts and crafts, games, and storytelling. The Ritz Kids is open only to guests of the Ritz-Carlton, Kapalua (808-669-6200). You can get here via either Lower or Upper Honoapi`ilani Highway, although the lower route is easier and more scenic. Ecotourist families love the hiking and environmental programs of the Kapalua Nature Society, based at the Kapalua Resort. $$–$$$$

Central Maui: Wailuku

Wailuku is also accessible from Lahaina, from which there are two routes that cross Central Maui. Route 30, a continuation of the Honoapi`ilani Highway, travels to Iao Valley and Wailuku. Route 35, the Mokulele Highway, leads to Kahului, where it branches off to Upcountry and Haleakala or changes to Route 36, the Hana Highway.

Coming from Lahaina, the Honoapi`ilani Highway continues through the central plains of Maui to Wailuku, passing the small village of Waikapu.

Maui Tropical Plantation (all ages)

1670 Honoapi`ilani Highway, Waikapu; (808) 244-7643 or (800) 451-6805; www.mauitropical plantation.com. Open daily 9:00 a.m. to 5:00 p.m. Admission is free, but there is a charge for the tram ride. $–$$

The Maui Tropical Plantation is a model of a working plantation and is a great place to visit for a glimpse into the lives of agricultural workers. Kids will love the forty-five-minute tram

Area **Beaches**

The first beach you'll arrive at along Lower Honoapi`ilani Highway is **Napili Bay.** This is a good site for swimmers and just-learning surfers, and the beach is beautiful. To get to the beach, follow the beach-access signs near the condominiums.

There are restrooms, showers, and concession stands at popular **Kapalua Beach.** It's a good spot for snorkeling, although better fish sightings will be had farther down the road at Fleming's. The crescent-shaped beach is truly beautiful and, in the absence of heavy winds or storms, is a safe spot for kids of all ages. To get there look for the public parking lot near the Napili Kai Beach Club. You'll have to walk through the short tunnels to get to the beach.

If you keep traveling up Lower Honoapi`ilani Highway, you can't miss **Fleming's Beach Park,** where the scenic beauty is not even the best part. The beach is ideal for snorkeling along the edges of the coast, surfing the outside break, and, for toddlers, wading in the gentle shorebreak. Use caution when trying any of these activities in winter, when storms create dangerous currents and pounding surf. There's plenty of parking, showers, and barbecue grills—a great place for a picnic.

Farther down the road, **Mokuleia** and **Honolua Bays** are Marine Life Conservation Districts, which means that fishing is prohibited, and therefore they are colorful, lively spots for snorkeling. However, as calm and tranquil as this area is in the summer, it gets equally choppy and dangerous in the winter. To find the bays, look for a trail about 250 yards from mile marker 32 on the highway. The trail for the beach is on the left; it's a bit of a hike down, so it's not recommended for small children unless you can carry them. But even if you choose not to walk down to the water, it's still a picturesque spot to stretch your legs and watch the surfers gliding through the sparkling blue Pacific.

ride that takes you through the taro patches surrounding the village. There are fields of pineapple and sugar cane and groves of banana, mango, macadamia nut, and papaya trees. An abundance of tropical flowers gives the place a rich fragrance. On-site facilities include a restaurant, gift shop, and nursery that will ship merchandise home for you.

Kaahumanu Church (all ages)
Route 30 eventually turns into High Street, and the church is easy to find, located right off High Street, Wailuku. It's usually closed on weekdays. Sunday services are held here at 9:00 a.m.

Kaahumanu Church is Maui's oldest stone church that's still standing. It was built in 1837 and continues to hold Sunday services. Many of the hymns are sung in Hawaiian.

Tropical Gardens of Maui (all ages)

200 Iao Valley Road, Iao Valley; (808) 244-3085; www.tropicalgardensofmaui.com. The gardens, gift shop, and nursery are open Monday to Saturday 9:00 a.m. to 5:00 p.m. $, children younger than 8 years old are admitted free. From Route 32, take Route 320 leading to Iao Valley and Iao Needle.

This is a delightful little garden filled with tropical fruits and flowers. The gift shop has a variety of homegrown plants, fruits, and flowers, along with information about how to ship these beauties home and grow them successfully.

Continuing on the way to Iao Valley, stop at Kepaniwai Park, a historic spot that's been turned into a great picnic site with plenty of tables and pavilions. Kamehameha won an important battle against Maui's warriors here during his mission to gain control of the islands. Today you can walk among a Hawaiian grass shack, a Portuguese villa, a Chinese pagoda, a New England–style house, a bamboo house, and a Japanese teahouse.

Iao Valley and Iao Needle (ages 6 and up)
From Route 32, take Route 320 about 5 miles.

Iao Needle is a 2,250-foot cinder cone, around which are several popular hiking trails that are great for families. You can't miss the large stone monolith rising up from the lush valley. This was also the site of a great fight between Kamehameha and the Maui warriors. Historical accounts say the battle was so intense, the soldiers' blood turned the stream red.

From the parking lot an easy walk is the Tableland Trail. It climbs for about 2 miles, and the beautiful views encompass all of the valley. If swimming in the pools is on your agenda, simply walk down to the valley floor and follow the stream. (*NOTE:* If it has rained lately, this area may be muddy and hard to navigate. Bring clothes that you don't mind getting dirty and plenty of mosquito repellent.) If altitude changes are too difficult for your group, try the Waihee Trail, which stays level and journeys over two suspended bridges to the stream.

Bailey House Museum (all ages)
2375–A Main Street, Wailuku; (808) 244-3326; www.mauimuseum.org. Open Monday through Saturday 10:00 a.m. to 4:00 p.m. $.

Just behind Kaahumanu Church sits Bailey House Museum. It's situated in the old Bailey House, named after the former manager of the Wailuku Sugar Company, Edward Bailey. It was built in 1833 and contains the biggest collection of Hawaiian artifacts in all of Maui.

Maui Trivia

Two-thirds of the humpback whale population in the North Pacific winters in Hawaii—between 2,000 and 3,000 whales.

You'll find displays of Hawaiian tapa (a cloth made from the bark of mulberry trees) and quilts, lots of memorabilia from the sugar days, and an extensive exhibit on missionary lifestyles.

Kahului

From Wailuku, Route 32, Kaahumanu Avenue, leads toward the town of Kahului.

Most visitors drive right through this area after landing at the airport, on their way to the popular resort sites of Kaanapali, Kapalua, Kihei, or Wailea. But a lot of great sites are packed into this little town.

Hawaiian Alii Coral Factory (all ages)
804 Keolani Place; (808) 877-7620. Open daily 8:00 a.m. to 2:00 p.m.

You can watch as coral that's been harvested from local waters is transformed into colorful jewelry.

Kanaha Fish Pond (all ages)
At the junction of Routes 36 and 37, less than 2 miles from the airport. There is an observation shelter at Route 37. free.

The Kanaha Fish Pond is not only a stopover for migrating Canada geese and ducks, it's home to two species of endangered Hawaiian birds, the stilt and the coot. You'll probably need binoculars to see them clearly. The coot looks almost like a duck; it's dark gray or black and can be seen in its floating nests on the pond. The stilt is a long, skinny bird with sticklike pink legs, a white stomach, and a black back.

Alexander and Baldwin Sugar Museum (all ages)
At the intersection of Hanson Road and Route 350 (Puunene Avenue), Puunene. Open Monday through Saturday 9:30 a.m. to 4:30 p.m.; (808) 871-8058; www.sugarmuseum.com. $

At the Alexander and Baldwin Sugar Museum in Puunene, the exhibits detail not only the sugar industry but also the lifestyles of the immigrants who arrived on Maui to harvest the cane. Particularly interesting are the explanations of how the rainfall was funneled into irrigation systems to ensure healthy crops.

Kanaha Beach County Park (all ages)
Follow Hobron Avenue toward the water and turn right on Amala Street. Signs will lead you right to the park.

From Kahului Route 36 heads northeast to Hana. Kanaha Beach County Park is a wonderfully scenic place for a picnic and is an ideal spot for beginning sailboarders. The wind and waves are gentle here, creating a safe environment in which to learn the basics of this fun activity.

Flight-seeing Maui

Maui's biggest airport, in Kahului, is not only the site of most visitors' inter-island arrivals and departures, it's also the headquarters for many helicopter and aerial tour companies. A variety of flight-seeing opportunities are available, from daylong sojourns over all of Maui to shorter, hourlong flights that highlight a certain geographical or natural wonder. Shorter trips fly to Haleakala Crater and remote spots of West Maui Mountains, where inaccessible valleys open up before your eyes. Other tours offer such niceties as a champagne brunch in Hana or an excursion to the spectacular sea cliffs and remote beaches of Lanai or Molokai. Prices vary depending on the trip.

- **Paragon Airlines.** (808) 244-3356; www.paragon-air.com, offers hourlong narrated trips over the whole island in ten-seater planes.

Helicopters can get passengers into even more remote spots than airplanes. Passengers are usually given headphones to drown out the noisy whir of the blades and to enjoy piped-in music and a narration explaining the sights below. Some companies even offer a video of your flight that you can take home as a souvenir. Well-known Maui companies that fly out of Kahului include:

- **Sunshine Helicopters.** (808) 270-3999 or (866) 501-7738; www.sunshine helicopters.com
- **Blue Hawaiian Helicopters.** (808) 871-8844 or (800) 745-2583; www.blue hawaiian.com
- **Alex Air.** (808) 871-0792 or (888) 418-8455; www.helitour.com

Prices range from $125 for a thirty-minute ride to $250 for an hourlong ride. Children ages two and up must pay full fare because the Federal Aviation Administration requires that they occupy their own seat.

Where to Eat

Haliimaile General Store. 900 Haliimaile Road, in the old Haliimaile General Store building; (808) 572-2666; www.haliimaile generalstore.com. Lunch is served weekdays, and dinner nightly. Just a few miles uphill of Kahului, don't miss a meal at Haliimaile General Store, which features such international entrees as Szechuan barbecued salmon, rack of lamb Hunan style, paniolo ribs, and blackened chicken with corn and roasted pepper sauce. Dessert delicacies include super-smooth piña colada cheesecake and chocolate macadamia fudge pie. Without a doubt, one of the best meals our family has ever eaten! $$$–$$$$

Where to Stay

Old Wailuku Inn at Ulupono. 2199
Kahookele Street, Wailuku; (808) 244-5897;
www.oldwailukuinn.com. This seven-room inn
is filled with vintage Hawaiiana (the floors are
the original ohia and eucalyptus). The location
gives you easy access to the Iao Valley, the
Hawaii Nature Center, antiques shops, and
nontouristy restaurants. $$–$$$

Paia

East of Kahului via Route 36.

Beyond the airport, a few minutes' drive east on Route 36, the Hana Highway, Spreck-lesville is a little secluded spot that's great for children. Part of the beach is sheltered by lava-rock piles on one side and a long reef in the water, making the setting tranquil and scenic. It's easy to find; just look for directional signs on the side of Route 36.

Continuing on Route 36, H. P. Baldwin Beach County Park is about 7 miles past Kahu-lui, and well-marked signs make it easy to find. The park contains full picnic facilities, rest-rooms, and showers. The protected swimming area is great for kids of all ages, and the sands framing the beach are fun for shell collecting.

Paia and Hookipa Beach are the next two must-stops on the road east of the airport. They are easy to find; just follow the well-marked signs off the Hana Highway. Paia is full of local color, with old-fashioned storefronts that house a variety of boutiques, coffee shops, and restaurants. If you're heading all the way to Hana, Paia is a good place to stock up on gas and supplies; some restaurants in town will even offer to pack your lunch in a dispos-able cooler. You can shop for authentic souvenirs at the Maui Crafts Guild (43 Hana High-way 808-579-9697; www.mauicraftsguild.com), which is open seven days a week.

Sailboarding Lessons

Sailboarding is now a multimillion-dollar industry, with many of the biggest, most reputable companies headquartered here in Paia or in Kahului. If watch-ing the sailboarders slice through the water is not your style and you'd rather join the crowds in the ocean, you can rent equipment and take lessons from **Maui Wind Safari** (in the High-Tech Surf Sports Store at 425 Koloa Street; 808-871-7766) or **Maui Windsurf Company** (22 Hana Highway; 808-877-4816 or 800-872-0999; www.maui-windsurf.com). Many of the companies offer hotel pickup, lunches, and lessons from world-class athletes.

Hookipa Beach (all ages) 🏊

Off Route 36, about 10 miles from Paia.

Paia is most noted for Hookipa Beach, where top-rated sailboarders come from all over the world to enjoy the hefty tradewinds. Bring binoculars, because you're sure to see at least a dozen colorful sails bobbing about in the water. It's a great place to sit and watch the sailboarders' athletic maneuvers. Several contests are held here throughout the year, the best of which is the O'Neill International Windsurfing Championship every spring.

Where to Eat

Mama's Fish House. 799 Poho Place; (808) 579-8488; www.mamasfishhouse.com; lunch and dinner daily. Mama's Fish House, a seafood gourmet's heaven easily found on the side of the road before Hookipa Beach, has a spectacular beachfront location. The papio in the Hana ginger teriyaki sauce is merely sensational, as is the papaya seed dressing on the chilled salad. $$$$

Where to Stay

Most visitors tour this area in day trips but stay in the resort towns of Kaanapali, Kapalua, Kihei, or Wailea.

The Road to Hana

Just as a sunrise on Haleakala is a must-do for any Maui vacation, so too is the Road to Hana. A stay on Maui simply would not be complete without taking your family over the 54 miles and fifty-plus one-lane bridges that lead to one of the most beautiful spots on Earth.

This is the tropical Hawaii that everyone imagines. The road leads through rain forests where waterfalls plummet down craggy cliffs into isolated pools framed by fragrant tropical flowers. At periodic turnoffs you can dip your toe in these little pools or jump completely in and let the waterfalls tumble over you, as a sort of hydro-gravity-powered massage!

The road begins just after Paia, as Route 36 leads into Route 360, the daunting yet beckoning Hana Highway. Actually, the road is more impressive, interesting, and scenic than the town itself. There reportedly are more than 600 hairpin turns in this curvaceous coastline, but the views are so captivating it's hard to keep count. The going is definitely slow, but the scenery is spectacular, and you wouldn't dream of speeding by. From Kahului it takes about four hours to get to the town of Hana and four hours to get back, so either start early or plan to spend the night. You can do it all in one day, but it's a bit much, and you may be navigating the curves in the dark on the way home.

The Road to Hana has earned an undeserved bad reputation. Throughout Maui, you'll see tank tops, T-shirts, sweatshirts, golf hats, and water bottles all imprinted with the famous slogan: I SURVIVED THE ROAD TO HANA. What began as a joke has become a misleading deceit. There's really nothing to "survive" about the road. It's a safe, well-maintained route that is never scary, just long and winding. It does rain often, however (the lush rain forests got that way for a reason), so the road can get a bit slippery. And make sure you bring plenty of mosquito repellent—the little pests are quite fierce in this damp area.

It's impossible to list every stopping place and name every waterfall on the way, but what follows are some highlights.

After Hookipa, you'll pass the minuscule towns of Huelo and Kailua. The entrance to the Waikomoi Ridge Trail and Nature Walk isn't very well marked, but it's definitely worth a stop. Look for a bunch of picnic tables in a clearing above the road and a metal gate. You can pull over and park here. The short trail travels into a bamboo grove. If you remain quiet, you can hear Mother Nature singing as the wind whistles among these tall, hollow trees.

Just past Waikomoi, you'll see Puahokamoa Falls and Haipuaena Falls, two consecutive waterfalls streaming down the mountain. You can park a bit beyond the falls at Kaumahina State Wayside Park. You'll see Puahokamoa first, and a short trek from the road leads to its pool base at the bottom of a large cliff. If you walk upstream for a few minutes, you'll find Haipuaena Falls and another pool.

The first "town" on the road is Keanae, a small agricultural community and a good place to rest your engine and stretch your legs. The scenic vistas from here are delightful, with native rain forests growing in wild contrast with neatly sculpted taro farms. Stop for a picnic at Puaa Kaa State Wayside Park. There are grills here for a do-it-yourself barbecue. Various trails lead to small waterfalls and idyllic pools, but don't let kids wander off. The earth is damp, and it's easy to slip and slide into potentially hazardous rocks.

The next town is Nahiku, identifiable by its small church, serving the local congregation since 1867. If you happen to be driving this road during the summer, look for a pod of dolphins swimming offshore. Locals say the graceful animals perform spontaneous shows of acrobatics, like a real-life version of Sea Life Park on Oahu.

Once you've reached the town of Hana, you'll be amazed at the sense of "civilization" you feel, even at this isolated spot. After such a long drive through wild, lush greenery, you'll be happy to see some buildings, homes, and stores. But don't expect too much; Hana epitomizes life in a small town, where residents all know each other and life moves very slowly. Both the local attitudes and the lush scenery create an atmosphere that's captivating and alluring. Famed aviator Charles Lindbergh became so entranced with Hana, his last wish was to be buried here. His gravesite is near the Hoomau Stone Church.

In Hana be sure to visit Hasegawa General Store. Even if you don't need any supplies, this local institution is surely something to see. It stocks everything from clothing to fishing lures to camera equipment—it's truly an all-in-one spot.

The town of Hana is so small it's impossible to miss the Hana Airport. Yes, you can skip that beautiful drive and fly here directly from Kahului. Pacific Wings (808-873-0877 or 888-575-4546; www.pacificwings.com) offers two flights daily.

Maui Trivia

Hawaii's first irrigation system was built on Maui in 1878, the 50-mile Hamakua Ditch that tunneled and bridged its way across Haleakala's rainy windward gulches to tap millions of gallons of water.

Hana Cultural Center (all ages)

The center is on Uakea Road, Hana; (808) 248-8622. Open weekdays 10:00 a.m. to 4:00 p.m. $

Among the attractions at Hana Cultural Center are wonderful examples of Hawaiian quilts. Anyone who has ever attempted to create a quilt will appreciate the intricacies and time involved in the Hawaiian styles. The center also has a great collection of shells, stone implements used in precontact times, and tapa cloths. There are ancient Hawaiian brooms made from coconut fronds and clothing made from mulberry bark. The center is a small, one-room museum that imparts a feeling of visiting someone's home. Guests can get really close to all the exhibits; there are no formal glass display cases here.

Piilanihale Heiau and Kahanu Gardens (all ages)

Past Hana Gardenland Nursery and leading left is Ulaino Road. Here, the road gives way to a rough track that leads to Kahanu Gardens, in Hana. Open Monday through Friday 10:00 a.m. to 2:00 p.m., but the schedule changes weekly, so it's best to call ahead. For more information call (808) 248-8912. $$

Even if you've seen enough plant life on the drive to Hana, it's still worth it to visit Kahanu Gardens to see Hawaii's largest heiau, Piilanihale, built in a.d. 1400. Piilani was one of the greatest rulers of Maui, the island's chief for more than forty years. The huge walls of the heiau are more than 50 feet high. The 120-acre gardens are part of the National Tropical Botanical Garden network and surround the heiau like a fragrant lei. Within the garden confines are an extensive variety of imported and domestic plants, including a large section of medicinal plants. It's fascinating to learn how the Hawaiians used plants, flowers, and herbs to heal.

Waianapanapa State Park (all ages)

3 miles from Hana on Route 360.

A bit farther down the road is 120-acre Waianapanapa State Park, a great place for snorkeling and swimming on a black-sand beach. With black-as-night lava jutting out into the deep blue sea, the sights here are breathtaking. But enter the water only on calm days; when the surf is strong, the sandy shore drifts away quickly. The park is great for picnicking and exploring nearby caves, but keep an eye on your children and keep them away from wet and slippery places.

The Legend of **Waianapanapa Caves**

There is a well-marked trail leading to Waianapanapa Caves, two small indentations that look like oversize bathtubs. An old Hawaiian legend tells of Popoalaea, a beautiful princess who ran away from Kakae, her mean husband, and hid in these caves. When Kakae found her, he was so angry that he viciously killed her there. Hawaiians say the waters periodically turn bright red in memory of the ancient bloodshed. Scientists, however, have reported that the red tinge in the water is caused by several thousand tiny red shrimp that drift this way during various weather and wind patterns.

Oheo Stream and Seven Pools (all ages, but for sightseeing only, as it is too dangerous for small children to swim) 😊 🏕️
On Route 360, about 12 miles from Hana.

If you haven't had your fill of the road, a slightly longer drive leads to the picturesque Oheo Stream and Seven Pools. The stream spills over the mountain, forming a series of pools that eventually empty into the ocean. You can walk and swim in each of the naturally formed pools, and the scenery is spectacular. Parts of the area are very slippery, so keep a tight rein on wandering children. Also, keep an eye on the sky for sudden rainstorms. This area is prone to flash floods, during which the stream rises quickly and can trap people on the cliffs. Most people swim in the pool just under the bridge. Only truly rugged and fit hikers should attempt to climb up the mountain.

Where to Eat

Hana Ranch Restaurant. At the Hotel Hana-Maui; (808) 248-8211. After a long drive through paradise, it's time to stretch your legs. The perfect lunch stop is the Hana Inn. The patio seating is close enough to the great outdoors that you feel the spirit of the tropics as you dine. Lunch fare includes upscale entrees of fine quality; however, prices also are upscale. $$$

Where to Stay

If you want to go beyond Hana to the Oheo Stream, Seven Pools, and Kipahulu, it's best to spend a night. Rooms at the **Hotel Hana-Maui** (808-248-8211; www.hotelhanamaui .com) start at $495 per night.

Heavenly Hana Inn. 4155 Hana Highway, Hana; (808-248-8442; www.heavenlyhanainn .com). The inn is a sleek Japanese-style hostelry of three suites under one roof. Plumeria trees and hibiscus surround the studio, suites, and the grand dining room. $$–$$$

Southwest Maui: Olowalu and Kihei

Starting from Lahaina, head east on Honoapi`ilani Highway, then take Route 31 to Kihei.

Driving east from Lahaina, you'll soon come to the town of Olowalu, which features a good swimming and snorkeling beach. The waters are so abundant with colorful fish that many commercial snorkel tours from Kaanapali to the west and Maalaea to the east anchor offshore from Olowalu.

Views from here are expansive; you can see Molokai, Lanai, Kahoolawe, and the tip of the Big Island to the far south.

Heading down Route 31, the first stop in Kihei is Maalaea Bay, which, along with Lahaina, is a major embarkation point for whale-watching and snorkeling tours. Additionally, on any given day you'll see dozens of sailboarders decorating the water with their colorful sails. This windy bay is an ideal spot for them to ply their boards across the water. The strong winds don't make it a great place for general swimming, but don't fear, the beaches improve farther down the road in Kihei and Wailea.

Almost one hundred condominiums grace the shore at the town of Kihei, about a thirty-five-minute drive from Lahaina. Although overbuilt, it's not as crowded as Lahaina, and the variety of condos means good values for vacationers. The string of beaches that make up this 6-mile section of the coast is ideal, offering everything from beachcombing to snorkeling, sailboarding, and bodysurfing.

Kalama Beach County Park (all ages)
You can't miss Kalama Beach County Park, in the middle of town.

Although the beach itself isn't ranked among the island's best, and it often disappears in the winter, it's a great place for a family picnic. (Beaches often lose their sand in the winter, when strong currents pull it out to sea, but the sand returns in the summer.) The thirty-six acres include barbecue pits, pavilions, tables, basketball courts, volleyball nets, a soccer field, and a baseball diamond. Local families frequent the area, and the views of Haleakala looming behind you and Kahoolawe sparkling offshore are beautiful.

Horseback Riding Tours

The **Hotel Hana-Maui** (808-270-5258) offers horseback rides throughout the area for $60 to $120 an hour, depending on the length. It's recommended that you make a reservation ahead of time, because hotel guests are given first priority. Riders must be at least nine years old.

n Excursions

The following are a small sampling of the different companies operating from Maalaea or headquartered in Kihei. There are several rental facilities for snorkeling, surfing, kayaking, boogieboarding, or bicycling. Just as in Lahaina, it's best to walk around the harbor to find the ideal excursion for your budget and family.

- **The Pacific Whale Foundation.** 300 Maalaea Road; (808) 249-8811; www .pacificwhale.org. The foundation offers educational tours via cruises and snorkel trips.
- **Snorkel Bob's.** In Kihei, at 2411 South Kihei Road, (808) 879-7449; and 1279 Azeka Mauka, (808) 875-6188; www.snorkelbob.com. Snorkel Bob's rents snorkel gear (plus a fish identification card) and boogieboards. There are four outlets on Maui and others scattered throughout the islands. You can rent from one Snorkel Bob's, drive around and snorkel to your heart's content, and return the equipment at any other Snorkel Bob's location.
- **South Pacific Kayaks.** At the Rainbow Mall; (808) 875-4848 or (800) 776-2326; www.southpacifickayaks.com. Offers a half-day introductory trip for $99, which includes lunch and lots of chances for great snorkeling. More advanced trips are also available. There's a discount for kids eleven and younger. The Turtle Reef Tour is ideal for kids as young as five—it's a leisurely paddle around Makena Bay, suited for first-time kayakers or experienced paddlers. Highlights include snorkeling with the endangered green sea turtle and wonderful views of Haleakala. You can rent a single or double kayak and venture out on your own as well.
- **Four Winds.** (808) 879-8188 or (800) 736-5740; www.mauicharters.com. Offers SNUBA tours for kids to Molokini Crater. No, that's not a typographical error. SNUBA is a sport that lets you explore the underwater world without becoming a full-fledged certified scuba diver. In SNUBA the tank is strapped to a small inflatable raft that floats on the surface above the diver. As the diver swims around, the raft follows. SNUBA divers breathe compressed air through a regulator, and the views awaiting them are much more detailed, colorful, and expansive than the views afforded to snorkelers. Kids must be at least eight years old. The trip itself costs $84 for adults, $49 for kids three through twelve; the SNUBA activity is an additional $49, regardless of age. The ride includes a full continental breakfast, an open bar for the adults, and a barbecue lunch.

Kamaole Beach Parks (all ages)

Signs point you toward the three-part series of Kamaole Beach Parks, bl/ expanses of sand and picnic tables.

Bodysurfing and swimming are great along this whole stretch of coast. Between Beaches I and II, a coral reef is home to many colorful fish, making conditions wonderful for snorkeling. There is a miniature playground, for the mini-size kids in your family, at Beach III.

Maui Ocean Center (all ages)

192 Maalaea Road; (808) 270-7000; www.mauioceancenter.com. Open daily 9:00 a.m. to 5:00 p.m. $$

This five-acre marine park has sixty exhibits, one a life-sized whale model. Don't miss the shark feeding in the 54-foot, walk-through tunnel aquarium.

Where to Eat

Buzz's Wharf. Located on Honoapi`ilani Highway, at the head of Maalaea Harbor; (808) 244-5426; www.buzzswharf.com. The upstairs dining room gives sweeping views of southwest Maui and Kahoolawe. Buzz's Wharf is a fine spot to visit for lunch and dinner. Fishing and tour boats parade in and out of the harbor. Buzz's offers great steaks, fine seafood, and good salads with excellent service. $$$–$$$$

Da Kitchen. 2439 South Kihei Road; (808) 875-7782; www.da-kitchen.com. Try this place for a true slice of local-style life. The menu is authentically Hawaiian, so you'll need a sense of adventure, but the servings are hearty and the prices are very reasonable, at about $5 a plate. $–$$

Wailea

The Wailea area comprises beautiful resort properties fronting five pretty, crescent-shaped beaches: Keawakapu, Mokapu, Ulua, Wailea, and Polo. All have great facilities and are relatively calm. Additionally, all have public access, so if you're just visiting the area and not staying in one of the hotels, you can still enjoy the beach. The complimentary Wailea Shuttle runs every thirty minutes daily, 6:30 a.m. to 10:30 p.m., between the major hotels, golf courses, tennis courts, and Wailea Shopping Village.

Hawaii Trivia

Just offshore from all Wailea beaches sits Molokini, which looks like a tiny, half-moon-shaped islet but really is a submerged cinder cone. It's also a marine preserve and one of the best snorkeling spots in all Hawaii. There are a variety of commercial outfits that will take you there; some offer picnic lunches, and most offer snorkeling instruction and equipment rental. It's best to pick an early-morning cruise, when the waters are the most clear. Too many snorkelers kicking around tends to create murky, sandy water.

To get to Keawakapu, the first Wailea beach, keep going on South Kihei Road until it dead-ends. Although there are no restrooms or picnic tables here, there are showers and plenty of parking, and the sandy beach is wonderful, calm, and great for swimming.

Mokapu and Ulua Beaches are off Wailea Alanui Drive, the main street in the resort. Turn right immediately past the Aston Wailea Resort. Signs point you to the beaches, where there are showers and restrooms. Being so close to the resort means these beaches are well tended, and they're definitely worth a stop. The two beaches are adjacent to each other, separated by a lava promontory that supports great snorkeling. The ocean is sheltered by this rocky point and therefore offers great swimming.

Wailea Beach is less than a mile from the Wailea Town Center, a small shopping area with boutiques, restaurants, and a general store. The turnoff is on the right on a well-marked access road. The facilities are fine, and the sandy beach offers great conditions for swimming, but the absence of rocks makes snorkeling fairly futile here.

There's never a crowd at pristine Polo Beach. Swimming is safe, and the snorkeling is illuminating. The water is brimming with colorful fish near the rocks that separate Polo from Wailea. Visitors will find restrooms, picnic tables, and grills but no lifeguard. To get here keep on Wailea Alanui Drive and follow the sign marked POLO BEACH.

At the road's end sit the Maui Prince Resort and Makena Beach. Makena actually consists of Big Beach and Little Beach. With children, it's a good idea to stick to the first, Big Beach, as the other is frequently a "clothing optional" hangout for locals. Big Beach is quite picturesque, and the waters are optimum for snorkeling, bodysurfing, and swimming.

If it's whale season (November through April), keep one eye peeled on the horizon, because Makena is a popular whale-sighting locale. In fact, if you swim a little bit away from the shore and keep your head underwater for a few seconds, you may even hear the shrieklike songs of the whales.

Sunsets are especially beautiful from Makena. The expansive vistas include Kahoolawe, Lanai, and the West Maui Mountains, which have the appearance of an entirely separate island.

Be sure to bring some water and snacks along, since the closest facilities are back at the Maui Prince Hotel. The beach is easy to find, with well-marked signs. Don't leave anything in your car.

On the way to Makena, look for Keawalai Congregational Church, built in 1832. Services are still held here every Sunday at 9:30 a.m.

Ahihi-Kinau Natural Area Reserve (all ages)
At the end of Route 31.

The scuba diving and snorkeling here are among the best in all of Maui. Although the beach is narrow, the waters are crystal clear, and there are lots of tide pools to explore.

La Perouse Bay is just beyond Ahihi-Kinau Reserve. In 1786 Jean-François La Perouse became the first westerner to land on Maui, and this bay was where he disembarked. It's a popular snorkeling site, but the beaches are fairly small.

King's Trail (all ages)
The remains of the King's Trail are a bit south of La Perouse Bay.

This 5½-mile trail goes from La Perouse Bay over Maui's last lava flow, which dates from 1790. Beyond La Perouse the road gets quite rough and is not recommended for cars, but it's an easy hike. The trail leads over the same path used by the king's tax collectors in Old Hawaii. At one point the path heads inland, past old stone foundations and walls, signs of an earlier civilization. Little offshoots of the main trail lead down to the ocean, where you'll be treated to a wonderfully scenic view of Cape Hanamanioa and the Coast Guard lighthouse.

Makena Stables (ages 13 and up)
8299 Makena Road; (808) 879–0244; www.makenastables.com. $$$$

Guides well versed in local plants and legends will take you on the slopes of Haleakala, over the old lava flows to pristine views. The horses are well kept, and the folks are friendly.

Where to Eat

Bistro Molokini. 3850 Wailea Alanui Drive; (808) 875-1234 or (800) 888-6100. An open-air, Italian-style cafe in the center of the Grand Wailea Resort and Spa offers mouth-watering pizzas made on the spot in a wood-burning pizza oven, plus sandwiches, salads, pupus, and ocean- and pool-front views. One of several restaurants in the Grand Wailea, the Bistro serves lunch and dinner. $$$

Caffe Ciao. At Fairmont Kea Lani Hotel, 4100 Wailea Alanui Drive; (808) 875-4100 or (800) 257-7544. This alternative eatery is patterned after a Sicilian delicatessen. Along with shelves full of take-out munchies, Ciao has lunch, and dinner specialties that you can eat on the spot, take to outside tables, or carry back to your suite. Pizza and pasta appear frequently on the menu. Fresh-baked specialties washed down with espresso, cappuccino, or other heavy-duty coffees will help parents recover from a midday slump. $

Mala. 3700 Wailea Alanui Drive; (808) 879-1922. This pool- and ocean-facing terrace restaurant in the Wailea Beach Marriott Resort & Spa mixes 1930s ambience with good food and comes out a winner all around. If it's a nice evening, dine outside under the stars. The restaurant features a super do-it-yourself salad bar, great steaks, fine fresh fish, a kids' menu, and sweet serenades by local entertainers. $$

Humuhumunukunukuapua`a. 3850 Wailea Alanui Drive; (808) 875-1234 or (800) 888-6100. Named for Hawaii's state fish, the restaurant is freestanding amid waterfalls and its own lagoon. It features a thatched roof, wood floors and railings, and a tropical, open-air design. Bronze statues of mermaids and Hawaiian fishermen add to the Polynesian atmosphere. Seafood is a specialty here, prepared in the style of Pacific Rim cuisine. A nighttime visit to "Humu" transports you back to old Hawaii, Tahiti, or Fiji. $$$$

Nick's Fishmarket Maui. At Fairmont Kea Lani Hotel, 4100 Wailea Alanui Drive; (808) 879-7224 or (800) 257-7544. Fresh seafood includes lobster and snapper in several preparations. Open for dinner. $$$$

Ferraro's Bar e Ristorante. At Four Seasons Resort, 3900 Wailea Alanui Drive; (808) 874-8000. This fine place for lunch or dinner overlooks the pool area and ocean. The Italian cuisine is referred to as *cucina rustica*, and features seafood, fish, and pasta. Plus, there is a kiawe wood-burning oven that brings pizzas-to-die-for. There is a children's menu and, get this, an "I'm not a kid anymore" teen menu. Cute, but pricey. $$$$

Where to Stay

The Fairmont Kea Lani Maui. 4100 Wailea Alanui Drive; (808) 875-4100 or (800) 257-7544; www.fairmont.com /kealani. Offers a Keiki Lani program for children ages five to thirteen, 9:00 a.m. to 3:00 p.m. daily. When children join, they receive a **free** Keiki Lani T-shirt, lunch, and a cool craft to take home. Activities change every day but include such things as erupting volcanoes by the beach, looking for lizards, sandcastle contests, learning the hula, fruit tasting, and much more! Kids can also enjoy their favorite movies. $$$$

Four Seasons Resort Maui at Wailea. 3900 Wailea Alanui Drive; (808) 874-8000; www.fourseasons.com/maui. The kids' program is called Kids for All Seasons, ages five to twelve, 9:00 a.m. to 5:00 p.m. daily. This complimentary guest program includes hula classes, flower lei making, Hawaiian legends and storytelling, arts and crafts, games, kite flying, and swimming. Children twelve and over are invited to a complimentary scuba clinic. Evening theme outings include children's luau and sea safaris. $$$$

Grand Wailea Resort Hotel & Spa.
3850 Wailea Alanui Drive; (808) 875-1234
or (800) 888-6100; www.grandwailea
.com. Camp Grande is for kids ages five to
twelve, 9:00 a.m. to 4:00 p.m. daily. There
is also a nightly camp offered from 5:00 to
10:00 p.m. Camp Grande offers children's
and family workshops, and it features
an arts and crafts room, Nintendo room,
video arcade, and much more. Workshops
include hula and ukulele lessons, lei making, lauhala bracelet weaving, and com-
puter graphics T-shirt design. $$$$

Maui Prince Hotel. 5400 Makena Alanui
Drive; (808) 874-1111; www.mauiprince
hotel.com. The Prince Keiki Club, ages

five to twelve, runs 9:00 a.m. to 3:00 p.m.
Monday to Saturday. Half-day sessions are
available from 9:00 a.m. to noon and noon
to 3:00 p.m. Kids from around the world
share fun activities such as net fishing,
sandcastle building, swimming, Hawaiian
arts and crafts, golf putting, table tennis,
shuffleboard, movies, and video games.
Activities also include whale watching in
season and scavenger hunts on the spa-
cious grounds. $$$–$$$$

Wailea Beach Marriott Resort & Spa.
3700 Wailea Alanui Drive; (808) 879-1922;
www.marriotthawaii.com. Recently reno-
vated; no specialized children's program at
press time. $$$–$$$$.

A Backpacking Trip for Active Parents and Teens

Even avid hikers are tested on this trip, but backpackers on the **Kaupo Gap Trail** stay in cabins. You have to carry water, food, personal gear, and a sleeping bag. These cabins ($75 per night for up to twelve people) each have twelve padded bunks, utensils and dishes, big wood-burning stoves, long refectory tables and benches, firewood, and outhouses. You spend the first night at Kapalaoa on the cinder-bottom floor of Haleakala Crater and the second night at Paliku beneath a rain forest cliff. For the cabin lottery, information, and updates on ranger-led Kaupo Gap trips, contact Haleakala National Park, P.O. Box 369, Makawao 96768; (808) 572-4400. Request a cabin two months before the first day of the month you want to visit. Each month a lottery is held for use of the cabins. Winners are notified by telephone, but you can get more information online at www.nps.gov/hale/.

Upcountry: Pukalani, Kula, Makawao, and Olinda

You'll hear the term *Upcountry* often on Maui. There are no real boundaries setting off this region, but locals use the name to refer to the towns and villages surrounding Haleakala. By this definition the area is huge, reaching from Ulupalakua Ranch in the south to Kipahulu Park in the east and Makawao in the north.

A series of picturesque, lush green towns surround Haleakala like a fragrant lei. The soil in these areas is rich and heavily cultivated; farms and nurseries dot the landscape, and herds of cows and horses munch contentedly in acres of tall grass. Undulating roads meander through hills and valleys carpeted in velvety green, looking decidedly untropical, almost like the back roads of England instead of a South Pacific island.

Different routes lead to Upcountry. The Haleakala Highway, Route 37, leads through Pukalani and Keokea and ends at the 30,000 acres of Ulupalakua Ranch. About midway, Route 377 branches off the Haleakala Highway and heads into Kula, home to several nurseries and protea farms. Or Baldwin Avenue off the Hana Highway leads to Makawao and Olinda.

You'll arrive in Pukalani when Route 37 intersects with Route 377. This is the largest town in the area, and a good place to stock up on gas and supplies if you're heading up to Haleakala. No doubt the kids will notice the tall golden arches of McDonald's.

Don't miss a visit to the charming cowboy town of Makawao (on Route 365, which veers off of Route 37, a thirty-minute drive from Kahului). You'll notice fine-dining establishments sitting side by side with hitching posts and saddleries. The town was settled by paniolo (cowboys) who moved here in the late 1800s to work on the local ranches. Many of the stores are family-run businesses that have been handed down for generations. The Oskie Rice Arena here is the site of the state's largest rodeo, usually held in July, and during the polo season the arena hosts weekend tournaments. Makawao is known statewide for its annual Fourth of July parade, and if you happen to be on Maui then, don't miss it.

Picturesque Kula is the heart of Upcountry, and a drive through this town offers the best of the region's sites. You'll see farm after farm of colorful crops, including potatoes, pineapples, grapes, lettuce, strawberries, sweet Maui onions, and cabbages. Nurseries are everywhere as well, growing beautiful protea, carnations, roses, and more.

Getting to Kula involves the same roads that lead to Haleakala. From Pukalani take the Haleakala Highway (Route 37), turn on Route 377, and then again on Route 378, a curv-

Maui Trivia

Haleakala National Park has more endangered species than any other park in the National Park collection throughout the United States. These even include species that are listed as endangered by the U.S. Fish and Wildlife Service but are not native to the park.

ing road that leads up to the crater. Kula is a great resting spot before venturing up the mountain.

Enchanting Floral Gardens of Kula (all ages)

The gardens are just outside of Pukalani, off Route 37; (808) 878-2531; www.flowersof maui.com. Open daily 9:00 a.m. to 5:00 p.m. $, children 5 and younger are admitted free.

At Maui Enchanting Gardens you can walk among eight acres of exotic plant species from all over the world as well as native Hawaiian plants.

Hui No`eau Visual Arts Center (all ages)

2841 Baldwin Avenue; (808) 572-6560; www.huinoeau.com. Open daily 10:00 a.m. to 4:00 p.m. free.

The Hui No`eau Visual Arts Center is an active artists' haven that brings a bit of sophisticated culture to an otherwise cowpoke town. The center is actually a nine-acre estate that used to be called Kaluanui. Within the two-story, Mediterranean-style home are beautiful displays of local artists' works. The center also offers art classes and lectures, studio space, kilns, and pottery wheels. Visiting artists often host free lectures.

Pony Express (ages 10 and up)

This outfit offers one- and two-hour trail rides across the Haleakala Ranch; (808) 667-2200; www.ponyexpresstours.com. The Crater Ride lasts about four hours, includes lunch, and delves deep into the volcano. (Nine-year-olds with lots of riding experience are allowed.) $$$$

Horseback Riding Tours

Horseback riding options in Maui include the following companies.

- **Pony Express Tours.** (808) 667-2200; www.ponyexpresstours.com. Children must be at least ten years old, and pregnant women are not allowed to participate. Pony Express features a variety of four-legged trips through the crater.
- **Charley's Trailride and Pack Trips.** (808) 248-8209. Children must be at least six years old. For guided overnight camping, Charley's will organize cabins and meals. The rates vary according to how extensive a trip you'd like and the number of riders in your group.
- **Thompson Ranch Riding Stables.** (808) 878-1910; www.thompsonranch maui.com. Thompson Ranch specializes in families and offers scenic rides on the slopes of Haleakala. They offer a variety of rides based on preferences and abilities. Times are flexible according to reservations; children must be at least five.

Maui Trivia

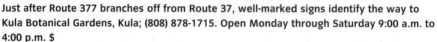

Rare Hawaiian nene geese, on the endangered species list, descended from off-course Canada geese.

Kula Botanical Gardens (all ages)

Just after Route 377 branches off from Route 37, well-marked signs identify the way to Kula Botanical Gardens, Kula; (808) 878-1715. Open Monday through Saturday 9:00 a.m. to 4:00 p.m. $

This is a great spot for a picnic. The six acres of plants and trees are all identified with signs and easy directions for a self-guided tour. A gift shop is on site, as are clean picnic tables for a relaxing respite.

Keiki Zoo Maui (all ages)

370 Kekaulike Avenue, Kula; (808) 878-2189. The zoo is very small, so admission and guided tours are by appointment only. $

For Mainlanders used to zoos with extensive collections of wild animals, this site may seem like kids' stuff. But that's exactly what it is. Kids love it here because most of the facility is a petting zoo, designed especially for children. (Keiki means child.) It's an interactive zoo, where children can hug, kiss, and cuddle with the animals. A few of the animals present are Woolite and Lambchop (sheep), Louie (llama), Harley (hog), and Rosie (Shetland pony).

Haleakala Crater National Park Trails (ages 8 and up)

From Route 377, take Haleakala Crater Road (Route 378). Visitor center open daily from sunrise to 3:00 p.m.; (808) 572-4400.

At the park's entrance, there's a small trail to the left of the headquarters; take it. It leads to two spectacular overlooks: Leleiwi and Kalahaku. Of the two, Kalahaku is the better because you get a good view of rare silversword plants from here. You can follow the signs for the Silversword Loop Trail; it's less than ⅒ mile and will offer up-close views of these beautiful plants.

NOTE: On any hiking trail it's important to stay on the well-worn paths. With a slight misstep or detour, a hiker could unknowingly crush the roots of an endangered plant, not only killing the plant, but also eventually killing the insects that feed off of the plant. Please explore with caution and be aware that the ecosystem here is very fragile.

Several companies offer guided hikes throughout the park. Hike Maui, operated by naturalist extraordinaire Ken Schmitt, features a veritable menu of hiking options designed to accommodate different ages and skill levels. Many of his hikes include a picnic lunch, and all of them offer a great chance to learn about the biological, environmental, and geographical particulars of the area. In addition to Haleakala, Schmitt leads hikes in the remote areas of Hana, La Perouse Bay, Polipoli Springs, and Iao Valley. Don't miss a chance to join

Day Trip to Explore **Haleakala Crater**

All Upcountry roads lead to Haleakala Crater, a trip that Maui visitors should include on their itinerary. Its naturally sculpted features and vast dimensions rank right up there with the Grand Canyon and Painted Desert in Arizona. Although some 22,000 feet of the mountain sits below sea level, it is the world's largest dormant volcano. It last erupted in 1790, and scientists, while reluctant to label it extinct, don't believe it's going to blow again within the next few hundred years.

Not only is Haleakala Crater remarkably beautiful, it's also home to two native Hawaiian species that exist only here and on the Big Island: the brilliant-when-blooming silversword plant and Hawaii's state bird, the nene goose. (Recently, nene populations have been bred successfully in captivity on the Big Island at Volcanoes National Park.) The silversword plant is very rare. It can take up to twenty years to bloom, and when the flowers do open up, they shine gloriously for a short while, from June through October; then the plant dies. Please appreciate the silversword plants from a distance.

The 30,183 acres of Haleakala were designated a national park in 1961 to help preserve the unique plants and animals here and to provide a safe, educational environment for visitors.

The drive up the mountain is almost as breathtaking as the views from the final destination at the top. Ever-changing vistas appear at each curve in the road, and each new view is like opening another window. You'll see forests of introduced and indigenous trees, including flowering jacaranda, eucalyptus, and cactus, and you'll pass through virtually untouched tropical rain forests, dry forests, and desertlike environments.

Don't feel pressured to explore the entire park in one visit—that's impossible. The park encompasses more than 30 miles of hiking trails, but the most exquisite feature is the crater. It's 7½ miles long, 2½ miles wide, and an unbelievable 3,000 feet deep. At the crater floor what looks like a small mountain range is really a series of cinder cones, ranging in height from 600 to 1,000 feet.

Hosmer Grove is the first stopping point along the curvaceous Route 378. It's actually a forestry project left over from the 1800s. In the hope of finding a marketable wood for the region, certain trees, such as pine, cedar, sugi, and juniper, were planted here. It's a scenic place to stop and stretch your legs, but don't think you've gotten anywhere close to seeing the best the park has to offer.

The **Park Headquarters** is just a few minutes past Hosmer Grove on Route 378, at the 7,000-foot elevation level. The facility is open daily 8:00 a.m. to 4:00

p.m. and is where visitors must pay $10 admission to get into the park. A free map is available at headquarters that will explain the degree of difficulty for each trail, so you can pick the route best suited to your family's abilities.

You may notice a few white dome structures at the very top of the mountain. This area is off-limits to visitors. It's known as **Science City** and encompasses solar tracking stations, U.S. Air Force solar observatories, and laser-ranging tracking stations.

If you have a four-wheel-drive vehicle, by all means venture to **Polipoli Springs State Recreation Area.** A variety of short hiking trails here lead through remote wilderness and offer some of the best views in all Maui. To get there take Highway 377 (Kekaulike Avenue) to Waipoli Road. You'll reach the Kula Forest Reserve about 10 miles outside of Kula, and from there Polipoli Springs will be easy to find.

his living classroom—it's educational, fun, and beautiful all at the same time. For more information call (808) 879-5270 or (866) 324-6284; or visit www.hikemaui.com.

The park's visitor center is at the end of the road, about 10 miles beyond the headquarters. The center features informative displays that explain the nearby natural wonders. Every hour, the staff rangers provide a short, interesting lecture about the geological wonders of Haleakala. The rangers also host a variety of hikes, during which they take time to explain certain outstanding features of the flora, fauna, or landscape. For more information call the center at (808) 572-4400.

Maui Mountain Cruisers (ages 12 and up)

15 South Wakea Avenue, Kahului; (808) 871-6014; www.mauimountaincruisers.com. The sunrise tours leave at 2:15 a.m. and return by noon. The midday rides leave at 7:00 a.m. and return by 2:00 p.m. Children must be at least 4 feet, 10 inches tall and older than 12, and pregnant women are prohibited from participating. $$$$

You're certain to spot groups of people riding bicycles down the mountain (much smarter than attempting to pedal up). For families with older children, this offers a way to absorb the beauty of the mountain with minimal physical activity. If your children are too young to participate in the downhill ride, they can buy a ticket to be a van passenger and still join in the fun. (Unfortunately, they have to pay full price.) Both rides offer a continental breakfast and full lunch. Hotel pickups are available.

Haleakala Skyline Tour, Skyline Eco-Adventures (ages 10 and up)

Located in Upcountry, Pukalani, (808) 878-8400; www.skylinehawaii.com. Kids must be 10 years old and weigh at least 80 pounds; adults must weigh less than 260 pounds. $$$$

NOTE: The newest skyline adventure is in Kaanapali (see description below).

Ziplining is the hottest new adventure in Hawaii, and there are new tour companies on Maui and Kauai. Imagine yourself soaring over gulches and through the trees along the slopes of Haleakala. The Haleakala Skyline Tour blends a short hike with five zipline crossings, an Indiana Jones–style swinging bridge, and an introduction to Hawaii's unique and fragile landscape. It's an adventure you're sure to remember long after you've returned home. The new Kaanapali adventure features eight ziplines that take you soaring high above streams and waterfalls to lunch served atop a 1,000-foot overlook. The views are truly spectacular, but this is adventure travel—not for the faint of heart, or for those of us whose stomach churns a bit when looking down from an elevated (though very scenic) perch.

Where to Eat

Komoda Store and Bakery. 3674 Baldwin Avenue, Makawao; (808) 572-7261. It's worth waking up early just to drive up to Makawao and savor a tasty cream bun from this bakery. Local favorites for more than fifty years, the cream buns are usually sold out by midmorning. Doors open at 7:00 a.m. $

Kula Lodge. On Haleakala Highway, Kula; (808) 878-1535 or (800) 233-1535; www.kula lodge.com/restaurant. Breathtakingly high on the road to the summit of Haleakala, the Kula Lodge offers good food plus picture windows that provide a view of the whole northern half of the island. Stop in on the return from a sunrise visit to the summit for mouthwatering omelets or Belgian waffles loaded with raspberries. $$$

Where to Stay

Haiku Plantation Inn. 555 Haiku Road; (808) 575-7500; www.haikuleana.net. Set in secluded Upcountry, the inn features charming guest suites decorated in Hawaiian style and reflect the vintage feel of the plantation era. All rooms have their own private bath with fluffy white towels, Hawaiian soaps, hair dryers, and full amenities. Each room has its own signature feel, with large plantation windows, ceiling fans, tropical quilts, and a comfy sitting area. Upcountry's cool breezes whisper through the original hand-blown plantation windows, making evenings delightful and carrying memories of "Romantic Old Hawaii." NOTE: At press time, the inn was closed temporarily due to new B&B regulations for Maui County. Please check the Web site for status of permits. $–$$

Hale Hookipa Inn. 32 Pakani Place, Makawao; (808) 572-6698. The gracious plantation home was built in 1924 and is on the Hawaii State and National Historic Registers. The craftsman-style home is reminiscent of a bygone era, with high ceilings, wood floors, and two separate wings. The interior is invitingly warm and rich in color, local art, and antique furnishings. The grounds feature a feast of tropical fruits, dazzling flowers, and old trees. (Children must be nine and older.) $$–$$$

For More Information

Maui Visitors Bureau. 1727 Wilipa Loop, Wailuku 96793; (808) 244-3530; www.visit maui.com.

Watching the Sun Rise atop **Haleakala**

You can tour this area by air, foot, car, horse, and bicycle—all are great and offer fantastic scenery. But watching the sun rise as a new day dawns is free and by far the most spectacular sight in all Maui, ranking up there with the best sights in the entire state.

The best place to watch the sun rise is at the **Puu Ulaula Observatory,** a glass-enclosed structure at the very top of the mountain. If you're deterred by the thought of dragging the kids out of a warm bed at 4:00 in the morning and driving up 10,023 feet to below-freezing temperatures, don't be. Although you'll need warm clothes, the experience is guaranteed to be unforgettable. Besides, you can let the kids sleep in the car on the way up and sightsee on the way down after the sun has risen. You'll no doubt see a few dozen cars parked and waiting, the people huddled together inside for warmth. As the sun emerges, so do the people, and the chorus of "oohs" and "aahs" begins.

You're above the cloud cover here, so you get to watch the sun eke its way through the puffy clouds. Streaks of light flash across the sky, as the sun cooks the cloud color to a rosy, blush pink, then a burnt orange, and then a fiery red as it rises. Soon it begins to reflect off the natural formations surrounding the crater, and the whole landscape adopts this pinkish-orangish-reddish hue. It's breathtakingly beautiful.

Pretty soon the sun is officially up, and the weather warms significantly. Sunscreen is important and should definitely be applied liberally. Even if you're not hot, at this high altitude where the atmosphere is thinner, you can burn more easily. Beware of blistering lips and noses! Additionally, the oxygen level drops a bit up here, and precautions are advised for anyone prone to respiratory or cardiovascular problems.

From Kahului the ride up to the visitor center will take about one and a half hours, excluding any stops for gas or food. If you're staying in Kaanapali or Wailea, tack on an additional forty minutes. Because you'd hate to wake up that early and miss the sunrise, plan on being there a half hour before. You can look in the daily newspaper for specific times or listen to the recording provided by the National Weather Service at (808) 877-5111.

The
Big Island

Hawaii, commonly referred to as the Big Island, is appropriately named, as it's the biggest of the six major Hawaiian Islands and accounts for 63 percent of the state's total landmass. It's 4,038 square miles and, as long as lava continues to spew out of Kilauea, still growing. About 150,000 people live on the Big Island (it's the second-most populated island after Oahu), but it has the lowest population density, barely twenty-five people per square mile. It's almost twice the size of all the other Hawaiian Islands put together.

Julie's
TopPicks for Family Fun on the Big Island

1. Exploring the rain forests at Hawaii Tropical Botanical Garden

2. Delving into Thurston and Kaumana Lava Caves

3. Visiting the ancient structures at Pu`uhonua O Honaunau National Historical Park

4. Snorkeling at Kealakekua Bay

5. Horseback riding at Parker Ranch in Waimea

6. Watching the lava flow from Kilauea into the sea

7. Swimming with the dolphins at Hilton Waikoloa

8. Traveling to the depths of Waipio Valley

9. Hiking to the floor of Pololu Valley

10. Watching the macadamia nuts being processed at the factory in Honoka`a

THE BIG ISLAND

Hawi

Pololu Valley
Lookout

Kapa`au

270

North Kohala

250

Waipio Valley

Kukuihaele

Hamakua

Honoka`a

Kawaihae

Waimea

19

Mauna Kea
Forest Reserve

Laupahoehoe

190

19

Kohala
Coast

Waikoloa

19

▲ Mauna Kea

Honomu

200

190

19

Kona
Int'l. Airport

200

Kailua-Kona

Saddle Road

Hilo Int'l.
Airport

19

Hilo

Holualoa

Keaau

Mountain View

130

Kealakekua

Hawaii Volcanoes
National Park

137

Kona
Coast

Captain Cook

Pahoa

11

11

▲ Mauna Loa

Volcano

130

Puʻuhonua O Honaunau
National Historic Park

Kilauea
Caldera

Kalapana/
Kaimu

Ho`okena

Pahala

11

11

Na`alehu

Ka Lae

South Point

Of all the islands, the Big Island is the most ecologically diverse, with natural environments ranging from the desert plains of Ka`u to the rain forests above Hilo to snowcapped Mauna Kea. Small towns, passed over by time, contrast with high-tech scientific communities housing world-renowned telescopes and observatories. Steaming molten lava pours from Earth's center and flows to the sea, creating fresh new land that's still too hot to walk on, while just a few miles away, rain forests thrive in lush valleys.

Within its 300 miles of coastline, the Big Island offers spectacularly colored beaches, from the snowy-white sands of Hapuna to the black and green sands of the southeastern coast.

The Big Island can be divided into two parts: the Kona side and the Hilo side, worlds apart in personality. The Kona side bustles with activity. The weather there is sunny and dry, and the beaches are wonderful, full of colorful marine life, and ideal for snorkeling. The Hilo side is quiet, often rainy, and lush with flower farms, gardens, and hidden black-sand coves. Tiny one-street towns dot the coastline, rich in history and picturesque sights.

The Big Island is so vast, it's impossible to explore every nook and cranny in just one visit. There are two airports serving both sides of the island: Kona and Hilo. Whichever one you choose, a rental car is essential because the island begs to be explored, and sights are spread quite far apart. The Kona International Airport accepts many direct flights (United, American, Hawaiian) from the Mainland; another option is to land first in Honolulu and hop on a commuter flight.

The island is dominated in the center by its two enormous peaks, Mauna Kea and Mauna Loa. The Saddle Road, Route 200, cuts across the island, but you can also drive almost completely around on Routes 19 and 11. The island is so large, however, that it doesn't make sense to drive a circle island tour. It's more feasible and rewarding to explore one side at a time. This chapter begins in Kona and continues north to Kohala and the tip of the island at Hawi. Then it will look at the Hilo side, from where you can venture north up the Hamakua coast to Waipio Valley and south to Kilauea Volcano and South Point.

South Kona: Kona and Kailua-Kona

Take the Queen Kaahumanu Highway, Route 11, south of the airport, and turn right on Palani Road. Palani goes straight to the ocean and leads to Kailua Bay and Alii Drive.

Most of the entire 90-mile coastline composing the Kona district is low and flat, while the mountains just east of town feature forests, ranches, and residential homesteads. Kona can usually be separated into two regions: north and south, with the border being the town of Kailua-Kona. It doesn't matter which way you go, but for purposes of easy orientation, this guide will cover Kailua-Kona, then proceed south to Ka Lae, then north

Kona **Beaches**

The beaches in Kona central aren't great for swimming; better conditions are found in South Kohala at the luxury resorts. However, continuing south, past the strip of hotels and condominiums, **White Sands Beach** is a popular local place in the summer. It's also referred to as "Magic Sands" or "Disappearing Sands" because winter storms often consume the beach. Boogieboarders flock here on swell days.

Kahaluu Bay is just south of Magic Sands, and some locals claim its designation as a nature preserve makes it the best snorkeling beach on the whole island. It's great for beginners because many of the snorkeling sites are close to shore, where it's shallow and protected. Be sure to warn your kids to stay within the bay, because the currents are strong outside. There are lots of turtles to see, but not to touch; it's against the law, as they are an endangered species. Keep a respectful distance.

to Kapaʻau. Some say Kailua-Kona is what Waikiki looked like some forty years ago. The hotels are plentiful but not built too close together. Although the Big Island's major visitor hub, it still has a small-town appeal and is the sort of place where restaurant workers "talk story" with fishermen and hoteliers.

Most sites, restaurants, hotels, and attractions are located within a close proximity to Alii Drive, the main drag.

The Kona Historical Society offers walking tours several times a week, based on reservations. Tours last seventy-five minutes and cost $15 per person, regardless of age. For more information call (808) 938-8225; www.konahistorical.org.

Kailua Pier will be the first structure you notice upon arriving in Kailua-Kona. It's bordered by a long seawall that offers a great spot to sit and watch the traffic. The pier really comes alive every October when thousands of participants churn up the water at the start of the Ironman Triathlon. The pier is also the embarkation point for many oceangoing tours, including snorkeling, whale-watching, fishing, and submarine excursions.

Just south of Kailua Pier, the opposite direction of Ahuena Heiau, you can't miss Mokuaikaua Church, the tallest structure in town. The land was given by King Liholiho to the first Congregationalist missionaries who arrived on the *Thaddeus* in 1820. The church was built from coral blocks in 1838 and is the oldest church on the island. It is across the street from the ocean, at the south end of Kailua Pier. It's open daily 7:30 a.m. to 5:30 p.m., and volunteer docents are on hand from noon to 1:30 p.m. to offer a bit of local history. **free**.

Waterfront Row on Alii Drive is a mini shopping center with gift stores, boutiques, and restaurants. Be sure to check out "Granders Wall of Fame." Kona is known as the billfish capital of the world because the local waters are chock-full of marlin. At the Granders Wall people who have caught fish weighing more than 1,000 pounds earn themselves a place on the wall with a picture of their catch.

Farther south on Alii Drive, you'll see the Little Blue Church, more commonly known today as St. Peter's Catholic Church. Within a short walking distance are the ruins of Kuemanu Heiau, Kapunaoni Heiau, Hapai Alii Heiau, and Keeku Heiau. Although these historic sites are not restored, they still represent a great deal of the spiritual importance of the Keauhou area.

OTEC Natural Energy Labs (all ages)

Just south of the airport; (808) 329-8073. Guided tours are given every Monday through Thursday at 10:00 a.m. $. free for ages 8 and under.

Before you get into town, you'll pass the OTEC Natural Energy Labs. It's worth a small side trip to tour this fascinating facility. Here, cold water is pumped from thousands of feet below the ocean's surface, mixed with warm water, and used to generate electricity and provide a suitable environment for aquaculture. Strawberries, lobsters, kelp, and abalone are being cultivated here.

King Kamehameha Beach (all ages)

Near the pier and the King Kamehameha's Kona Beach Hotel.

King Kamehameha Beach is very gentle and, therefore, ideal for children. Here, you can rent kayaks, paddleboats, boogieboards, and snorkeling gear from a little shack on the beach.

Ahuena Heiau (all ages)

On the north end of Kailua Bay, Kona. Admission is free, and the heiau is open daily 9:00 a.m. to 4:00 p.m.

The completely restored Ahuena Heiau is where King Kamehameha the Great retreated to spend his remaining days after conquering all the islands. The nearby King Kamehameha's Kona Beach Hotel (808-329-2911) offers free guided tours of the heiau grounds Monday through Friday at 1:30 p.m. Although you must get permission from the security guards to enter the grounds, you needn't visit as part of a tour.

Within the heiau grounds is a temple dedicated to the god of fertility, Lono. The oracle tower, or anuu, is the tallest part of the heiau and is where the high-ranking priest would meditate and receive messages from the gods.

Big Island Trivia

Wao Kele O Puna is the only remaining lowland rain forest in the United States.

Oceangoing Tours

It's almost sacrilegious to visit Kona and not take advantage of the clear, beautiful ocean surrounding it. Many of the hotels can arrange for a snorkeling, scuba diving, or fishing excursion, and many offer snorkeling equipment, either complimentary or for a small price. If you're staying in a condominium, however, or if you decide to venture into the ocean when you're driving around, the following Kona-based businesses rent snorkel and scuba gear:

- **Dive Makai.** At Kailua Pier; (808) 329-2025; www.divemakai.com. Rents equipment if you're participating in its charter trips, which leave daily from Kailua Pier.
- **Jack's Diving Locker.** 75-5819 Alii Drive; (808) 329-7585 or (800) 345-4807; www.jacksdivinglocker.com. About a mile from the King Kamehameha Beach Hotel; open daily 8:00 a.m. to 9:00 p.m. They even have special activities for children.
- **Big Island Divers.** In the Kaahumanu Plaza; (808) 329-6068 or (800) 488-6068; www.bigislanddivers.com. Rents equipment and arranges charters, mostly for scuba divers.
- **Snorkel Bob's.** Next to the Royal Kona Resort off Alii Drive; (808) 329-0770; www.snorkelbob.com. There's also a new location closer to the airport at 73-4976 Kamanu Street; (808) 329-0771. Rents snorkeling equipment and boogieboards. Open 8:00 a.m. to 5:00 p.m. daily.
- **SNUBA.** Off Kailua Pier; (808) 326-7446; www.snubabigisland.com. SNUBA is a sport that lets you explore the underwater world without becoming a full-fledged, certified scuba diver. In SNUBA the tank is strapped to a small inflatable raft that floats on the surface above the diver. As the diver swims around, the raft follows. SNUBA divers breathe compressed air through a regulator, and the views awaiting them are much more detailed, colorful, and expansive than the views afforded to snorkelers. Minimum age is eight for SNUBA, four for "Snuba Doo" (a modified version of the real thing, but with a flotation vest).

If you're interested in a guided scuba, snorkel, or SNUBA excursion, check out the following companies. *NOTE:* Again, most of these trips can be booked through your hotel activities desk.

- **The Fair Wind.** Reservations, (808) 345-0268 or (800) 677-9461; www.fair-wind.com. Sails on two cruises daily from Keauhou Bay. The fun thing about the *Fair Wind II* boat is the 15-foot water slide and high jump platform from the top deck—older kids will love it. The morning cruise lasts from 9:00 a.m. to 1:30 p.m. and includes a continental breakfast, barbecue lunch, and snorkeling or SNUBA diving at Kealakekua Bay. Admission is $119 for adults, $75 for children ages four to twelve, $29 for kids three and younger. The afternoon cruise, offered on Tuesday, Thursday, and Saturday (during the busy seasons) from 2:00 to 6:30 p.m., also goes to Kealakekua Bay for underwater fun, and lots of snacks are offered, as well as a late barbecue lunch. Prices are $109 for adults and $69 for children, free for kids three and younger.

- **Kamanu Charters.** Reservations, (808) 329-2021 or (800) 348-3091; www.kamanu.com. Hosts snorkeling and sailing cruises that cost $80 for adults, $50 for children twelve and younger.

- **Ocean Sports.** Reservations, (808) 886-6666 or (888) 724-5234; www.hawaii oceansports.com. Offers a morning snorkel and lunch cruise that costs $99 for adults, $49 for children between twelve and five, under five years old are free. There is also an evening sunset cruise for $90 and $45, respectively. Cruises include equipment and towels and run Monday, Wednesday, Friday, and Saturday.

- **The Body Glove.** Reservations, (808) 326-7122 or (800) 551-8911; www.bodyglovehawaii.com. Charges $73 for adults, $53 for kids ages six to seventeen for the 1:00 to 4:00 p.m. tour; kids younger than five are free. Kids enjoy the 15-foot water slide, high dive, and scores of water toys. It's primarily a snorkeling cruise, and it leaves from Pawai Bay. An 8:00 a.m. to 12:30 p.m. daily tour costs $112 for adults and $72 for ages six to seventeen.

- **Sea Quest.** Reservations, (808) 329-7238 or (888) 732-2283; www.seaquest hawaii.com. Six-person rafts leave from Keauhou Bay, at the south end of Alii Drive. Trips cost $89 for four hours and $69 for three hours. Children's prices (ages five to twelve) are $72 and $59, respectively. The boat stops at two snorkeling spots.

- **Kona *Atlantis* Submarine.** For a glimpse into the colorful underwater world without getting wet, this submarine may suit your family. This craft dives to 100 feet, where passengers gaze out windows and watch a scuba team interact with the colorful creatures of the deep. The coastal cruise has views and narration of Kona's historic sights. Tickets are $80.10 for adults, $40.50 for children twelve and younger; call (808) 329-6626 or (800) 548-6262, or visit www.goatlantis.com. (Kids must be at least 3 feet tall.)

Hawaiian **Entertainment**

For a full-scale luau while in Kona, the **King Kamehameha's Kona Beach Hotel** (808-326-4969) hosts a longstanding luau that is well reputed among locals. Performances are every Sunday, Tuesday, Wednesday, Thursday, and Friday at 5:00 p.m. Admission is $65 for adults, $29 for children ages five to twelve.

The **Royal Kona Resort** (808-329-3111), also located in Kailua-Kona, hosts a "Drums of Polynesia" luau every Monday, Wednesday, and Friday evening. Tickets are $60 for adults, $23.20 for children ages six through twelve, and children younger than six are admitted free. Up the coast in Kohala, most of the larger resorts offer their own Polynesian revue.

Hulihee Palace (all ages)

In the center of Kona, on Alii Drive; (808) 329-1877; www.huliheepalace.org. Open Monday through Saturday 9:00 a.m. to 4:00 p.m., Sunday 10:00 a.m. to 4:00 p.m. $

Hulihee Palace, built in 1838, is a two-story building commissioned by John Kuakini, Hawaii's first governor. It was used as a summer retreat for ruling monarchs until 1916. Tours offer a chance to see the period furniture and learn about the lifestyles of Hawaii's monarchs. Although Iolani Palace on Oahu was the formal headquarters for kings and queens, Hulihee was a place they came to for relaxation and recreation.

NOTE: Hulihee Palace suffered extensive damage from the October 2006 earthquake. At press time, tours have been suspended due to the repair and restoration process. Updated information can be found on the Web site.

Where to Eat

Kona Beach Restaurant. 75–5660 Palani Road; (808) 329-2911; www.konabeachhotel .com. The King Kamehameha Hotel's breakfast and lunch restaurant is open 11:00 a.m. to 9:00 p.m. and serves up plenty of good food in that time. All the favorites are here, but the banana bread is a special breakfast treat. $

Buns in the Sun. In Lanihau Shopping Center; (808) 326-2774. "Buns" features a great selection of bakery goods and sandwiches. $

Drysdale's Two. On the west side of Keauhou Center, Alii Drive and Keauhou Highway; (808) 322-0070. Set up like a "Cheers" type of sports bar, Drysdale's Two features big-screen televisions in every corner for watching sports events, movies, and so on. Along with an incredible number of tropical drinks, the restaurant serves very good sandwiches and suppers. Plus, there are unusual menu items sure to bring about a lively discussion with your family, e.g., buffalo and ostrich burgers. $$

O's Bistro. 75–1027 Henry Street (at Mamalahoa Highway); (808) 327-6565; www .osbistro.com. You'll certainly find something for everyone—it's noodles every which way you can imagine them. Not only does Chef

Amy Ferguson-Ota produce culinary delights for lunch and dinner, but also you can buy prepackaged noodles to cook at home! $$$

Where to Stay

ResortQuest Kona by the Sea. 75–6106 Alii Drive; (808) 327-2300 or (877) 997-6667; www.resortquesthawaii.com. (Condominiums) $$–$$$

King Kamehameha's Kona Beach Hotel. At the pier, next to Ahuena Heiau; (808) 329-2911 or (866) 228-9009; www.konabeach hotel.com. $$

Keauhou Beach Resort. 78–6740 Alii Drive; (808) 322-3441 or (800) 688-7444; www.outrigger.com. $$–$$$

Pu`ukala Lodge. P.O. Box 2967, Kailua-Kona 96745; (808) 325-1729 or (888) 325-1729;

www.puukala-lodge.com. Hosts Ron and Tom of Pu`ukala Lodge will steer you to great restaurants, hidden beaches, and worthwhile tourist adventures. Families can rent the first-floor suite with full kitchenette. $–$$

Royal Kona Resort. 75–582 Alii Drive; (808) 329-3111 or (800) 222-5642; www.royalkona .com. $$–$$$$

Holualoa, Kealakekua, and Captain Cook

Heading south from Kailua-Kona, Alii Drive leads toward the mountain and joins Highway 11.

You'll pass through the small towns of Honalo, Kealakekua, Captain Cook, Honaunau, and Keokea en route to the southern coast of the island and Milolii. Before heading down the coast, however, take a detour on Hualalai Road, Route 182, which leads to Route 180 and the charming town of Holualoa.

Route 182 leads straight up the mountain to Route 180, where you'll run into Holualoa. This is a small town that's recently become a haven for art galleries. The views from here are expansively scenic, encompassing all of Kailua-Kona and the harbor. It's much cooler here compared to the coastal towns surrounding Kona. The vegetation is lush with coffee trees, macadamia nut groves, and banana, mango, and papaya trees.

Continuing south on Route 11, another group of historic sites surrounds Keauhou Bay. A monument marks the 1814 birthplace of Kamehameha III. Nearby is a *holua*, a grassy hill that was used as a makeshift water slide during rainstorms. Hawaiians of yesteryear would slide down the hill on wooden sleds.

A few miles from Keauhou is the little town of Honalo, really nothing more than a junction for Routes 180 and 11. The Daifukuji Buddhist Temple is an interesting attraction located here. It's **free** and open daily 9:00 a.m. to 4:00 p.m.

Big Island Trivia

Kauna`oa Beach was named the best beach in the world twice by *Condé Nast Traveler.* To keep the beach clean, pristine, and full of coral and fish life, the Mauna Kea Beach Hotel limits access to thirty passes at a time. Try to be there by 9:00 a.m. to get in right away, or wait until someone leaves. It is located near the Mauna Kea Beach Hotel, about 31 miles north of Kona

Kona Historical Society Museum (all ages)

Off Route 11 (follow the sign for Kona Meat Company Market) in Kealakekua. Located in the old Greenwell Store, built in 1875 by H. L. Greenwell, a local entrepreneur; (808) 323-3222; www.konahistorical.org. Open 10:00 a.m. to 2:00 p.m. Monday through Friday. $

The first attraction worth stopping at as you pass through the South Kona towns of Kealakekua and Captain Cook is the Kona Historical Society Museum. It's on the National and Hawaiian Registers of Historic Places. Here, exhibits show what life was like in Kona in the early part of the twentieth century. There are artifacts, manuscripts, and lots of old photographs depicting the Kona community.

The museum also offers several tours in the community, but our favorite is the Uchida Coffee Farm; $20 for adults; $7.50 for children five through 12. Here you can tour a working farm that has been producing coffee since the 1930s. It brings the coffee pioneer's story to life by depicting the daily lives of early Japanese immigrants who came to these islands in the mid-1920s. You can walk through the coffee and macadamia orchards, tour the historic farmhouse, and visit with the donkey and chickens. Along the way, docents dressed in costume are available to offer a personal explanation and answer questions. (Reservations required.)

The museum also sponsors a variety of jeep tours of the surrounding countryside and a historical boat tour, usually in late January, that travels south from Kailua-Kona along the coast. There's really no fixed schedule, but it's certainly worth investigating. It's a wonderful opportunity to explore the area with knowledgeable guides.

King's Trail Rides (ages 8 and up)

Off Highway 11 at mile marker 111, Kealakekua; (808) 323-2388 or (808) 345-0616; www .konacowboy.com. Children must be older than 7 and have previous riding experience. $$$$

For tours of the four-legged persuasion, in the outskirts of Kealakekua, King's Trail Rides offers a two-hour tour for $135 on weekdays, $150 on weekends and holidays. The tour includes a two-hour horseback ride to Captain Cook's monument in Kealakekua Bay, then a long break for a gourmet picnic lunch and time for snorkeling. They even provide the mask and snorkels! There are no discounts for children.

Royal Kona Coffee Mill (all ages)

On Route 11, Captain Cook; (808) 328-2511. Open daily 7:30 a.m. to 5:00

In Captain Cook, Napoopoo Road branches off Route 11 and leads to the Royal Kona Coffee Mill. The mill has been fashioned into a museum of sorts, with displays portraying life in the old-fashioned coffee plantations. There also are **free** coffee samples and a souvenir shop.

Amy Greenwell Ethnobotanical Garden (all ages)

In the town of Captain Cook, off Highway 11; (808) 323-3318; www.bishopmuseum.org /greenwell. Open weekdays 8:30 a.m. to 5:00 p.m. Donations ($4) requested. Guided tours are offered Wednesday and Friday at 1:00 p.m. for $5 per person.

The fifteen-acre Amy Greenwell Ethnobotanical Garden is a wonderful place to walk around. The gardens focus on education, conservation, and research of traditional Hawaiian plants and land use. You will see more than 200 species of plants that grew in traditional farms and native forests of Kona before Captain Cook arrived in the late 1700s. Don't forget sunscreen, hats, and mosquito repellent.

Pu`uhonua O Honaunau National Historical Park (all ages)

Off Route 11, Keokea, past Honaunau. Follow Route 160 as it veers toward the ocean; (808) 328-2326; www.nps.gov/puho. The park is open daily from 7:00 a.m. to 8:00 p.m. The visitor center is open daily from 8:00 a.m. to 5:00 p.m. $5 per vehicle. The visitor center has maps and brochures detailing a self-guided tour. *NOTE:* You can also take the coastal road that leads south for about 4 miles from Kealakekua Bay. If you're traveling on Route 160, notice the quaint, castle-like St. Benedict's Painted Church.

The 180-acre Pu`uhonua, or Ancient Place of Refuge, is one of the most important historic sites in all the islands. Some archaeologists claim this sacred temple was used in the mid-1500s, while others say it was used at least 200 years earlier. Places of refuge were an integral part of old Hawaiian culture. Within these areas, absolution was granted to opposing armies, *kapu* (taboo) breakers, or anyone guilty of disobeying common law. If the miscreants could reach a *pu`uhonua* before being caught, they were safe within its boundaries. Kahuna lived here for the sole purpose of granting salvation to the inhabitants; they alone had the power to cleanse the wrongdoers' *mana,* or spirits. This temple at Honaunau is the largest of its kind in all Hawaii.

The temple was completely restored and earned national park status in 1961. During the restoration local artists studied old records and drawings from ancient voyaging ships to give the site as much authenticity as possible. They used traditional techniques and tools to carve the renditions of the gods from large *ohia* logs.

Big Island Trivia

Queen Ka`ahumanu once swam a great distance to the Pu`uhonua after an argument with her husband, Kamehameha I. She hid under a large stone, but her barking dog gave away where she was hiding. Her husband soon found her and the two made up.

Ho`okena

To get to Ho`okena follow the well-marked road leading off Highway 11 just a few miles south of the Pu`uhonua O Honaunau exit.

Continuing south, after Keokea, the next towns are Kealia and Ho`okena, the latter a charming coastal town with a wonderful beach. The beach park offers picnic tables and showers, and the long black-sand beach is ideal for swimming and bodysurfing. The rest of this area is known as South Point, but since most people head to South Point after visiting the volcano, and most people go to the volcano from the Hilo side of the island, South Point is covered in detail in the Hilo section of this chapter.

NOTE: There are few accommodations and restaurants in this area. Most visitors stay (and dine) in nearby Kona or Kohala.

Fishing Trips

Kona is ranked among the world's best sites for deep-sea fishing, particularly for marlin. There are a few different ways to go about trolling for that "big one." Usually boats are available for either a full-day or half-day trip and can be rented as a private or shared charter. Rates vary from $85 for a half day on a shared charter to $400 for a full day on a private charter. The gear is usually included in the price, and no licenses are required.

There are a few booking agencies that will arrange a fishing trip according to your family's size and budget: Charter Services, (808) 334-1881; Kona Activities Center, (808) 329-3171; Kona Charter Skippers Association, (808) 329-3600; and Jack's Kona Charters, (888) 584-5662.

Also at the harbor is the headquarters for Captain Zodiac (www.captainzodiac.com), which provides oceangoing tours and snorkeling along the Kona Coast, combined with a light picnic lunch. The advantage of traveling in a Zodiac, a tough, virtually unsinkable motorized rubber boat that holds up to sixteen people, is that its small size enables it to explore the nooks and crannies, including sea caves. The adventure lasts four hours and costs $90 for adults, $80 for children ages four to twelve; younger than age four prohibited. For more information call (808) 329-3199.

North Kona

North on Highways 180 and 19.

Just north of Kailua-Kona and the King Kamehameha Kona Beach Hotel is the site of the old Kona Airport, which has been turned into a beach park called Old Kona Airport State Recreation Area. Facilities here include picnic tables, showers, restrooms, and lots of parking. The beach is somewhat rocky and therefore not great for swimming, but the snorkeling is good. Beware of rough waters during high surf.

Kona Coast State Park (all ages)
About 2 miles north of the airport, off Route 19, between mile markers 91 and 90.

This beach park offers picnic tables and restrooms. Swimming is safe here during calm weather. The dirt road is a bit rugged but passable, and it's only about 1½ miles to the beach. On the way look for a well-defined path that leads to the right. A five-minute walk will take you to scenic and secluded Mahaiula Bay.

Honokohau Harbor is between Kailua-Kona and the airport and is the departure point for the majority of deep-sea fishing excursions. If a fishing expedition is too daunting with young children, at least visit the weigh station at the harbor. It's **free** and often exciting to watch. When the fishing boats come back, the large catches are hoisted off the boat, measured, and photographed. The Harbor Hut Restaurant, easily found at the harbor, has excellent food and lots for the kids to look at during lunch.

Dan McSweeney's Whale-Watching Adventure (all ages)
Trips depart from Honokohau Harbor; (808) 322–0028 or (888) 942-5376; www.ilovewhales .com. $$$$

The humpback season runs from November through April, but during the rest of the year you can always find other types of whales in Hawaii's waters, such as false killers, pygmy, and sperm whales. Visitors are guaranteed a sighting, or else they're invited to come back for **free** next time. On every trip Capt. Dan McSweeney takes a photo of a whale, and all passengers get a souvenir copy.

Kohala

North of Kona on the Queen Kaahumanu Highway.

The Kohala coastline north of the Kona International Airport is divided into North and South Kohala. South Kohala features the best and the most beautiful swimming beaches on the island, and North Kohala stretches to Hawi, the northern tip of the island.

Traveling north on the Queen Kaahumanu Highway, Highway 19, you'll get a sense of why Hawaii is known as the Big Island. There are no structures at all; just black, barren lava. Driving through this desolate lava desert, beware of the "Kona Nightingales," wild donkeys that were originally brought to this area to carry saddlebags full of coffee. They

akekua Bay

Highway 11 continues to **Kealakekua Bay,** a wonderful underwater playground and one of the best snorkeling sites on the island. Dozens of commercial charters flock here on picnic, snorkel, and sail trips. Although the bay can get crowded, there's still plenty of room for travelers who venture here on their own. For those independents, access to the bay is via **Napoopoo Beach Park,** where there are restrooms, showers, and picnic tables.

Not only is Kealakekua Bay regarded as a prime snorkeling locale, it's also an important historic site. If you do drive, notice the Hikiau Heiau at the parking lot. This heiau is dedicated to the fertility god, Lono, who Hawaiians of olden days believed would be resurrected and return to this bay. The well-preserved heiau is carved into the steep cliff, where the priests were afforded an expansive view of the ocean so that they might spot Lono's arrival. The cliffs above the heiau are reported to contain numerous gravesites of ancient chiefs.

History played havoc with the Hawaiians' belief in Lono's return in a particularly ironic way. In January 1779 Capt. James Cook sailed his ships, *Resolution and Discovery*, into the tranquil waters of Kealakekua Bay. It just so happened that the locals were in the midst of their Makahiki celebration, an annual festival dedicated to rejoicing and thanking the gods for a fruitful harvest. Imagine their surprise when these two majestic ships appeared, full of never-before-seen Caucasian men.

It's understandable that the Hawaiians mistook Captain Cook for a personification of their sacred Lono. (Some Hawaiian scholars dispute this claim.) They showered the surprised captain and crew with accolades and gifts. Unfortunately for Cook, a variety of miscommunications and cultural insults ensued within a few weeks, and the Hawaiians no longer believed he was a benevolent god. A fierce battle followed, and Cook was killed at this very bay.

In 1874 a 27-foot marble pillar was built in the northern end of the bay as a memorial to Cook and his courageous forays into uncharted oceans.

now roam the area freely, including the highway. They have become quite a road hazard, especially at night.

Notice the Hawaiian-style graffiti that borders each side of the road, where local families or couples spell out their love and devotion with light-colored rocks that contrast sharply with the dark lava. Feel free to pull over and create your own message.

The string of hotels and resorts situated on this coastline begins about 30 miles from the airport. Here are some of the finest ultra-deluxe resort properties in all Hawaii. From the first property, Kona Village Resort at Kaupulehu, to the last, Mauna Kea Beach Hotel at Kauna'oa Beach, there is really no designated town, in the sense of a post office and main street. It's almost as if each resort occupies its own little town. The first official town in the Kohala district is Kawaihae, a few miles north of the Mauna Kea Beach Resort.

The coastline has a lot more to offer than nice hotels. There are a series of fishponds, petroglyph fields, tide pools, and rarely visited archaeological sites. The area is full of historic and natural wonders, and nonguests are encouraged to tour the grounds of each hotel. Most of the hotel activity desks distribute **free** maps and brochures listing walking tours and important stops. All of the properties are on well-marked roads leading down to the ocean from Highway 19.

Anaehoomalu Bay is part of the grounds of the Waikoloa Beach Marriott and Hilton Waikoloa Hotel and a great place to watch sailboarders. The beach is open to the public, and although the sand may be a bit rough, it's still wonderful for swimming, snorkeling, scuba, and sailboarding.

A few minutes' walk north along the bay leads to well-formed tide pools and ancient fishponds. Hawaiians of old constructed fishponds with gaps so that young mullet could swim in and feed in the protected area, but once they ate a lot and grew to a certain size, they could no longer swim back through the gaps to freedom in the open ocean. These particular fishponds were solely for the chiefs of this area.

There are well-marked trails surrounding the bay that lead to petroglyph fields and the lava path known as the King's Highway. In old Hawaii, the king's tax collectors would follow this path to collect payment in the form of fresh fish from oceanside dwellers.

Kona Village Resort Luau (all ages)

In Kona Village Resort, off Highway 19; (808) 325-5555 or (800) 367-5290; www.konavillage .com. The resort hosts an authentic luau, complete with an imu ceremony, every Wednesday and Friday. Nonguests are welcome to attend, but reservations are required. $$$$

Even if you're not staying at the Kona Village Resort, take the road down from Highway 19 to walk around the property. Hotel rooms are authentic hales, or grass huts. There are no televisions or telephones; this resort is for people who really want to get away from it all. You can take a **free** tour of the resort and its surrounding historic sites daily at 11:00 a.m.

Paniolo Riding Adventure (ages 8 and up)

In Kawaihae, at mile 13.2 Kohala Mountain Road, Highway 250; (808) 889-5354, www .panioloadventures.com.

Paniolo Adventures offers horseback riding, mountain biking, and hiking tours—all throughout Ponoholo Ranch, an 11,000-acre, environmentally friendly working cattle ranch in the historic Kohala Mountains.

There are lush pasturelands, native woods, cool mountain air, and spectacular views of the coastline, surrounding volcanic peaks, and often the island of Maui in the distance.

Big Island Trivia

It takes 345 pounds of pressure to crack the macadamia nut's outer shell.

Ponoholo Ranch and Kahua Ranch, its sister ranch, are among the oldest ranches on the Big Island. Ponoholo ranges from the rim of Pololu Valley in the rain forest to nearly sea level in the Kohala desert. The land was once a training ground for Kamehameha's troops and bears the ruins of ancient Hawaiian agricultural fields, settlements, and other prehistoric sites. Its 11,000 acres cover three climate zones and stretch from the rain forest at 4,800 feet above sea level to the ocean. Ponoholo has the second-largest herd of cattle on the island.

The guided tours stay on ranch land at all times and include rest stops at points of interest or sites for great photos. On all tours visitors learn about ranch operations, local plants, wildlife, geology, and a bit of Hawaiian history and legend. These adventures offer great views, moderate exercise, lots of fresh air, and fun.

Guides greet and outfit visitors with proper equipment for their tour (raincoats if needed, boots, and so on). A safety and basic skills demonstration gives beginners and novices guidance and reminders for proper riding techniques so they can thoroughly enjoy their adventure.

Waikoloa

Head inland on Waikoloa Road for 7 miles.

The little town of Waikoloa contains a small shopping center with a grocery store, a few boutiques, and restaurants, mostly serving residents in the local community. A few rental condominiums are also here. There is **free** entertainment at the King's Shops, the local center that features shopping, dining, and entertainment. Your kids will appreciate the great food pavilion with a good choice of food.

Waikoloa Stables (all ages)
In Waikoloa Town; (808) 883-9335.

The stables offer a number of trail rides as well as a few rodeos. Rides are available by appointment only and groups must have at least eight people. An excursion features a trail ride that lasts for a half hour, and the rest of the time is spent on fun activities, such as barrel and relay races. Prices vary according to group size.

Vog and **Laze**

You may notice the presence of vog and laze, two atmospheric conditions that are by-products of volcanic eruptions. Vog is a volcanic fog that is caused by sulfur particles and sometimes makes the sky look more like southern California than Hawaii. Laze occurs when lava flows into the ocean and reacts with the saltwater, creating hydrogen chloride gas. The gas dissolves in water droplets and forms hydrochloric acid, which can cause stinging eyes and sore throats. These unpleasant conditions usually are blown out to sea with normal trade winds.

Puako Petroglyph Field (all ages)

In the Mauna Lani Resort Area, composed of the Mauna Lani Resort and the Fairmont Orchid at Mauna Lani.

The best way to see the petroglyphs is to take the well-marked, 1½-mile path that leads through the field. It's a short hike and, although the heat can be stifling, it's very easy and suitable for young children. (Be sure to wear hiking shoes and bring some water along. Hot lava radiates heat like a lit barbecue pit.)

It's a fascinating experience to walk among the 3,000-plus etchings on the rocks in this 233-acre park. These are considered some of the oldest, finest, and most extensive petroglyph examples in all Hawaii. Look for circles outlining a small hole. Families placed their infants' umbilical cords in the hole to forever connect them to the land, *aina,* and ensure a long and healthy life.

Holoholokai Beach Park (all ages)

Part of the grounds of the Orchid at Mauna Lani. Open from 6:30 a.m. to 7:00 p.m.

Although quite scenic, the beach offers limited water access because it's full of rocks. The picnic tables and beautiful surroundings provide an ideal spot for a shady respite and wonderful tide-pool exploring.

Pu`ukohola Heiau National Historic Site (all ages)

In Kawaihae, where Highway 19 intersects with Route 270; (808) 882-7218; www.nps.gov /puhe. Open daily 7:30 a.m. to 4:00 p.m. free.

The Pu`ukohola Heiau National Historic Site encompasses a whopping seventy-seven acres. It was built between 1790 and 1791 by Kamehameha I. The area is composed of the Mailekini Heiau and the nearby John Young House. John Young was an English seaman who settled in Hawaii and became a close friend and advisor to Kamehameha the Great. It was Young who taught the Hawaiians how to use muskets and cannons, which helped Kamehameha in his quest to conquer all the islands.

Each August Pu`ukohola Heiau hosts the Hawaiian Cultural Festival, where visitors experience native customs and traditions. Demonstrations and cultural workshops allow visitors to learn about Hawaiian crafts, dance, music, and games.

The site is maintained by the National Park Service. A free map at the visitor center highlights specific points of interest.

Kohala Divers (ages 12 and up)

Off Route 270, in Kawaihae Shopping Center; (808) 882-7774; www.kohaladivers.com. Open daily 8:00 a.m. to 6:00 p.m.

Kohala Divers' PADI Five Star Center offers an array of diving and snorkeling equipment for rent. The well-trained staff can assist you in selecting the right equipment at the right price and even direct you to the coolest spots around the island. All of their rental gear is state-of-the-art with the safety of the diver foremost. Their tanks are aluminum with 3,000 PSI. Besides renting equipment, they also offer a variety of dive charter rides, ranging

Big Island Trivia

The island's peaks are home to the world's biggest telescope and more scientific observatories in one place than anywhere else in the world, representing nine nations.

from $59 seasonal whale-watching tours to $179 introductory scuba diving class, with prices in between.

Spencer Beach County Park (all ages)

It's just a few miles north of Pu`ukohola Heiau, off Highway 19.

Spencer Beach County Park is a great place to snorkel, swim, and picnic. There are restrooms, showers, picnic tables, tennis courts, and even electricity for campers. An offshore reef around Kawaihae Bay protects the waters and helps keep them calm, providing great swimming conditions for kids. The reef also is home to many colorful species of fish, making for great snorkeling. Trails lead from this beach park up to the Pu`ukohola Heiau.

Where to Eat

Brown's Beach House. One North Kaniku Drive; (808) 885-2000. Offers Pacific Rim favorites for lunch and dinner such as steamed opakapaka laulau, plus music and hula. $$

The Grill Restaurant and Lounge. One North Kaniku Drive; (808) 885-2000. Features fresh seafood and grill specialties (dinner only) with a special kids' menu. $$$$

The Ocean Bar and Grill. One North Kaniku Drive; (808) 885-2000. Has traditional island favorites such as smoked-chicken pizza, Oriental chicken salad, and Puna goat cheese salad. $$

Canoehouse. 68–1400 Mauna Lani Drive; (808) 885-6622. A visit to Mauna Lani would be incomplete without sampling the innovative Hawaii Regional Cuisine at Canoehouse. The views are spectacular and the flavors sublime. $$$$

**Pahu i`a.** 72-100 Kaupulehu Drive, Kaupulehu, Kona; (808) 325-8000. The signature restaurant for Four Seasons Hualalai, Pahu i`a

is certain to be a memorable dining experience. Signature items include Keahole lobster, Dungeness crab, and fire-roasted Kona Kampachi—all harvested from the nearby OTEC Labs. (see page 99). The open-air eatery offers sweeping ocean views, with gentle rolling surf at breakfast and dinner. $$–$$$$

Where to Stay

Four Seasons Resort Hualalai. 72–100 Kaupulehu Drive, Kaupulehu, Kona; (808) 325-8000 or (888) 340-5662; www.fourseasons .com/hualalai. This 243-room, low-rise, bungalow-style resort has a spa for parents and educational programs for children, including celestial navigation. The complimentary Kids for All Seasons program runs daily from 8:00 a.m. to 5:00 p.m. and is filled with exciting adventures such as treasure hunts, canoe lessons, sand sculpting, swimming, and even volcano building. $$$–$$$$

Hapuna Beach Prince Hotel. 62–100 Kauna`oa Drive; (808) 880-1111; www.hapuna beachprincehotel.com. Mauna Kea Beach

Hotel and the Hapuna Beach Prince Hotel share grounds. The beach is one of the prettiest in all Hawaii; it's long, sandy, crescent-shaped, shallow, calm, and great for children during summer months. Families with young children gravitate toward the north end, where a small cove provides year-round calm waters. In winter, however, Hapuna's rough waters can be dangerous, so use caution when entering the water. The Prince Keiki Club offers a variety of activities including Hawaiian-style arts and crafts, sandcastle building, hula dancing, T-shirt painting, beach treasure hunts, and movies. Full- and half-day rates are available. $$–$$$$

Hilton Waikoloa Village. 425 Waikoloa Beach Drive; (808) 886-1234; www.hilton waikoloavillage.com. Guests can cruise around the resort on mahogany boats or an air-conditioned Swiss-made tram. The resort encompasses a whopping sixty-two acres with three pools, two of which have waterfalls and waterslides. The Camp *Menehune* program for kids is available as a day or night camp. It's for ages five through twelve and can accommodate non-Hilton guests. The camp even has its own Web site: www.hilton waikoloavillage.com/camp. $$–$$$$

Kona Village Resort. Queen Kaahumanu Highway; (808) 325-5555 or (800) 367-5290; www.konavillage.com. An all-inclusive property where accommodations are Hawaiian-style shacks. Each shack, or hale, reflects the Polynesian style of architecture. This is among the oldest resorts on the coast but is one of the very best—it epitomizes the

Swimming with the **Dolphins**

A truly wonderful attraction at the **Hilton Waikoloa Resort** is the dolphin pool, where people can actually swim and play with Atlantic bottlenose dolphins. Before any animal-rights activists begin to worry, the dolphins live in a specially built saltwater pond that's sixty-five times larger than federal regulations deem necessary. The dolphins come from Florida, where in their natural habitat they swim in lagoons and bays not more than 20 feet deep. Here, their pond is 350 feet long and 22 feet deep in the center, and contains 2½ million gallons of seawater.

The program was started by two well-respected veterinarians, and the experience is designed to be educational and safe, for both humans and dolphins. You don't get to sit astride the dolphins and ride them like a horse, and there are no acrobatic tricks performed. Instead, chosen participants are given a short lecture on marine life, and then they stand in the shallow part of the pool. If the dolphins want to be touched, they stop; if not, they glide right by. Guests of the resort and nonguests who want to participate are chosen via a lottery system.

For more information about the **Dolphin Quest** at Hilton Waikoloa, call (808) 886-2875 or (800) 248-3316; www.dolphinquest.org. There are a variety of programs, with different prices. Children must be five years old. Programs may be booked online or by phone up to two months in advance.

Big Island Trivia

The profitable macadamia nut industry began in Honoka`a when John MacAdams harvested the first batch of these tasty treats in 1892.

aloha spirit and offers a truly Hawaiian vacation. The complimentary children's program is offered daily (except May and September) for ages six through twelve. There are fishing contests, coconut painting, net throwing, and Hawaiian crafts, mixed with pool visits and ball games. $$–$$$$

Mauna Kea Beach Hotel. 62–100 Mauna Kea Beach; (808) 882-7222 or (800) 882-6060; www.maunakeabeachhotel.com. The Mauna Kea Beach Hotel is currently closed for an extensive renovation and is expected to open in December 2008. In the meantime, the beach remains open (do visit—it's one of the best) as well as a few restaurants. $$$$

Mauna Lani Resort. 68–1400 Mauna Lani Drive; (808) 885-6622; www.maunalani.com. Mauna Lani has the distinction of being the only beach resort in the United States to be named one of the "World's Top Earth Friendly Getaways." The resort has made great strides in the implementation of solar energy and golf course water systems. Camp Mauna Lani is offered for kids five through twelve. Counselors take them throughout the resort, exploring the fish, secret ponds, caves, tide pools, and petroglyphs. Cost is $50 a day per child. $$$$

Fairmont Orchid at Mauna Lani. One North Kaniku Drive; (808) 885-2000 or (800) 257-7544; www.orchid-maunalani.com. An absolutely wonderful luxury resort, with every amenity under the sun, including a

wide array of activities, golf, restaurants, etc. The Keiki Aloha Adventure Program is offered year-round for either a full or half day. Daily adventures for kids ages five through twelve include hikes to petroglyphs, tide pools, shell hunting, Hawaiian crafts, shark tour, and koi feeding. $$$–$$$$

Waikoloa Beach Marriott. 69–275 Waikoloa Beach Drive; (808) 886-6789. Part of the statewide Marriott chain, this property has been newly renovated. For kids, there are lots of Hawaiian cultural activities on site, including lei-making classes, hula and ukulele lessons, and walking history tours. There is also a children's pool on the property that has a partial sand bottom and a water slide. $$

North Kohala: Hawi and Kapa`au

Highway 270, known as the Akoni Pule Highway, continues up the coast for what is among the prettiest drives in all Hawaii.

You'll pass through North Kohala's two major towns, Hawi and Kapa`au, and the road ends at Pololu Valley. The road leads into an area that's damper than dry, desertlike Kona; trees with hanging mossy vines stand vigil at the roadside next to boldly colored flowers, palms, and banana trees. Time and modern lifestyles haven't changed secluded North Kohala too much, as witnessed by the old homes and stores still functioning for the small group of people who call Kohala home.

An alternative road, Route 250, cuts inland from Waimea to Hawi and offers expansive views. It meanders through miles of green grass, an occasional cactus, and small old-fashioned shacks. About halfway to Hawi the Von Holt Memorial Park is a great spot for a picnic. As you get closer to Hawi, you'll find huge panoramic vistas of rolling hills and sparkling seas.

Highway 270 eventually curves around the tip of the Big Island and leads to a junction with Highway 250 at Hawi, a former booming sugar town that's relatively deserted today. Local residents are trying to revive the area, and there's been slow growth of new stores, restaurants, and art galleries. There's a charming old-fashioned theater in town that still runs movies.

You can get **free** maps, information, and a chance to "talk story" with the old-timers at the Kohala Visitor Center in the center of town.

If you're heading all the way to the end of the road at Pololu Valley (and if you've come this far, you might as well go all the way to Pololu), Kapa`au will be the last chance to stock up on food, gas, and supplies.

NOTE: Beyond the hotels along the Kohala Coast, the choices for accommodations and restaurants for families are limited.

Lapakahi State Park (all ages)

About 12 miles north of Kawaihae; well marked from Highway 270. Open daily 8:00 a.m. to 4:00 p.m.

Lapakahi State Park is a must-visit attraction, full of historical significance. This ancient fishing village has been restored and reconstructed to look just as it did before westerners

Hawaii Trivia

The coconut tree was an important resource in Hawaii. It served as a source of food and water, provided material for building and rope making, and was made into drums. Cutting down the coconut grove of another person was considered an act of war.

arrived. It's a living museum, with exhibits you can actually touch and feel, that let you learn firsthand about local history.

The different stations are numbered and include canoe sheds, a salt-making area, and a fishing shrine dedicated to Ku`ula, god of fishing. Children will love learning how to play *ulumaika* and *konane*, Hawaiian games similar, respectively, to bowling and checkers.

The Koai`e Cove Marine Life Conservation District is next to Lapakahi and offers good snorkeling, weather permitting. It's rough and isolated here, so only expert swimmers should enter the water.

Mahukona is a few minutes' drive past Lapakahi, and Kapa`a Beach is a few minutes beyond Mahukona. Although the beach is rocky at Kapa`a, it's a great place for a quiet picnic and expansive views.

During the heyday of the sugar industry, Mahukona was a busy port from which the Kohala Sugar Company shipped its harvest. Today all that's left are abandoned warehouses and buildings. During the summer months the bay and pier are good for swimming and snorkeling, but stay out of the water during the winter.

Mo`okini Heiau—The Most Important in all Hawaii (all ages)

To get to Mo`okini Heiau from Highway 270, turn left toward Upolu Airport at mile marker 20. This one-lane road will end at the runway. Turn left and continue on a rough, bumpy dirt road for about 2 miles to the isolated site. Look for a tall transmission tower that marks the road to the heiau. When you come to a closed gate, it's just a five-minute walk up to the temple.

Mo`okini Heiau is the oldest, most important heiau in all Hawaii, and in 1963 it became the first Hawaiian site to be included on the National Register of Historic Sites. There are genealogical charts that can trace the origins of this place to A.D. 480 and the High Priest Kuamo`o Mo`okini. It was designed and constructed only for the ali`i (chiefs), who came here to purify themselves. The temple is shaped as an odd-sized rectangle, 125 by 250 feet. The walls are 30 feet high and 15 feet thick. One legend says the heiau was built in a single night; stones were passed hand to hand by a 14-mile chain of 18,000 men that stretched here from Pololu Valley to the east. Today the site's caretaker, Kahuna Nui Leimomi Mo`okini Lum, is a direct descendant of the first Mo`okini priest.

The heiau was the point of convergence for religious life in Kohala. Kamehameha the Great was born in approximately 1758 right near the heiau, and historians believe he was taken here for his birth rites, returning as a young man to worship here and gather spiritual strength before he rebuilt Pu`ukohola Heiau in Kawaihae.

Just a few minutes' walk beyond Mo`okini Heiau, a small plaque marks the spot where Kamehameha the Great was born, Kamehameha Akahi Aina Hanau. Kamehameha the Great was raised in North Kohala, and it was here that he began his mission to unite the islands under one rule.

A Tale of **Two Statues**

Just beyond Hawi is the sleepy town of **Kapa`au,** best known for its huge statue of King Kamehameha. The statue was commissioned by King Kalakaua in 1878, and the kahuna (priests) of the time felt it was best to situate it in the community where he was born. If you happen to be visiting the Big Island on June 11, Kamehameha Day, be sure to drive up to Kapa`au to see the thousands of leis that are draped on this statue.

You may have noticed a similar statue in downtown Honolulu, on Oahu. This is because the two statues were created by the same person. The original, as soon as it was completed, was sent to Paris to be bronzed. The freight ship carrying the statue back from Paris to Honolulu sank, and everyone thought the nine-ton statue was lost forever. So, with the insurance money, King Kalakaua commissioned a new statue, which arrived in Honolulu in 1883. Soon after, a British ship arrived in Honolulu carrying the original statue, which had somehow been salvaged and unceremoniously dumped in a Port Stanley junkyard in the Falkland Islands.

Kamehameha County Park (all ages)
In Kapa`au, down a well-marked side road. free.

The park is definitely worth a stop if your children are itching to be active. It has a 25-yard pool, basketball and tennis courts, a driving range, weight rooms, and a little kiddie area, all **free** and open to the public.

Kalahikiola Congregational Church (all ages)
A few minutes' drive beyond Kapa`au. A sign points down a formal driveway, framed on both sides by pines and well-manicured stands of macadamia and palm trees.

The picturesque church was built in 1841 by the Reverend Elias Bond and his wife, Ellen. On the way to the church, you'll pass the weatherbeaten buildings of the old Bond Estate.

Pololu Valley (ages 12 and up)
Highway 270 ends at Pololu Valley Lookout.

From the Pololu Valley Lookout, you can see the astounding beauty of the Hamakua Coast. A series of trails here transcend five lush, relatively uninhabited valleys to Waipio, the most well known. By all means, do take the short trail to the bottom of the valley, where a beautiful black-sand beach awaits you. The trail takes about fifteen minutes and can be slippery if recent rains have fallen. But, slippery or not, this is one of the prettiest hikes in all Hawaii.

The beach is a series of sand dunes that offer safe swimming only during the summer months.

Waimea

Inland of South Kohala. A few routes lead to Waimea. If you're coming from Kailua-Kona, the quickest way is via Route 190, the Hawaii Belt Road, also known as Mamalahoa Highway. If you're coming from Kohala, the Kawaihae Road heads inland from Kawaihae straight to Waimea. From Hilo you can either travel up the Hamakua Coast on Highway 19 and head inland at Honoka`a or take the Saddle Road, Route 200, across the island and up to Waimea.

Waimea is a great *paniolo* (cowboy) town and the center of Parker Ranch, which encompasses 200,000 acres of Mauna Kea's western slopes and is one of the largest privately owned ranches in the United States. It was started in the 1800s by John Parker. Today 40,000 head of cattle and about 300 horses are raised here. This is picturesque country; the rolling, green, grassy hills contrast sharply with the desolate black lava fields of Kona.

Waimea is one of the few remaining towns in Hawaii that has maintained its old-fashioned paniolo heritage, the other most famous one being Makawao on Maui. Various rodeos and paniolo events are held in Waimea year-round. Kids will love the Anuenue Playground in the center of town. It was constructed by local residents and is the pride of the community. It's very unusual and certain to please kids of all ages.

Kamuela Museum (all ages)

On Route 19, just west of the junction with Route 250. Actual address: 66-1655 Kawaihae Road; (808) 885-4724; www.hawaiimuseums.org. Open daily 8:00 a.m. to 5:00 p.m. $

The Kamuela Museum is the largest privately owned museum in all the islands. It houses rare stone idols, some of the first Hawaiian bibles, and a collection of furniture handed down from various members of the old monarchy. There are antiques from all over the world and a wonderful set of old photographs depicting life on Parker Ranch from back in the 1800s to modern times.

Puuopelu (all ages)

A few minutes south of central Waimea, along Route 190; (808) 885-7655; www.parker ranch.com. Open Monday through Saturday 10:00 a.m. to 5:00 p.m. $–$$ (Cheaper prices are available by combining a tour with the Parker Ranch visitor center; description follows.)

You may not expect to find artworks by Degas or Renoir here in the midst of cattle country, but a visit to Puuopelu will prove you wrong. Richard Smart, heir to the Parker Ranch, was a longtime supporter and collector of fine art. He opened this museum before he died in 1992. It features the works of more than one hundred artists, some internationally acclaimed, some local superstars. This ultraclassy establishment is worth a visit.

Parker Ranch Visitor Center and Museum (all ages)
Across the road from Puuopelu; (808) 885-7655; www.parkerranch.com. Open Monday through Saturday 9:00 a.m. to 5:00 p.m. $$$

The center comprises both the Historic Home (Puuopelu, with its original homestead artifacts) and the Visitor Center Museum (with a video and an entire exhibit of the family history).

A visit to the Parker Ranch Visitor Center and Museum will give you a complete history and overview of the Parker Ranch and Waimea town. There are two museums and a wonderful slide show that demonstrates how today's ranch hands hold fast and proud to their important place in history.

Horseback Riding (ages 7 years and older)
Parker Ranch Stables, (808) 885-7655 or (877) 885-7999; www.parkerranch.com. All rides begin at the Blacksmith Shop on Pukalani Road. $$$$

Riders will feel like paniolo as they ride through old stone corrals over the 150,000-acre working ranch. The terrain is gentle and scenic—rolling green hillsides with majestic Mauna Kea soaring as a backdrop. Two rides are offered daily, 8:15 a.m. and 12:15 p.m. Each ride lasts for two hours.

Hilo

Hilo has the dubious distinction of being one of the rainiest cities in the United States, with more than 135 inches of annual rainfall. But don't let the rainy weather deter you from visiting. All that moisture has helped foster a beautiful, green, lush community full of waterfalls, gardens, and nurseries. In fact, Hilo is the orchid capital of the world and the only major town on the Big Island's windward coast.

The majority of Big Island visitors blindly head for Kona, missing the old-fashioned charms and natural scenery in Hilo. Although Kona is growing, fast-paced, and modern, Hilo has remained mostly unchanged. A few vegetarian eateries, coffeehouses, and art galleries have sprouted up in recent years, but for all intents Hilo is a small-town, slow-moving residential community.

Most of the buildings in downtown Hilo are two stories with raised wooden sidewalks and charming old-fashioned facades. Downtown boasts various gardens, natural phenomena, museums, and lots of riverbank fishing.

Merrie Monarch **Festival**

At one time, all of Hawaiian culture, mythology, and history were passed down through the movements and chants of the hula. Christian missionaries banned the hula in the early 1800s, effectively cutting Hawaiians off from their past. In 1883 King David Kalakaua, also known as the Merrie Monarch, requested that the hula be performed in public at his coronation, an act that revived the study and practice of hula, still thriving today.

At the **Merrie Monarch Festival,** twenty-five to thirty halau, or hula dance groups, perform the kahiko (ancient) and auana (modern) hula. During the festival, local hotels are 100 percent occupied, and restaurants can't prepare the food fast enough. Obtaining tickets is difficult, so unless you've planned ahead, don't expect to be admitted just because you happen to be in town during this spring festival. In fact, unless you're lucky enough to be attending the festival, it's better to plan a Hilo visit for another time. To get tickets you must write well in advance of your trip to Merrie Monarch Festival, 101 Aupuni Street, Suite 1014-A1, Hilo, HI 96720. Because the event is so popular and thousands of people send away for tickets, the event's organizers mandate that requests be sent after a certain date (usually in late December). It's best to check the Web site for ticket information: www.merriemonarch festival.org.

Walking Tour of Downtown Hilo (all ages)

Hilo Main Street offices are at 329 Kamehameha Avenue; (808) 935-8850; www.downtown hilo.com. Open 8:30 a.m. to 4:30 p.m. Monday through Friday. free.

Armed with a detailed map from the Hilo Main Street Program, you can take a **free** self-guided walking tour that highlights the important historic sites and leads you down streets and lanes that demonstrate Hilo's architectural diversity. The **free** pamphlet, Hilo Downtown Walking Tour, is also available at most local shops, restaurants, and hotels.

Banyan Drive (all ages)

The road follows the edge of Waiakea Peninsula, which occupies the east end of Hilo Bay.

The young and the old will be awed by a short walk down historic Banyan Drive. Each majestic tree is named after a famous politician, movie star, athletic hero, or other celebrity and was dedicated when its namesake visited Hilo. Some of the more famous trees were planted by Richard Nixon, Franklin D. Roosevelt, Babe Ruth, and Amelia Earhart. The series of banyans forms a green canopy that's quite picturesque.

Liliuokalani Gardens (all ages)

At the west end of Banyan Drive. Open daylight hours. free.

Liliuokalani Gardens is named after Hawaii's last reigning monarch. These formal Oriental-style gardens are a quiet, scenic place good for a meditative stroll, but it may not be exciting enough for energized children.

Hilo Farmers Market (all ages)

At the corner of Mamo Street and Kamehameha Avenue in downtown Hilo; (808) 933-1000; www.hilofarmersmarket.com. Open Wednesday and Saturday from dawn 'til it's gone!

Proclaimed the best farmers' market in all Hawaii, the Hilo Farmers Market is a must-see. Choose from the finest, freshest variety of exotic fruits, vegetables, and flowers, including lychee, starfruit, coconut, papaya, orchid, anthurium, heliconia, bird-of-paradise, protea, and even gardenia and roses. Be prepared to purchase more fruits and flowers than you'll ever need. Residents of other Hawaiian islands fly in regularly to Hilo just to shop here.

Nautilus Dive Center (ages 12 and up)

382 Kamehameha Avenue; (808) 935-6939; www.nautilusdivehilo.com. Open 9:00 a.m. to 4:00 p.m. Monday through Saturday.

If there are any scuba or snorkeling fans in your family, this is one of few dive shops on the Hilo side of the island that not only rent equipment but will take visitors on guided cruises. You also can pick up a free map detailing nearby dive sites.

Wailoa State Park (all ages)

On Piopio Street between Pauahi Street and Kamehameha Avenue; (808) 933-0416. The center is open Monday through Friday 8:30 a.m. to 4:30 p.m., except Wednesday, when it's open noon to 4:30 p.m.; the center is closed weekends. free.

At Wailoa State Park, you'll want to stop by the Wailoa Information Center for all sorts of free information on local sights and activities. There are also historical exhibits and artworks by local artists that rotate every month.

The East Hawaii Cultural Center (all ages)

141 Kalakaua Street; (808) 961-5711; www.ehcc.org. Open Monday through Saturday 10:00 a.m. to 4:30 p.m. free.

The center displays revolving exhibits by local and international artists. If you're on the Big Island in July, by all means come to the center for the annual Shakespeare in the Park Festival. Local performers design, direct, and stage various plays, performed under the banyan tree.

Lyman Mission House Museum (all ages)

276 Haili Street, across Waianuenue Avenue from the library; (808) 935-5021; www.lyman museum.org. Open Monday through Saturday 9:30 a.m. to 4:30 p.m.; closed Sunday. Guided tours offered at 11:00 a.m., 1:00 p.m., and 3:00 p.m. $

View life in Hawaii in the 1800s at the Lyman Mission House Museum, an old missionary

nd Trivia

home that's been converted into a living museum with wonderful artifacts such as old canoe paddles and stone implements. The home, built in 1839, is the oldest frame building on the whole island. Guided tours by docents offer a glimpse into the local history. Displays include period furniture and missionary artifacts.

Wailuku River State Park and Rainbow Falls (all ages)
Heading inland on Waianuenue Avenue. The park is well marked and easy to find.

The falls are colorful and beautiful as they cascade over boulders into a large pool and spray rainbow-colored plumes of water in the air.

Pe`epe`e Falls and Boiling Pots (all ages)
Continue inland on Waianuenue Avenue a few miles past Hilo Hospital and look for a sign for Pe`epe`e Falls and the Boiling Pots.

It's said that Mother Nature likes to enjoy a Jacuzzi bath in the Boiling Pots. A small path leads to an overlook where you'll see a series of naturally formed holes. The water in some of these holes actually bubbles as if it were a Jacuzzi. The scenic falls are just upriver from here.

Panaewa Rain Forest Zoo (all ages)
A few miles south of Hilo proper, at 25 Apuni Street. To get there continue on Route 11 toward Hawaii Volcanoes National Park. Open daily 9:00 a.m. to 4:00 p.m.; (808) 959-9233; www.hilozoo.com. Petting zoo is on Saturday, 1:30–2:30 p.m. free.

The Panaewa Rain Forest Zoo is the only tropical rain forest zoo in the United States. An international assortment of animals, including an extra-large anteater from Costa Rica, pygmy hippos from Africa, and a wide assortment of birds live here. The zoo hosts many endangered birds indigenous to Hawaii, such as the Laysan albatross, Hawaiian coot, pueo (owl), and Hawaiian gallinule. There are some iguanas, mongooses, and lemurs, and an aviary section with exotic and colorful birds. It doubles as a botanical garden, and much of the growing plant life is labeled. Most kids are drawn to the center of the facility, where a white Bengal tiger roams in a large fenced-in area with a pond. Kids love to watch the tiger feeding, daily at 3:30 p.m.

Mauna Loa Macadamia Nut Mill (all ages)
The mill is easy to find; just look for the signs for Macadamia Road off Route 11, just 6 miles outside of Hilo; (808) 966-8618. Open daily 8:30 a.m. to 5:30 p.m. free.

No doubt the macadamia is Hawaii's most famous nut. Visit the Mauna Loa Macadamia Nut Mill for the opportunity to see how the machines crack the tough hull and harvest this tasty treat. You can watch a **free** video that fully explains the process and then take a self-guided tour among the orchards. Especially wonderful are the macadamia treats at the snack shop.

Kaumana Cave (all ages)

Just a few minutes' drive from Hilo on Route 200; the way to Kaumana Cave is well marked. Open during daylight hours.

Lava caves, also known as tubes, are formed when the flowing lava turns into a molten river. Similar to the top layer of water crusting into ice on a freezing Mainland lake, the top layer of lava hardens. Underneath, the lava continues flowing, creating a tube. When the volcano ceases erupting and the lava stops flowing, the lava eventually drains out of the tube. Sometimes the lava on the top of the tube is too heavy to be unsupported and the tube crushes into itself, but other tubes remain intact and offer an amazing look at the underground environment, navigable of course only after the tube is significantly cooled off.

This cave has had plenty of time to cool since it was formed in 1881. A staircase leads down a hole that looks as if you're entering a wild forest. Flowers and ferns bloom everywhere, creating a misty, ethereal green.

You can walk only about 50 yards into the cave without a flashlight. If you bring flashlights, you'll see quiltworks of color, owing to white, yellow, and orange mineral deposits. Be sure to explore with caution and wear good, closed-toe shoes, as the lava is rocky and uneven in many sections.

Local **Gardens**

Hilo is like one big flower bouquet; fragrant blooms grow everywhere. Some nurseries have become living galleries where visitors can stroll along paths surrounded by delicate tropical petals.

The **Hilo Arboretum,** on Kilauea Avenue between Lanikaula and Kawili Streets, is a nineteen-acre garden established in 1920. It's filled with most of the different types of trees (native and introduced) that thrive throughout the state. You can take a self-guided tour with a **free** map that's available at the office. The arboretum is well maintained by the Department of Natural Resources's Division of Forestry. Admission is **free**, and it's open weekdays 7:45 a.m. to 4:30 p.m.

At the east end of town, off Route 11, the **Nani Mau Gardens** are the largest, most renowned in town. Guided tours lead you along wide pathways, bordered on both sides by flowering trees, shrubs, and vines. The special features of all plants are explained in detail. Nani Mau is open daily 9:00 a.m. to 4:30 p.m. and is located at 421 Makalika Street; (808) 959-3500; www.nanimau. com. Admission is $10 for adults, $4 for children ages four to ten; children younger than four are admitted **free**.

Area Beaches and **Coconut Island**

- Although the long expanse of black sand at **Hilo Bayfront Park** makes this an interesting site, the swimming isn't great here. Fishing and picnicking, however, are top-notch.
- At the end of Banyan Drive, **Reeds Bay Beach Park** is another idyllic picnic spot. Swimming is safe here, although the water is often chilly.
- Just offshore of Hilo Bay, **Coconut Island** is a tiny speck of land that used to be a place of refuge, or *pu`uhonua*, in precontact Hawaii and has since been turned into a picturesque park. Once you've crossed the footbridge that connects Waiakea Peninsula to Coconut Island, you'll feel as if you've entered a Japanese meditative garden. There are pagodas, stone lanterns, torii gates, and a meandering series of streams shadowed by little crescent-shaped stone bridges. It's a wonderful place to enjoy a picnic and the panoramic views of Hilo. A cozy little natural pool here, complete with a diving tower, offers a sheltered area ideal for small children.
- Heading east of Hilo Bay on Kalanianaole Avenue, you'll soon pass Kuhio Bay and Puhi Bay. Head straight to **Onekahakaha Beach Park,** where a wonderful, large, sandy pool is sheltered by the reef and is great for children. Don't swim too far out, however, because the currents can be strong here.
- Just past Onekahakaha is **James Kealoha Park,** frequented by snorkelers and anglers. The tiny island just offshore is called Scout Island, as it's a frequent camping spot for local Boy Scouts.
- **Leleiwi Beach Park** is a great black-sand beach that's really a series of small coves, perfect for swimming and snorkeling during calm-weather days. Beware, however, of heavy storms that can create strong currents. The waters are shallow and clear, and a nearby retaining seawall helps keep the ocean calm. The park facilities include pavilions and restrooms. The park is at the eastern tip of the island.
- Snorkelers will definitely want to walk past Leleiwi to **Richardson Ocean Park,** another black-sand beach and the most popular snorkeling area on this side of the Big Island.
- **Lehia Park** sits at the end of the road. In winter the sandy beach disappears and the waters are rough. In the summer, however, the series of pools are safe. To get there follow the dirt road after the pavement ends, and you'll run right into the park.

Where to Eat

There are plenty of good restaurants in town, and this is by no means an attempt to list them all, just some of the many that are great for families.

Cafe Pesto. On Kamehameha Avenue, fronting Hilo Bay; (808) 969-6640; www.cafepesto.com. The whole family will love Cafe Pesto (also located on the Kona side of the Big Island, in Kawaihae Shopping Center; (808) 882-1071. The menu is diverse, with something to please everyone, and it's full of traditional favorites, blended with local flavors. $$–$$$$

Don's Grill. 485 Hinano Street (Kekuanaoa Street); (808) 935-9099. A great casual, all-in-the-family, kind of place. $

Harrington's. Overlooking scenic Hilo Bay at 135 Kalanianaole Street; (808) 961-4966. Harrington's has to be the best dinner restaurant on the east side of the island. Fish, steaks, chicken, and veal are specialties of the house; there's a kids' menu. Reservations are advised. $$$

Restaurant Osaka. 762 Kanoelehua Avenue; (808) 961-6699. Lunch and dinner menus feature many local favorites and Japanese-American selections. $$

Where to Stay

Dolphin Bay Hotel. 333 Iliahi Street; (808) 935-1466; www.dolphinbayhotel.com. $

Naniloa Volcanoes Resort. 93 Banyan Drive; (808) 969-3333. $$

Hilo Hawaiian Hotel. 71 Banyan Drive; (808) 935-9361; www.castleresorts.com. $–$$

Uncle Billy's Hilo Bay Hotel. 87 Banyan Drive; (808) 935-0658 or (800) 367-5102; www.unclebilly.com. $

Pahoa

If you take Route 130, you'll travel directly south to Pahoa. Here, you can veer east on Route 132 to Lava Tree State Park.

At one time Pahoa's claim to fame was that it housed the largest sawmill in the United States. The town and sawmill were destroyed in a 1955 fire, but local residents have been trying to rebuild and restore. It's a quaint town that's enjoying a renaissance of sorts. Locals are trying to join the nationwide Main Street USA program, which will help designate historic sites and bring new vitality to old buildings. It's fun to stroll along the streets, framed on both sides by old-fashioned false-front shops, mostly housing produce and flower stands.

The Legend of the
Naha and Pinao Stones

In front of the Hilo Library, off Waianuenue Avenue, sit two large stones. The bigger of the two is called the Naha Stone; the smaller, Pinao. In Old Hawaii royal infants were placed upon the Naha Stone; if they remained silent and did not cry, they were true *ali`i*, members of the Naha clan. If they cried, they did not earn the Naha status.

The Naha Stone is also important because legend dictated that the man who could pick it up and move it would be the one great king of all the islands. Kamehameha the Great, as a young man, astonished the town by moving the colossal stone, thus fulfilling the prophecy, and became Hawaii's most powerful ruler of all time.

Lava Tree State Park (all ages)
Off Route 132, about 5 miles from Pahoa. Open during daylight hours.

Lava Tree State Park is an unusual geological formation that's definitely worth a detour. It was formed in 1790 when a quick-moving lava flow slammed into an ohia forest. The lava crept up the tree trunks, but the interiors of the trunks were too moist and cool to become engulfed in flames as one would expect. Instead, the lava cooled and solidified, covering up all the land that held the roots of the ohia trees. What's left is the site you see today. Huge trees stand like ominous statues, looking like fearsome guards forbidding you to enter. The hike here takes about a half hour and is well suited for children.

Cape Kumukahi (all ages)
At the eastern tip of the island, at the end of Route 132. Open during daylight hours.

The picturesque lighthouse at Cape Kumukahi is notable because in 1960, when the last big lava flow destroyed the surroundings, the cape and lighthouse were spared. Local superstition explains the phenomenon with the following story: Madame Pele, the Hawaiian goddess of the volcanoes, came to this area disguised as an old woman. She traveled door to door, asking for food and shelter, but the local townsfolk refused to take her in. The only person who did help was the keeper at the lighthouse, his goodwill thereby securing his safety.

Big Island Trivia

The oldest theater in the state is the Akebono Theater in Pahoa.

Kaimu and Kalapana

Routes 130 and 137 end at the two towns of Kaimu and Kalapana, former residential areas since destroyed by Madame Pele and her flowing lava. You can drive right up to the barricades, where the fresh lava is still steaming. A sign warns adventurous explorers from continuing on foot, and this warning should be strictly heeded. Not only are there spontaneous brush fires and toxic levels of methane gas, you may hit a patch of thin crust, slide right into a moving river of molten lava, and never be seen again!

The lava has been advancing almost continuously since 1983. More than 600,000 cubic yards of lava have been pouring from the volcano daily, hitting the sea like a slow-moving fireball. While it's added more than 500 new acres of land to the Big Island, it's annihilated almost 20,000 acres, including homes, schools, and ancient heiau, causing more than $25 million in property damage. (For more about the volcano's devastation, see the section "Hawaii Volcanoes National Park," which follows.)

An old church sits on the side of the road, looking awfully out of place in this black landscape. This is the Star of the Sea Catholic Church, more commonly known as the Painted Church, which was in danger from an advancing lava flow. Local people joined forces to move the church out of the way but have not been able to find a new home for the structure. So it sits at the side of the road, the lone surviving structure of a community lost to nature.

Area **Beaches**

Route 137 leads south from Cape Kumukahi and passes a series of fishponds. **Isaac Hale Beach Park** is less than 10 miles away from Pahoa, at Pohoiki Bay, formerly the commercial wharf for Puna Sugar Company. This is the only boat launching site for the entire southern coast and is therefore usually quite busy with private and commercial boaters. If you can avoid the seagoing traffic, this is a great scuba site, especially in the summer when the ocean is calm. A short walk on a well-worn path east of the beach leads to naturally formed hot springs that bubble like Jacuzzis.

MacKenzie State Recreation Area is a thirteen-acre park that may not be suitable for young children. It's framed on both sides by rugged fingers of lava, and the currents here have been known to pluck unsuspecting people who were walking on the lava and carry them out to sea. It's a popular fishing site, but swimming is unsafe. It is located in a grove of ironwood trees planted by forest ranger A. J. MacKenzie.

Volcano

Stay on the Belt Road, and you'll travel through the higher elevations and the communities of Kurtistown, Mountain View, Glenwood, and Volcano.

Don't miss a chance to experience the awesome powers of Madame Pele at Hawaii Volcanoes National Park, home of the most active volcano on our planet. Here your family can see new earth being formed as lava spits, chortles, and blasts from deep inside Earth's core. Whether you simply motor around the Crater Rim Drive or hike into the inner sanctum of the park, the experience is an amazing blend of science and legend and is guaranteed to be unforgettable.

There is a danger inherent in visiting here that's important to be aware of. No, it's not the chance of getting swept away by an approaching lava flow, but rather the risk of running over the endangered native nene goose. The nene are quite tame and often approach visitors and congregate in parking lots. They're short and brown, often blending in with the landscape and easy to miss if you're driving fast, so keep one eye peeled for the nene.

Hawaii Volcanoes National Park (all ages)

Stop at the Kilauea visitor center, where you can pick up a variety of maps and brochures and plan your exploring strategy; (808) 985-6000; www.nanimau.com. The center is open 7:45 a.m. to 5:00 p.m. daily. Entrance fee is $10 per vehicle.

The moving lava is just one of many attractions in the park. Extensive trails lead to steaming vents, fern forests, ancient petroglyphs, and even into old lava tubes. The best idea is to save visiting the flow for the end of the day, when you can watch the glowing lava hiss its way into the sea, creating a cloud of steam that turns an eerie purple color at sunset.

The lava flow moves slowly in predictable paths, and visitors often seek the most active areas instead of avoiding them. Don't be afraid to follow the signs to the flow.

The heavy fumes in the air may present problems for pregnant women, elderly people, and small children, but occurrences of respiratory problems aren't too frequent as long as people use common sense and know their limits.

Crater Rim Drive is a scenic 11-mile road that circles the summit of Kilauea, passing sulfur banks, recent flows, craters, and steam vents. Many of the most popular sites in the park are situated along this drive.

Hawaii Trivia

The state motto is "Ua Mau Ke Ea O Ka Aina I Ka Pono," which translates to "The life of the land is perpetuated in righteousness."

"Drive-In Volcano" Road (all ages)

In Hawaii Volcanoes National Park. A 2½-mile drive from Highway 130 leads to a mark᠁ path for the "Drive-In Volcano."

This road allows visitors to experience the beauty of earth-in-the-making as the lava flows, hissing and sputtering, into the sea, creating new land. This is nature at its most powerful and spectacular.

The short drive is an adventure over ancient lava that flowed from the mountains to the sea carved by the glory of Pele, Hawaii's Fire Goddess. The drive ends on a stretch of old highway where there is plenty of parking. Step out and immediately feel the excitement electrifying the air. County of Hawaii and Hawaii Volcanoes National Park officials are available to answer any questions. An informative kiosk provides additional safety considerations and geological information on the volcano activity. Then take off on a short, twenty-minute hike over sculptured lava fields so incredible only nature could have designed the landscape.

Halemaumau Trail (all ages)

In Hawaii Volcanoes National Park.

Although the Hawaii Volcano Observatory is closed to the public, an accessible lookout here offers a gaping view into the Halemaumau Crater. Plaques situated throughout the area offer information about the history and geological particulars of the park. Near the observatory, the short Halemaumau Trail travels for just ¼ mile around the rim of the crater.

Jaggar Museum (all ages)

In Hawaii Volcanoes National Park; (808) 967-7643. Open 8:30 a.m. to 5:00 p.m. daily. free.

The Jaggar Museum, located adjacent to the Hawaii Volcano Observatory, opened in 1987. The museum is the fulfillment of a dream of Dr. Thomas Augustus Jaggar, a scientist who adopted the Kilauea region as his home in 1912 and devoted his life to the study of volcanoes. As early as 1916, he proposed creating a museum to help visitors understand how volcanoes work. Today, more than a million and a half visitors a year tour the museum and learn about volcanoes through colorful and informative displays.

Devastation Trail (all ages)

In Hawaii Volcanoes National Park. From the visitor center, signs point the way to the Devastation Trail.

This paved path, well suited for children, travels for ½ mile through an ohia forest that was damaged by the lava but continues to hold fast to the landscape. The stark trunks and leafless stems contrast sharply with the black, desolate landscape, and this is among the most photographed sites in the park.

Hawaii Trivia

Only two butterflies are native to Hawaii—the larger and more colorful one is called the Kamehameha Butterfly.

Thurston Lava Tube (ages 6 and up)
In Hawaii Volcanoes National Park.

The Thurston Lava Tube is an amazing, 450-foot-long cave. The plant life surrounding the cave's entrance is vibrantly green and lush, its very existence a testimony to the tenacity of regenerating plant life. If you bring flashlights, you can walk far into the cave; for the first 50 feet the cave is illuminated with electric lights and is quite spacious. The remainder of the cave is about 15 feet in height and width. Be sure to wear sturdy, closed-toe shoes, as the lava is rocky and uneven in many sections, guaranteed to stub a sandal-footed toe! Explore with the utmost of caution, because getting lost in these caves means getting lost in a place that never sees the light of day. If your flashlight batteries were to expire, you would have to wait for another explorer to rescue you, whereas if you got lost on a hiking trail as the sun was setting, you'd simply have to wait until sunrise to find your way out.

Volcano House Inn and Art Center (all ages)
In Hawaii Volcanoes National Park; (808) 967-7321 for inn, (808) 967-7511 for art center. The art center is open daily 9:00 a.m. to 5:00 p.m. free, but you have to pay to get into the national park ($$).

Volcano House Inn is the first hotel ever built in the islands. It overlooks Halemaumau Crater and has been welcoming guests since 1866. It's definitely worth a stop to walk through the lodge, even if you're not spending the night. The inn serves breakfast from 7:00 to 10:30 a.m., lunch from 11:00 a.m. to 2:00 p.m., and dinner from 5:30 to 9:00 p.m. $$–$$$$

The Volcano Art Center is the original Volcano House Inn, which was converted into an art center in 1974. It's an educational center that functions as a minimuseum. Displays feature artwork created by local artists.

Chain of Craters Road (all ages)
In Hawaii Volcanoes National Park.

The Chain of Craters Road branches off the Crater Rim Drive and leads to the most recent lava flow that has seeped over the highway. It takes about a half hour to reach the end,

Big Island Trivia

The Big Island is home to Kilauea, the world's most active and largest volcano.

where a makeshift visitor station is staffed with rangers who offer the latest eruption scoop.

Puu Loa Petroglyph Field (ages 10 and up)

In Hawaii Volcanoes National Park. On the way to the end of the road, look for the sign kau puna trail. The Puu Loa Petroglyph Field is on the other side of the road.

The trail to the field is marked with little ahu, or triangular piles of stone. You can walk on a wooden path around the field, but please do stay on the path to protect the petroglyphs. The ancient markings are fascinating and offer a glimpse of what life was like for ancient Hawaiians. Etchings of warriors, canoes, and families are easily discernible. Look for etched circles with holes in the center. These are known as *puu loa*. Fathers would place the umbilical cords of newborns into these holes as offerings to the gods and to ask for a long life for their children.

Where to Eat

Kilauea Lodge Restaurant. Volcano; (808) 967-7366; www.kilaualodge.com. Open for dinner nightly, 5:30 to 9:00 p.m. $$$–$$$$

Volcano Country Club Restaurant. At Volcano Golf Course; (808) 967-8228. Serves breakfast and lunch daily. $$

Where to Stay

Kilauea Lodge. P.O. Box 116, Volcano Village 96785; (808) 967-7366; www.kilauea lodge.com. Charming family-owned bed-and-breakfast. They've been here so long, they're a local favorite. $$

Helicopter Tours

Touring Hawaii Volcanoes National Park is possible by car, by foot, and by air. No doubt you'll see a few helicopters flying overhead as you're driving around. Some visitors swear these mechanical birds offer the best (albeit expensive) sightseeing. They fly directly to the most active areas, over pools of bubbling lava and streams of red-hot flows—places impossible to reach by hiking, biking, or driving. Some pilots dip so low to the ground, your face becomes flushed with the heat.

In recent years, however, the helicopter industry on all Hawaiian islands has been mired in controversy. Safety and maintenance standards became suspect after a few fatal crashes. Additionally, hikers and naturalists object to the annoying whir of the engines disturbing otherwise pristine environments. But ask anyone who has ever soared in the skies above the volcano, the lush Hamakua Coast and Waipio Valley, Maui's verdant valleys, or Kauai's rugged Na Pali Coast, and they'll say the experience is incomparably incredible.

NOTE: Try to schedule a flight as early as possible. Late-afternoon trips often are plagued with fog and soot that prohibit optimum visibility.

My Island Inn. Volcano; (808) 967-7216 or (808) 967-7110; www.myislandinnhawaii .com. Just outside Hawaii Volcanoes National Park, this bed-and-breakfast has garden units, a self-contained studio, and several guest houses. Breakfast is served at the host's home, which also has B&B rooms. $–$$

Volcano Guest House. 11-3733 Ala Ohia Street, Volcano. (808) 967-7775 or (866) 886-5226. Ideal for families, the family-run place offers spacious accommodations— each family gets its own cottage. $$

Ka`u and Na`alehu

Beyond Hawaii Volcanoes National Park, the Belt Road continues to the Ka`u District and the area known as South Point.

The sights along this section of the Belt Road are among the most ecologically diverse in Hawaii, as green pastures abut desolate black lava fields. Most of the area can be reached by a normal car, but some of the secluded coastal spots are accessible only with a four-wheel-drive vehicle.

The next town is Na`alehu, the southernmost town in the entire United States, and the largest town in this area. It's a good place to refurbish your supply of gas and snacks if you're heading all the way up to Kona. There's also a fruit stand here that's a favorite place to stock up on fresh banana bread.

Area Beaches (all ages)

Shortly after passing through Pahala, look for Punalu`u Beach Park, which is well known for its expansive black-sand beach. There are restrooms, phones, showers, and a pavilion. Swimming is safe only during calm weather.

Punalu`u Beach Park is home to many green sea turtles and the legendary turtle princess Kauila. Please be aware that the turtles are endangered and prone to heart attacks when afraid. It's okay to view them from a distance, but you should never approach one up close.

Pele's **Fiery History**

Since January 3, 1983, when a huge explosion sent lava 1,500 feet into the air, Pele has been spewing her wrath from Kilauea. So far, 181 homes have been completely covered; 8 miles of public highway and several private roads are gone; and scientists say there's no end in sight. Those who believe in superstitions say that Madame Pele, the goddess of the volcano, may be appeased after several bottles of gin are offered to her in the most reverent seriousness. So don't think the many empty bottles of gin scattered throughout the park were left behind by careless party people. But after thousands of bottles have been poured into the crater, it seems she's still thirsty.

Big Island Trivia

King Kamehameha the Great was born and raised on the Big Island.

Beyond Punalu`u the coastal drive is lush and beautiful. Whittington Beach County Park is about 5 miles past Punalu`u, but it's a little difficult to find because it's not very well marked. The turnoff comes before you cross a bridge and head up a hill toward Na`alehu. The beach offers full amenities, including restrooms, phones, and drinking water. Nearby Honuapo Bay used to be a busy port for transporting sugar, and the surrounding area is home to many old ruins from that era.

South Beach (all ages)

About 6 miles beyond Na`alehu, the Hawaii Belt Road leaves the coastline and cuts inland toward Kona and the western side of the island. After the tiny town of Waiohinu, look for a turnoff labeled South Point Road. This road leads straight south for 12 miles, ending at Ka Lae, South Point. Open during daylight hours.

South Point is the southernmost tip of the United States. Its latitude is 500 miles south of Miami, Florida. Many scholars believe that this is where the migrating Polynesians first landed, as early as A.D. 150; others claim it wasn't until A.D. 750.

Don't be alarmed if you see a sign claiming the land is controlled by the Hawaiian Homeland Agency and trespassing is not allowed. This means that you shouldn't park your car randomly on the side of the road and explore the surrounding area on foot. But you have complete right-of-way if you're traveling on the road, and it's frequented heavily by tourists. Veer right when the road splits; there's a parking lot at the end of the road. The views are captivating, and you'll be able to say you walked on the southernmost tip of the United States.

Green Sand Beach (ages 10 and up)

East of Ka Lae, a 3-mile trail leads to Pohakuloa and Green Sand Beach.

Yes . . . green sand. The green is a dull olive shade, not a vibrant grassy color. It's formed by olivine present in the lava. Olivine is a semiprecious stone, and here it has been weathered into sandlike pieces. The trail that leads to the beach is beautiful, but be sure to bring plenty of water and venture this way only if the weather is sunny and dry.

Kipuka (all ages)

On Route 200, across from the sign pointing to Kaumana Cave.

Continuing along the Saddle Road, you'll see certain areas lush with green life that look

Big Island Trivia

South Point, Ka Lae, is the southernmost point in the whole United States.

markedly out of place in the dry lavascape. These are called *kipuka* and are formed when the lava simply goes around an area instead of covering it, creating an isolated little mini-ecosystem. You can explore the kipuka, but be considerate of the fragile environment; many rare and endangered birds flit about.

Mauna Kea

The Saddle Road continues to skirt around the edges of Mauna Kea and climbs to the summit at 13,796 feet. A few well-marked side roads also lead to the summit.

As the serpentine road winds its way up the mountain, you'll rise above the cloud cover and feel as if you've left ordinary civilization behind. The landscape becomes barren; instead of the greenery of Hilo, you'll see a series of reddish volcanic cones.

While the sun may be beating down on the resorts of Kona, the temperature up here is always cold, so dress warmly. Be prepared for temperatures less than twenty degrees Fahrenheit and wind that blows up to 70 miles per hour. It's really, really cold. In the winter it snows atop Mauna Kea, and skiers flock to the mountain. If you don't have a four-wheel-drive vehicle, it's best not to attempt to reach the very top of the mountain. Not only is the road often closed due to snow, it's a windy, steep incline that would claim easy victory in a battle with ordinary rental cars.

Altitude sickness is a serious predicament for young children, the elderly, or pregnant women. In fact, because of the remoteness of the area and the inherent dangers of high altitudes, children younger than age sixteen are prohibited from venturing all the way to the top (but not many people want to, anyway). If health and age circumstances deem it

The **Saddle Road**

The Saddle Road, Route 200, goes directly from central Hilo across the middle of the island for 87 miles until it ends at the Mamalahoa Highway near Kona. Most car-rental companies try to forbid clients from venturing this way because it's pretty rocky for a few miles and there are many potholes. Also, it's very isolated; if you were to break down, there would be virtually nowhere to go for help. But it certainly is passable and offers some of the best views on the Big Island. Don't let the car-rental companies discourage you from exploring.

Mauna Kea towers at an elevation of 13,796 feet to the north, and Mauna Loa, at 13,679 feet, looms to the south. A road branches off from the Saddle Road and travels all the way to the top of Mauna Kea, where astronomical observatories house an international collection of scientists who gaze into the heavens and study the stars.

Big Island Trivia

Mauna Kea is the tallest mountain in the world (measured from its base at the ocean floor).

all right for members of your family to venture all the way up, however, it's recommended to use a four-wheel-drive vehicle and to spend about an hour at the Onizuka Center, at 9,300 feet, to acclimate to the altitude change.

Onizuka Center for International Astronomy (ages 16 and older on summit tour)

The entrance to the center is well marked off the Saddle Road; call (808) 961-2180 for a live person, or (808) 935-6268 for a recording detailing hours, various programs, and summit information or go to www.ifa.hawaii.edu/info/vis. Open 9:00 a.m. to 10:00 p.m. daily. Guided tours are offered on weekends. free.

Ellison Onizuka was a local Kona boy with big dreams that landed him a spot as a crew member of the ill-fated space shuttle Challenger. The center is dedicated to his memory. The center is at the altitude limit for young children, pregnant women, elderly individuals, and people with respiratory problems. There are free stargazing programs on the summit Friday through Sunday, 7:00 to 10:00 p.m. You must have a four-wheel-drive vehicle to get up here.

At the top of the mountain, astronomers from all over the world work in several different observatories. They can stay here only for four-day stints because the high altitude can cause brain malfunctions over a long period of time. These scientists are privy to exploring the heavens above 40 percent of Earth's atmosphere. The lack of light pollution and dust make this the best observatory site in the world. The W. H. Keck telescope, the largest in the world, sits atop Mauna Kea. It has thirty-six mirrors and is 33 feet in diameter.

Although the University of Hawaii manages the entire summit, teams from France, Canada, Japan, Great Britain, and the Netherlands have permanent outposts here. Visitors can tour the complex at the summit, but reservations are necessary. For more information call the Hilo-based Mauna Kea Support Services at (808) 961-2180.

Where to Eat and Stay

There are no accommodations or restaurants here; the nearest are in Hilo, an hour's drive away.

Journey to a Realm of Science Fiction and Ancient Hawaiian Lore

On Hawaii's Big Island visitors can start their day exploring the pristine underwater world of the coast and end up surrounded by stars atop the summit of Mauna Kea. There the skies are among the clearest, driest, and darkest in the world, revealing the most amazing show of stars, planets, nebulae, and more! No wonder Mauna Kea is home to thirteen world-class telescopes, representing nine countries. It's the closest way you can get to the stars without leaving Earth. The night sky never looked so clear or revealed such terrific sights as what visitors will see at the nearly 14,000-foot summit of Mauna Kea and at 9,300 feet at the Ellison Onizuka Visitor Center. At these altitudes the temperature and atmosphere are extreme, requiring strict adherence to proper physical activity and clothing. Choose from any one of the following stargazing and sunset tours, where safety and fun are the first priorities.

- **Arnott's Famous Sunset-Stargazing Adventure** departs every Monday, Wednesday, and Friday between noon and 3:00 p.m. and returns between 9:00 and 11:00 p.m., depending on the season. For more information on the tour, visit www.arnottslodge.com or call (808) 969-7097. $$$$

- **Hawaii Forest & Trail** takes the high ground to the stars with its Mauna Kea Summit & Stars Tour. The sunset and nighttime adventure starts with departure from the Kona-Kohala coast every afternoon. A naturalist guide provides excellent insight into the diverse and beautiful landscape from the coast to the summit of Mauna Kea. Guests learn the remarkable story of Hawaii's natural, cultural, and geological history. A picnic dinner stop provides just enough time to acclimate for the final summit ascent for a spectacular sunset show. Back down at the 9,300-foot elevation, guests use a personal telescope while the guide describes the brilliance of the Hawaiian sky with stories of the observable universe. For more information visit the Web site at www.hawaii-forest.com/adv-maunakea.html, or call (808) 331-8505 or (800) 464-1993. $$$$

- **Mauna Kea Summit Adventures Sunset and Stargazing Tours** provides professional guides for small groups to explore the natural wonders of space from one of the world's leading astronomy centers. On this tour visitors witness panoramic views of eerie landscapes reminiscent of an alien environment found in a science fiction book, as well as the spectacular color show when day fades to night. The guide reveals the treasures of the night sky through a personal, private telescope (conditions permitting). Guides pick up and drop off at Kailua-Kona or the Kings' Shops in Waikoloa. Warm hooded parkas and gloves are provided, along with a soup-and-sandwich supper and hot beverages. The trip lasts between six and eight hours. For more information visit www.maunakea.com or call (808) 322-2366. $$$$

• The **Visitor Information Station Stargazing Program** is a free program held every evening from 6:00 to 10:00 p.m. Transportation is not provided and guests are advised to use vehicles with four-wheel drive because of the windy, steep road. The program begins with a video followed by a discussion of astronomy and Mauna Kea. Then the program moves outside for the remainder of the evening, where guests can view the brilliant colors of the stars, star clusters, and other cosmic delights with a telescope. Hot drinks and snacks are available in the Visitor Information Station. For more information visit the Web site at www.ifa.hawaii.edu/info/vis/ or call the Visitor Information Station at (808) 961-2180.

Hamakua Coast

Take Route 19 north of Hilo to the town of Hamakua.

This route to the Hamakua Coast heads through some of the prettiest scenery in all Hawaii. Gorgeous rain-carved, velvety green valleys lush with tropical foliage contrast with black-as-night craggy lava promontories and foaming white water from pounding waves. For many years the Hamakua Coast was dominated by sugar plantations, and although those are now gone, the handful of towns formed to accommodate local workers still exists, virtually unchanged by time.

The Hamakua area encompasses Highway 19 and the entire northeast coast of the Big Island, from Waipi`o 50 miles to the north on Highway 19 to Hilo in the east. Although traveling on Route 19 offers many breathtaking views, the best vistas are inaccessible by car and best seen by soaring aboveground in a flight-seeing helicopter.

Small country roads occasionally veer off Highway 19, leading to one-lane towns where a few dozen people compose a whole community and life is so slow paced that pets lounge lazily in the middle of the road and families don't even lock their doors at night.

The Scenic Drive reconnects to Route 19 at the small sugar town of Pepeekeo. Just a few minutes' drive past Pepeekeo is Honomu. With a little imagination it's easy to picture the saloons, hotel, and bordello that used to be the focal points of entertainment in this now-forgotten town. The small town of Honomu prospered when sugar plantations dominated the coastline, but today it has become a mere shell of its former grandeur. The town is a worthwhile stop; you can walk down the main street, with its old-fashioned storefronts and raised sidewalks, and gather a sense of the charming atmosphere.

Although there's just one main street, Honoka`a is the largest town on the Hamakua Coast, with a population of about 2,000. The town features a few craft shops, boutique-type stores, restaurants, gas stations, and a general store.

Big Island Trivia

- The Big Island's highest peak, Mauna Kea, is often topped with snow every winter, while just a few miles away, at the Kona Coast, the average temperature in January, the coldest month, is sixty-three degrees Fahrenheit.
- Atop Mauna Kea, astronomers are studying Venus's eerie "ashen light." The observatory's Keck telescope is so powerful, with its 33-foot-wide mirror, the Venusian atmosphere is more distinct than it was to Russian space probes that flew past the planet.
- Lake Waiau, at 13,020 feet, is the third-highest lake in America and is almost at the summit of Mauna Kea.

Big Island Trivia

Mauna Kea's cross-island sister peak, Mauna Loa, is the densest mountain in the world. It's 60 miles long and 30 miles wide and is made of more than 10,000 cubic miles of lava. It weighs more than the entire Sierra Nevada range in California.

Hawaii Tropical Botanical Gardens (all ages)

Getting here is half the fun. A few minutes' drive from Hilo, you'll hit Papaikou. Look for a scenic drive sign leading to a right turnoff. This road is literally carved through a jungle; it quickly becomes narrow and winding, and you'll travel over a series of small bridges as you head toward the coast. Open daily 9:00 a.m. to 5:00 p.m.; (808) 964-5233; www.htbg .com. The self-guided walking tour takes about an hour, so guests are admitted only until 4:00 p.m. $–$$$; children age 5 and younger are admitted free.

Even if your kids aren't excited at the proposal of venturing to yet another beautiful garden, you should insist on including Hawaii Tropical Botanical Gardens on your itinerary. Here, you'll get to explore a true tropical rain forest up close. Facilities include restrooms and drinking fountains. (Bring mosquito repellent!)

The walking tours are self-guided and take about an hour. The various trails are well maintained and easily navigable. The Ocean Trail leads to the sea, where violently foaming waves crash into the jagged coastline. Even the sounds are impressive as the water sloshes in and out of submerged lava tubes.

The gardens were started when a transplant from San Francisco, California, wanted to do his part to save the endangered Hawaiian rain forests, so he purchased this land and set about caretaking and preserving it. It's said that the gardens house the world's largest selection of tropical plant species.

Akaka Falls State Park (all ages)

Route 220 leads from Honomu to Akaka Falls State Park. To get there take Route 220 inland from Highway 19 at Honomu. The falls are a short but scenic drive from Honomu, and there are signs directing drivers where to turn. Open during daylight hours. free.

There is an easy, well-maintained, short loop trail at Akaka Falls. The trail is suitable for children of all ages, and the majestic sights beyond each turn will delight everyone. You'll pass through groves of orchids, ferns, and bamboo and over small gurgling streams. The

Hawaii Trivia

When Hawaii became a state in August 1959, it meant redesigning the U.S. flag for the twenty-seventh time. The new flag, containing fifty stars, was first flown July 4, 1960.

Hawaii's **Newest Island**

Rising from deep within the Earth is a jet of molten rock that cuts gargantuan holes in the Pacific seabed, forming new volcanoes and eventually whole new islands. Although you can't see it, 23 miles southeast of the Big Island another volcano is erupting. Called **Loihi,** it's spewing lava from 3,000 feet below the ocean's surface. Scientists estimate that within the next 100 to 100,000 years, a new island will be born.

falls tumble 426 feet into a beautiful jungle pond. There are picnic tables and restrooms on-site.

Kolekole Beach County Park (all ages)
A sign points to the park a few minutes' drive past Honomu on Highway 19.

At one time many farmers and fishermen lived in Laupahoehoe Valley, and there was a boat landing here that bustled with activity. Today it's nothing more than a beach park that's frequented by local fishermen. The small road wiggles a short way down to a beautiful black-sand beach. The place is popular with local families, and facilities include pavilions, showers, barbecue grills, restrooms, picnic tables, and electricity for camping. This is a wonderful, well-equipped, and scenic picnic site, but the ocean can be quite treacherous here. Swimming isn't advised here, but you may see some brave surfers catching a ride offshore.

Kalopa State Recreation Area (all ages)
About 12 miles beyond Laupahoehoe, before Honoka`a.

This inland park offers a great chance to walk among lush native forest plants and trees. There are well-maintained hiking trails that will appeal to a variety of ages and abilities, and many of the plants are identified.

Where to Eat

Jolene's Kau Kau Korner. At the corner of Mamane and Lehua Streets in Honoka`a; (808) 775-9498. Be sure to stop at Jolene's Kau Kau Korner. This renovated old shop is clean and bright and offers a wide range of local-style plate lunch specials such as teriyaki beef and chicken, plus burgers, sandwiches, and snack items. $

Kukuihaele and Waipio Valley

Highway 240 ends at Kukuihaele, a charming one-street town that boasts a few gas stations, restaurants, and galleries. The lookout point over Waipio Valley is a truly beautiful spot for picnicking.

At road's end is the 1,000-foot overlook to Waipio Valley, a place so lush, green, and picturesque that no words can do it justice; it begs exploring. From the overlook you can see the terraced taro patches and gardens. Although today's inhabitants include just a few families, Waipio used to be home to thousands of Hawaiians who lived off this fertile land, and it was the largest cultivated valley in all Hawaii. Today only about fifty people live here, and the land has changed very little in the last hundred years. It consists mostly of taro farms, but there are a few horses and cattle as well. In the heart of the valley, passion fruit, bananas, coffee, avocados, coconuts, grapefruit, and a large variety of other fruits and vegetables thrive.

Unless you have a four-wheel-drive vehicle, don't try to navigate the road down to the valley—your car will never make it. Hikers in excellent physical shape will enjoy the hike, but remember that going down is the easy part—the hill is mighty steep.

Waipio Valley Wagon Tours (all ages)

For more information call (808) 775-9518 or go to www.waipiovalleywagontours.com. The one-and-a-half-hour tours leave at 10:30 a.m. and 12:30 and 2:30 p.m. Monday through Saturday. $$$$; children age 3 and younger ride free.

The tour takes about twelve people at a time on a surrey-type mule-drawn wagon.

Waipio Naalapa Trail Rides (ages 8 and up)

The rides last two and a half hours and are offered twice daily, at 9:30 a.m. and 12:30 p.m., Monday through Saturday. For more information call (808) 775-0419; www.naalapastables .com. $$$$

Along the ride, guides relate the fascinating history and legends of this region. The horses, which are descendants of the original herd given to the chiefs in the 1700s by Capt. George Vancouver, transport you to picturesque swimming holes, waterfalls, and a heiau.

The Waipio Valley Shuttle (all ages)

The tours last one and a half hours. For information call (808) 775-7121, $$$$

The shuttle offers valley tours in comfortable air-conditioned vans. For children too young to handle a long trail ride, this is a good way to see the valley sites.

Big Island Trivia

Hi`ilawe Falls, deep in Waipio Valley, tumbles 3,000 feet and is ranked among the highest falls in all Hawaii.

Big Island Trivia

The Big Island is the worldwide leader in harvesting macadamia nuts and orchids. Waipio is the largest valley on the Big Island: 6 miles long and 1 mile wide.

Where to Eat and Stay

There are no facilities in this area other than a few roadside fruit stands. For dining and accommodations, see nearby towns of Waimea, Hilo, or Kona.

For More Information

Big Island Visitors Bureau. 250 Keawe Street, Hilo 96720; (808) 961-5797; 250 Waikoloa Beach Drive, B–15, Waikoloa 96738; (808) 886-1655; www.bigisland.org.

Kauai

Kauai is the northernmost, oldest, and first-populated island in the Hawaiian chain. Its age has made it a grand natural spectacle—over time, wind and rain have sculpted great cliffs and valleys lush with picturesque foliage and tumbling waterfalls. Nicknamed "the Garden Isle," Kauai is known worldwide for its awe-inspiring beauty. Mt. Waialeale, in the island's center, is lined with velvety green landscaping, blessed with more than 450 inches of rainfall every year. The mountains have been carved over time to form deep crevices, from which waterfalls drop to isolated pools, and the damp fertile soil is home to many colorful flowers and fruits.

These pools have formed a series of streams, which in turn have created Hawaii's only navigable river. Of all the islands, Kauai is home to the most beaches per mile of coastline and the most miles of hiking trails.

From the craggy Na Pali Coast, rising 4,000 feet above the foamy waves, to the kaleidoscopic Waimea Canyon, Kauai is blissfully beautiful. Apparently Hollywood producers

Julie's
TopPicks for Family Fun on Kauai

1. Swimming at Poipu Beach

2. Exploring Waimea Canyon

3. Spending a day at Hanalei Bay

4. Hiking up to the Sleeping Giant

5. Waterskiing Wailua River

6. Learning to sailboard at Anini Beach

7. Taking a cruise up the Na Pali Coast

8. Touring Kokee State Park

9. Ziplining over Kipu Falls

10. Kayaking the Hanalei River

KAUAI

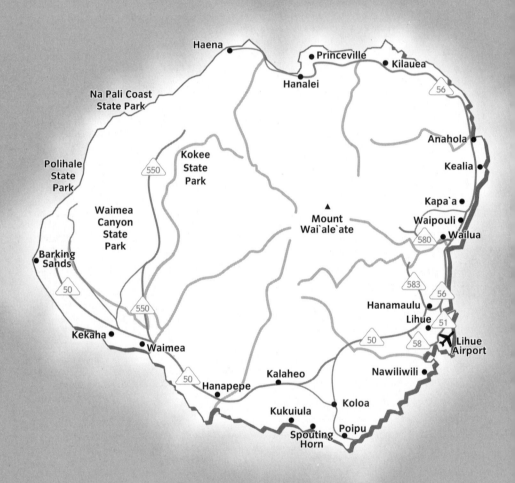

agree, for film crews habitually arrive, creating internationally famous flicks. The island has been used in *South Pacific* (1958), *Blue Hawaii* (1961), *Lord of the Flies* (1989), *Jurassic Park* (1992), *and Six Days, Seven Nights* (1998). And when Disney's notorious space alien Stitch met little Lilo, it was here on beautiful Kauai.

Some historians believe the first Polynesian explorers to settle on these islands made landfall on Kauai around A.D. 200, about 500 years before the rest of the islands were populated. *Menehune*, the mischievous leprechauns of the Pacific, made their home on Kauai. The island has a special magic that appeals to everyone's youthful heart, and special places that delight the young of all ages. Some things are just fun, while others have educational opportunities built in.

Kauaians have a distinctive spirit. This is the only island King Kamehameha could not conquer. During his campaign to unite the islands under one rule, Kamehameha could never get Kauai's King Kaumualii to concede. (The rough Kauai channel that separates Kauai and Niihau from the other islands claimed many of Kamehameha's soldiers and canoes and probably had a lot to do with Kamehameha's inclination to back off.) It wasn't until Kaumualii's death in 1810 that Kamehameha's dream was finally realized, for Kaumualii had agreed to let Kamehameha have Kauai upon his death.

Kauai ties with the Big Island as the third-most-visited island, after Oahu and Maui. United Airlines and American are the only airlines that fly directly from the Mainland into Lihue. Lihue is also serviced bycommuter airlines Hawaiian, (808) 835-3700 or (800) 367-5320; Island Air, (808) 484-2222; and GoAir, (808) 838-7900 or (888) 435-9462. Although the bigger resort properties offer airport pickup, a rental car is essential here—Kauai's beauty begs to be explored. The island is about 33 miles long and 25 miles wide, but you can't drive completely around because much of the northern coast is inaccessible by car.

Most of the resort and hotel properties are in Poipu and Lihue, with a few scattered in Kapa`a, Hanalei, and Princeville. Kauai is relatively underdeveloped compared to Oahu, Maui, and even the Big Island. The resorts here are built conservatively—instead of crowded condominiums and strings of hotels on a single street, the construction has been designed to be unobtrusive, to blend in with the beautiful landscape. Developers chose not to build sprawling, Disneyland-type accommodations, forgoing opulence for nature's grandeur. They must have known that no matter how beautiful a resort is, it can't compare with the lush, picturesque surroundings.

Unlike the other islands, it's very easy to self-navigate your way around Kauai. The main highway travels from Waimea in the southwest in a large U shape to Hanalei in the north. A few smaller roads branch off the main highway. This chapter begins in Lihue, the site of the main airport and the biggest city on the island. Then it goes south to Poipu and west to the end of the line at Waimea, then up the road to Waimea Canyon and Kokee State Park. The latter part of the chapter focuses on the towns north of Lihue: from Wailua to Hanalei and the magnificent Na Pali Coast.

Lihue

Although Lihue is the biggest city on the island, the place still exudes a small-town feel and appeal. The majority of the island's shops and restaurants are here.

If you're on the island during February, April, July, and November, be sure to call the **Kauai Community Players** to see if they're holding any performances ($$$). Shows are offered just four times a year, and it's best to call ahead, because sometimes the "on" months vary. This nonprofit community group has been producing well-known plays for

The Legend of the **Menehune Fishpond**

Just a short way beyond Kalapaki sits the Alakoko Pond, more commonly known as the *Menehune* Fishpond. It's one of the most famous archaeological sites on Kauai and was supposedly built by the *menehune*, Hawaii's mythological little people (similar to Ireland's leprechauns). Some historians believe the menehune actually existed, that they were the lost tribe of what may have been the first Polynesians to land on these islands. Living in isolation for many years, some scientists claim, they could have evolved with different physical characteristics. Whether their existence is a fact or a myth, they live forever in Hawaiian legends. According to the tales, the menehune work only at night, anonymously performing kind deeds or building great structures but never allowing themselves to be seen in daylight.

The legend about the Alakoko Fishpond says a royal prince and princess once asked the menehune to build this large pond for them so they could raise mullet. The menehune agreed, with the stipulation that the couple not try to see them or disturb their work. In one night the menehune formed a line to create a living chain for 25 miles and passed the stones needed to separate the pond from Huleia Stream. They used the stones to construct a wall that's 5 feet high and 900 feet long, creating a dam that trapped the fish inside.

The royal couple could not stifle their curiosity and climbed to the top of a nearby mountain to check the progress. The menehune spotted them, left the pond unfinished, and as punishment turned the couple into two stone pillars, still seen today, standing vigil on the mountainside overlooking the pond.

To find the pond follow Rice Street out of Lihue until it turns into Route 51. Turn on Nawiliwili Road and head toward the ocean. Turn left on Niumalu Road, following it to Hulemalu Road. A lookout offers scenic views of Nawiliwili Harbor and the Hoary Head mountain range. Huleia Stream is off Hulemalu Road. Many adventurers enjoy kayaking up Huleia Stream for a closer view of the fishpond. (See the sidebar on Water-Sports Rentals.)

more than thirty years, and it's definitely worth attending a performance for a great slice of Kauai life. The plays are usually in the Kapa Theatre in Puhi, across the street from Kauai Community College.. For more information call (808) 246-8985 or visit www.kauai communityplayers.org.

Kauai Museum (all ages)

4428 Rice Street; (808) 245-6931; www.kauaimuseum.org. Open Monday through Friday 9:00 a.m. to 4:00 p.m. and Saturday 10:00 a.m. to 4:00 p.m. $–$$, free for children younger than 5. The first Saturday of every month is family day, and admission is free. Guided museum tours are offered at 10:30 a.m. Tuesday through Friday.

The Kauai Museum is a charming site, right in central Lihue, that reveals Kauai's distinctive wildlife and cultural, geological, and social history. The displays focus on Hawaiiana and the missionary era. There are great examples of ancient Polynesian canoes, musical instruments, and feather capes.

The museum actually consists of two buildings. Visitors enter in the two-story Wilcox Building; the Rice Building is the site of the permanent exhibit "Story of Kauai." Both are named after prominent Kauai missionary families.

Grove Farm (all ages)

Kaumualii Highway; (808) 245-3202. Open Monday, Wednesday, and Thursday. Tours leave at 10:00 a.m. and 1:00 p.m. By reservation only. The trip involves a great deal of walking and may not be suitable for younger children. $

The Grove Farm Homestead is a wonderful place to visit and learn about the enormous impact of the sugar industry on Kauai. The Grove Farm, under the helm of missionary son George Wilcox, was once the most profitable plantation in all the islands. Wilcox engineered a series of aqueducts that let water flow around the surrounding eighty acres and produced large harvests. The plantation flourished from 1864 until the 1930s, when Wilcox died. Today the museum-like grounds are maintained by his descendants.

Guided two-hour walking tours pass through the various buildings and grounds, left much the way they were during the farm's working days. You'll see antique furniture made from Hawaiian koa wood, walk among gardens and fields where workers once toiled, and stroll through old homes and cottages that housed the staff.

Kilohana (all ages)

To get to Kilohana from Lihue, take the Kaumualii Highway (Highway 50) west toward Puhi for just a few minutes. The plantation is in front of the mountain, and well-marked signs point the way; (808) 245-5608; www.kilohanakauai.com. Twenty-minute carriage tours leave from the plantation house each hour between 11:00 a.m. and 6:30 p.m. daily. Hourlong sugar cane tours leave at 11:00 a.m. and 2:00 p.m. New tours also are offered via Kauai Plantation Railway (www.kauaiplantationrailway.com). Reservations required for both. $$$–$$$$

The beautifully elaborate 16,000-square-foot mansion at Kilohana Plantation was built in 1935 and still exudes an aura of grand class. It was built by Gaylord Wilcox to suit his wife Ethel's expectations of a Hollywood-type manor.

Today the home has been authentically restored, and various rooms have been converted into a small sampling of galleries and shops. The old living room looks like a museum with its period furniture, artifacts, and collectibles.

An optional hourlong horse-and-carriage tour pulled by Clydesdales is available, or you can simply park and walk around the grounds on your own for **free**. The horses pull tourist-filled wagons on other routes as well, through Lihue valley or sugar cane fields. Rates vary depending on the tour.

The newest attraction at Kilohana is Kauai Plantation Railway, which offers five tours daily, starting at 10:00 a.m. A vintage diesel train travels through fields of sugar, pineapple, banana, papaya, coffee, and tropical flowers.

Kalapaki Beach (all ages)

This is one of the most scenic beaches in all Hawaii. Its gentle waves make it a perfect playground for beginning surfers, sailboarders, boogieboarders, or just plain swimmers. There's a shack on the beach where you can rent surfing, snorkeling, sailboarding, and sailing equipment or arrange for lessons.

Where to Eat

Duke's Canoe Club. 3610 Rice Street; (808) 246-9599; www.dukeskauai.com. This oceanfront restaurant is adjacent to the Marriott and is a favorite eatery and watering hole for locals and visitors, with a special kids' menu. The view is grand and spacious, and the famous mud pie is a dessert institution on the island. $$$–$$$$

Gaylord's Restaurant. Off Kilohana Highway, next to Kauai Community College, 1 mile from Lihue; (808) 245-9593; www.gaylords kauai.com. Inside Kilohana Plantation, Gaylord's Restaurant is another island institution. It's a wonderfully scenic place for a meal and offers great continental food at reasonable prices. It's in the manor's original dining room, and some of the original furniture remains. Gaylord's menu features fresh fish and steaks and local-style specials. $$$–$$$$

Hamura Saimin. 2956 Kress Street; (808) 245-3271. Don't miss a chance for a family meal at Hamura Saimin, another famous local establishment that's been making its own noodles for generations. Saimin is a Japanese soup that comes with different variations of fish, meat, or vegetables but always includes long, spaghetti-like noodles. The food is cheap and the local ambience priceless. $

Where to Stay

Kauai Marriott Resort & Beach Club. 3610 Rice Street; (808) 245-5050. Even if you're not staying at the Kauai Marriott, do stop by and walk around the property. There are constructed lagoons dotted with tiny picturesque islands. The resort features one of the largest swimming pools in the state, and a multimillion-dollar art collection is scattered thoughtfully, unobtrusively, throughout the gardens, lobby, and grounds. The Marriott and its surrounding attractions are a five-minute drive from the airport and are easy to find, with well-marked signs pointing the way. The Kalapaki Kids program is available for children five to twelve years old. Activities include Hawaiian cultural lessons, garden explorations, hula lessons, Hawaiian crafts, ukulele lessons, and more. The program includes lunch, a snack, and a Kalapaki Kids T-shirt. $$$–$$$$

Poipu and Koloa

Continuing west from Lihue on the Kaumualii Highway, Route 50, look for Maluhia Road, Route 52, which veers left and heads toward the ocean and Koloa Town.

Maluhia Road is commonly referred to as the "Tunnel of Trees" because of the large trees growing on either side of the road; their uppermost branches and leaves join overhead to create a picturesque, living green tunnel.

As you arrive in town, note the stone chimney and adjacent cement structure. The chimney dates from 1835 and is a remnant of the Koloa Plantation, Hawaii's first sugar mill. The structure near the chimney is actually a permanent display dedicated to the birth of the sugar industry, the development of which is chronicled on plaques circling the monument.

The mill opened in 1837, thereby starting an industry that would forever change the people of these islands. As more plantations opened, there was a need for more workers, and immigrants arrived from Asia, Europe, and the Caribbean.

Not only has sugar been grown in these fertile lands, but Koloa is also home to one of Hawaii's first coffee plantations, started in 1836. Today the 4,000-acre Koloa Plantation is the largest coffee plantation in the state.

In Koloa there's a nice sampling of shops, restaurants, and businesses specializing in water-sports rentals and lessons. It's fun to walk through the small town, where most buildings are restored from original plantation structures.

Route 52 leads to the ocean and east to Poipu. On the way you'll see the tall steeple of Koloa Church, also known as the White Church, built in 1837. Nearby, St. Raphael's Catholic Church was built in 1841 and was the first Roman Catholic mission in the islands. To get there from Maluhia Road, turn left on Koloa Road, go right on Weleweli Road, then take Hapa Road to the church.

Maluhia Road ends at the coast, where a left turn leads to the string of hotels and condominiums composing the Poipu Resort area. A right turn leads to Spouting Horn.

If you turn right on Lawai Road instead of heading left to Poipu, you'll reach Baby Beach, a small protected cove that offers ideal conditions for young children. Soon after, look for Kuhio Park, which marks the birthplace of Prince Kuhio, Hawaii's first delegate to Congress. A statue and monument here are dedicated to the prince.

Captain Andy's Sailing Adventures   (ages 6 and up)
Reservations, (808) 335-6833 or (800) 535-0830; www.napali.com. Tour locations and prices vary. $$$$

Captain Andy's offers sunset catamaran rides along the south shore, and daytime cruises on the northern, Na Pali coast. Sunset cruises leave from Kukuiula Harbor in Poipu and include snacks and drinks. Tickets cost $69 for adults, $50 for children ages two to twelve; children younger than two ride **free** (Tuesday, Thursday, Saturday, and Sunday only). Also, a Na Pali tour leaves from Port Allen Small Boat Harbor daily, except Sunday, in season. It costs $139 for adults, $99 for kids two to twelve, and includes snorkeling and sailing. The trips are narrated by the captain and offer a wonderful insight into Kauai's history and a complete regaling of family-fun opportunities. This is one of the best oceangoing tours in all Hawaii!

The Kipu Falls Zipline Trek (ages 7 and up)

Reservations: (808) 742-9667 or (888) 742-9887; www.outfitterskauai.com. Children must be able to fit into the safety harness. $$$$

Ziplining is the newest adventure travel craze—better than a roller-coaster or even a trapeze! The zipline is designed, built, and operated according to the highest safety standards as set by the Association for Challenge Course Technology. The setting is magnificent: A quarter-mile foot trail through the jungle leads to a steep valley at the confluence of two streams, with a 150-foot waterfall tumbling over fern-covered boulders on one side

Water-Sports **Rentals**

- **Fathom Five Divers.** 3450 Poipu Road, next to Koloa's Chevron Station; (808) 742-6991 or (800) 972-3078; www.fathomfive.com. Offers scuba charters and certification courses and also rents snorkeling gear.
- **Sea Sport Divers.** 2827 Poipu Road, Koloa, (808) 742-9303; and 4–976 Kuhio Highway, (808) 823-9222 or (800) 658-5889; www.seasportdivers.com. Mostly offers scuba excursions but also holds certification classes for scuba wannabes. You can also rent boogieboards and snorkeling gear.
- **Snorkel Bob's.** 3236 Poipu Road, Koloa; (808) 742-2206 or (800) 262-7725; www.snorkelbob.com. When you rent from Snorkel Bob's and you're traveling to other islands, you can drop off at other Snorkel Bob's locations. There's another store on Kauai, in Kapa`a, at (808) 823-9433.
- **Outfitters Kauai.** Also at the Poipu Plaza, 2827 Poipu Road, Koloa; (808) 742-9667 or (888) 742-9887; www.outfitterskauai.com. You can rent kayaks and paddle upstream for an up-close view of the Alakoko Pond. Outfitters rents bicycles, too, and offers a huge variety of guided tours on both modes of transport. Most popular are the Waimea downhill ride, Kokee mountain-bike trip—in which guides explain the native plants, special geographic features, and local legends—and a bicycling/snorkeling tour. In addition to normal adult- and child-size bikes, they also rent trailers that hook up to a bike to accommodate a small child. See the entry on the Kipu Falls Zipline Trek for this unique adventure. Open daily 8:00 a.m. to 5:00 p.m.

and a huge stream on the other. Once you're "zipped" and "launched," you sail 50 feet above ground and over rivers, waterfalls, and treetops—all at a speed of 35 mph. Outfitters Kauai offers a number of tours, some including kayak trips, hikes, picnics, and so on.

Kiahuna Resort Gardens (all ages)

2253 Poipu Road, Koloa; (808) 742-6411. Nonguests are permitted to walk among the gardens during the day for free.

Kiahuna Plantation Resort is worth exploring—it's home to thirty-five acres of well-kept, colorful gardens, boasting more than 3,000 varieties of flowers, plants, and trees. Many of the plants are identified.

Poipu Beach (all ages)

Look for a well-marked turnoff from Poipu Road, between Kiahuna Resort and the Hyatt Regency.

Poipu Beach County Park, at the end of the road, is a well-tended park that's great for families and is the most popular beach on the south shore. The waters are quite clear here, ideal for close-to-shore snorkeling, as well as swimming and boogieboarding. Great for picnics too. There are restrooms, showers, a playground, picnic tables, and a pavilion. A naturally formed sheltered pool, surrounded by lava, is tame enough for toddlers and young, inexperienced swimmers. Poipu is one of the safest beaches on the island.

Shipwreck Beach (all ages)

Just past the Hyatt Regency Poipu Resort, off Poipu Road, Poipu.

Also known as Keoneloa, this secluded spot features a long, wide strip of sand and offers good sunbathing spots and swimming. Swim only during calm weather, however, because the beach is fairly deserted.

CJM Country Stables (ages 7 and up)

Situated just beyond Shipwreck Beach, past the golf course, Poipu; (808) 742-6096; www .cjmstables.com. Rides depart at 9:30 a.m. and 1:00 and 2:00 p.m. Children must be at least 7 years old. $$$$

A variety of horseback-riding trips are offered by CJM. A three-hour ride includes breakfast and costs $125 per person. A two-hour trip travels through the surrounding countryside and down to the beach and costs $98. (No special discounts for children.)

Mahaulepu Beach (all ages)

This beach sits at the east end of the Hyatt Regency Poipu Resort, in Poipu, just beyond Keoneloa Beach. It's a 2-mile trip, best done by car, from the end of Poipu Road. To get there turn right at the road's first fork, pass the first turnoff, and look for the McBryde Sugar Plantation's guard booth. You'll have to sign in; hours are 7:00 a.m. to 6:30 p.m.

There are some nice tide pools to explore here, but the undertow can be fierce, so swim with caution. Mahaulepu is actually three separate beaches: Kawailoa Bay, Ha`ula Beach, and Gillin's Beach.

This area is important to Kauai's history. In 1796 Kamehameha the Great sent 10,000 warriors in outrigger canoes from Oahu, across the channel, intending to land at Mahaulepu. Severe storms sank many of the canoes. The soldiers who did complete the journey were killed by King Kaumualii's warriors as soon as they landed here.

Centuries later, Mahaulepu was the site where George C. Scott portrayed Ernest Hemingway in the movie *Islands in the Stream*.

Spouting Horn Beach Park (all ages)

At the end of Lawai Road, Lawai; there's a large parking lot designed to hold several tour buses. Open during daylight hours.

It's almost impossible to miss the site of Spouting Horn. As with the Halona Blowhole on eastern Oahu, water spurts up from an open-ended lava tube that extends into the ocean. Depending on surf conditions, the currents can send fountains of water quite high.

Koloa Heritage Trail (all ages)

Maps and brochures are available free at numerous points of distribution throughout Kauai or by contacting Poipu Beach Resort Association, (808) 742-7444 or (888) 744-0888; www.poipubeach.org.

The Poipu Beach Resort Association created the new 10-mile Koloa Heritage Trail. It features fourteen stops with historical and cultural information at each location (marked by lava rock pedestals topped with bronze signs). The trail can be explored by foot, bicycle, or automobile. Stops along the trail in Koloa Town include the sugar monument, Yamamoto Store, Koloa Hotel, Koloa Jodo Mission, and the Koloa Missionary Church. Along the shoreline the trail continues with signs at Spouting Horn Beach Park, Prince Kuhio Birthplace and Park, Koloa Landing, Moir Gardens at Kiahuna Plantation, and Hapa Road.

McBryde and Allerton Gardens (ages 8 and up)

To get to both gardens from the Kaumualii Highway, turn down Route 530, then take Halima Road toward the right to Lawai; (808) 742-2623; www.ntbg.org. The visitor center is at the end of the driveway (beyond the dead-end sign). The interior of the McBryde and Allerton Gardens is open for guided tours only. The two-hour tours are in open-air sampans and include about 1 mile of walking. Daily tours are given hourly, beginning at 9:30 a.m. Last tour leaves at 2:30 p.m. They are led by horticultural specialists and are quite enlightening. Reservations are not required, but recommended. Guided tours not recommended for young children; they involve a one-and-a-half-hour walk. *NOTE:* Bring lots of mosquito repellent. $$$$

In Lawai, the 186-acre National Tropical Botanical Garden at McBryde is the only tropical-plant research station in the United States. Here you'll see lily pads the size of swimming pools, along with dozens of rare and endangered plants, including strawberry bananas and wild ginger.

The research station was founded by congressional charter in 1964 but is supported today through private donations. The National Tropical Botanical Garden also manages two off-site properties: 1,000 acres in Limahuli Valley in northern Kauai and 100 acres in Hana, Maui.

The neighboring hundred-acre Allerton Gardens was a favorite summer vacation spot for Queen Emma, wife of Kamehameha IV, in the 1800s. Today it's run by John Allerton, whose father, Robert, bought the property in the 1930s for the purpose of creating a beautiful garden. The father-and-son team certainly succeeded, and Allerton is a cornucopia of sights and smells.

More than 6,000 species of tropical plants flourish in this fertile land. The gardens are organized into sections, such as plants with medicinal value, plants of nutritional importance, endangered species, and herbs and spices.

As the world's rain forests are being destroyed at an alarming rate, this is an important facility where tropical plants are preserved and propagated and the public is educated about the role of each plant within its ecosystem.

Kukui O Lono Park (all ages)

To get there from Kalaheo, turn left at the little convenience store called Menehune Food Mart. The road leads uphill for about a mile; pass Puu Road and turn right at the second Puu Road, where you'll find the gates to the park. The gates are open from 6:30 a.m. to 6:30 p.m.

Although it's a little difficult to find, Kukui O Lono Park is a nice place to stop for a picnic or just to stretch your legs. The views are expansive and immensely beautiful. The park contains a Japanese-style garden and golf course.

Where to Eat

The Beach House Restaurant. 5022 Lawai Road; (808) 742-1424; www.the-beach-house.com. The Beach House's menu is exciting and innovative, one of the best examples of Hawaii Regional Cuisine on Kauai. Molten Chocolate Desire, with a hot chocolate tart, vanilla bean ice cream, and chocolate caramel sauce, is our dream dessert. There is a special keiki menu, complete with a wonderful selection of smoothies and "virgin" tropical drinks, such as Poipu Punch and Virgin Mango Mama. $$$–$$$$

Brennecke's. 2100 Hoone Road; (808) 742-7588; www.brenneckes.com. Has an open-air lanai that overlooks Poipu Beach Park. We kept going back for the grilled ahi (yellowfin tuna) burgers with fries. Open 11:00 a.m. to 10:00 p.m. daily. $$

Casa Di Amici. 2301 Nalo Road; (808) 742-1555. Lovely views and an outdoor dining terrace make for a wonderful, relaxing ambience. The menu, Italian in intent, is also colored by influences from France and the Far East. Pastas, ravioli, and risottos are perfectly cooked and flavored with pungent ingredients, while duck breast, grilled prawns, and fresh fish are adorned with succulent sauces that make perfect accents. A pianist regales diners with live music on Friday and Saturday night. $$$

Dondero's. 1571 Poipu Road; (808) 240-6456. This is Hyatt's upscale eatery. It offers regional Italian cuisine in an elegant setting of inlaid marble floor and ornately patterned tile work. $$$$

Ilima Terrace. 1571 Poipu Road; (808) 240-6456. This is the spot for meals at the Hyatt Regency. Breakfast and lunch daily includes a prime rib buffet for $36. The menu, complete with kids' specialties, includes Hawaiian, Asian, and American fare. The Sunday champagne brunches are colossally wonderful; be sure to make a reservation. It's popular with Poipu locals. $$

Plantation Gardens. At Kiahuna Plantation, 2253 Poipu Road; (808) 742-6411. Tasty Italian food served in an idyllic garden setting. You'll never leave hungry! $$$–$$$$

Where to Stay

The Point at Poipu. 1613 Pe`e Road; (808) 742-1888 or (800) 426-3350; www.sunterra kauai.com. Condominiums. $$–$$$$

Grand Hyatt Kauai Resort & Spa. 1571 Poipu Road; (808) 742-1234; www.kauai .hyatt.com. If you happen to be in this area, the Grand Hyatt Kauai Resort & Spa hosts different cultural demonstrations daily; **free** even if you're not a guest at the hotel.

The Hyatt also features a children's program known as Camp Hyatt. The program includes Hawaiian arts and crafts and lessons about Kauai's history, archaeology, and ecological preservation. The schedules vary daily but usually include a nature trek along the sand dunes near Shipwreck Beach, a visit with the wildlife manager, kite flying, snorkeling, face painting, and tennis. The program costs $70 per child, includes lunch, and runs daily from 9:00 a.m. to 4:00 p.m. and 4:00 to 10:00 p.m. (includes dinner); (808) 742-1234. Half-day camps are also available. Participants get a Camp Hyatt T-shirt. $$$$

Kiahuna Plantation. 2253B Poipu Road, Koloa; (808) 742-2200 or (800) 367–5004; www.outrigger.com. My kids enjoyed the airy bungalows on the beautifully landscaped twenty-eight acres. Outrigger Resorts, the management company, also offers one-bedroom suites that can sleep up to four. Oceanfront suites are expensive but include a basket with continental breakfast. A beachside concession rents bodyboards, snorkels, and fins. $$–$$$$

Poipu Kai Resort. 2827 Poipu Road; (808) 742-7400. Beachfront condominiums. $–$$

Poipu Kapili. 2221 Kapili Road; (808) 742-6449. Beautiful beachfront condos. $$–$$$$

Sheraton Kauai. 2440 Hoonani Road; (808) 742-1661; www.sheraton-kauai.com. Recently renovated in 2006. Kids will love the water slide. The Sheraton offers the Kauai Keiki Aloha Program, for children ages five to twelve on weekdays. Activities include arts and crafts, kite flying, fishing, storytelling, pool play, and more. The program is available on weekends during holiday seasons (December, spring break, etc.). It costs $50 for a full day, including lunch. Half-day schedules are also available. $$$–$$$$

Hanapepe

Beyond Kalaheo, the highway veers south and leads to Port Allen Harbor, then continues and travels through acre after acre of sugar cane, west to Hanapepe.

On the way to Hanapepe, look for a small sign that leads to Hanapepe Valley Overlook, a must-stop. The views from here encompass the picturesque valley, lush with sugar cane and taro farms.

Just before Hanapepe is the little town of Ele`ele. Stop here to sample such goodies as coconut krispies cookies and macadamia shortbread at the Kauai Kookie Kompany (808) 335-5003 or (800) 361-1126. The facility is at 1–3959 Kaumualii Highway and is open Monday through Friday 8:00 a.m. to 4:00 p.m. and weekends 9:00 a.m. to 4:00 p.m.; www.kauaikookie.com.

You'll know you're in Hanapepe when you see the sign reading KAUAI'S BIGGEST LITTLE TOWN. The town consists of "Old Hanapepe" and "New Hanapepe." To get to the old part, take Hanapepe Road right at the intersection where Green Garden Restaurant sits. It's a charming one-lane town that looks just as it did a hundred years ago, when sugar dominated the landscape and all the plantation workers lived here. Former plantation homes have blossomed into modern-day art galleries, boutiques, and restaurants.

The beaches in Hanapepe and Waimea, the next town west, not only are quite scenic but are among the best on the island, blessed with lots of sunny days and cooperative currents making for smooth swimming conditions.

Salt Pond Beach Park (all ages)

At the west end of Port Allen, just beyond the Port Allen runway. To get there take Route 543 from Route 50. A sign points the way to the beach.

Look for large basins carved into the red dirt. For centuries Hawaiian families have created salt from evaporated seawater here. The ancient practice has been continued through the generations, and the product is used for cooking and medicinal purposes.

Learn to **Surf**

Seven-time women's world surfing champ Margo Oberg started giving lessons on Kauai twenty-five years ago. Instructors with the **Margo Oberg Surf School** teach beginners inside the break at Poipu Beach, using a safe beginner's board to take you out when the waves are smaller than 4 feet and winds are moderate. Located just past the Sheraton Hotel, where the road ends; (808) 332-6100 or (808) 639-0708; www.surfonkauai.com. The price is $65 for two hours. Children ages eight and younger require parental supervision and assistance during the lesson.

This is the best spot on this side of the island for swimming, sailboarding, and snorkeling. There's even a calm area that's ideal for toddlers. Facilities include picnic tables, restrooms, showers, and a pavilion.

Where to Eat

Green Garden Restaurant. 1–3749 Kaumualii Highway; (808) 335-5422. This is somewhat of an institution in town, it's been here so long. A good all-purpose eatery and one of the few in town. $

Omoide Bakery and Delicatessen. Across the street from Green Garden on Kaumualii Highway; (808) 335-5291. Be sure to stop by the Omoide for a slice of the

famous lilikoi pie, coveted by locals and residents since 1956. Open Monday 7:00 a.m. to 3:00 p.m. and Tuesday to Sunday 7:00 a.m. to 9:00 p.m. $

Where to Stay

The closest accommodations are a few minutes' drive west, in Waimea, or back at Poipu.

Waimea and Kokee

Beyond Hanapepe, the Kaumualii Highway skirts along the coast and passes through the small sugar towns of Kaumakani, Olokele, and Pakala. Historic Waimea is a few minutes' drive from Pakala.

From Waimea the highway continues east to Kekaha and farther on to the end of the road at Mana Point and Barking Sands Pacific Missile Range. At Kekaha Route 55 leads north to Waimea Canyon State Park. A shortcut to Waimea Canyon is via Waimea Canyon Road, which leads inland from Waimea town, then joins with Route 55 coming from Kekaha.

Visitors should stop at the Waimea Public Library (808) 338-6848 or at the front office of Waimea Plantation Cottages (808) 338-1625 for a **free** map that highlights the town's historic hot spots. The town has joined the Main Street USA program in an attempt to revive local businesses and promote community-sponsored restoration and historic awareness.

Fort Elizabeth State Park (all ages)
Off Highway 50, 1 mile south of Waimea town. Open during daylight hours.

Upon arriving in town it may be surprising to see the remains of a Russian fort, here in the middle of almost nowhere. A sign points left to Fort Elizabeth State Park. In the early 1800s George Anton Schaffer, a visiting German doctor, constructed this fort and named it after Elizabeth, Czar Nicholas's daughter. Schaffer believed the strategic location of these islands in the middle of the Pacific Ocean was an important factor for Russia to consider and wanted to turn the fort into a trading post. (There are a few other Russian forts still

S

Packing Slip

Venue: Half
Ship Method: Standard
Order ID: 100002287270
Ship From: Best Bargain Books
65 Robinson Ave
East Patchogue, NY 11772

Order Date: 01/24/2012
Processed: 01/24/2012 06:43:57 AM
Batch: 20120124064237413-1538
Ship To: Chris Clarke
204 Oneida Ln
Malvern, PA 19355-3107
United States

76105351101

100002287270

SKU	Matched	Qty	ISBN	Title	Condition	Notes	Price
BP-11-01-1504	BP-11-01-1504	1	0762748591	Fun with the Family Hawaii, 7th: Hundreds of Ideas for Day Trips with the Kids (Fun with the Family Series)	Used - Good	A copy that may have been re....	$0.75

Subtotal:	$0.75
Shipping fee:	$3.49
Total:	**$4.24**

Seller Note:

Buyer Note:

Inspected By #13

Touring Na Pali By Sea

Boats provide fantastic perspectives of the towering jagged cliffs, deep valleys, and sea caves. You'll hear the lilting chorus of dozens of waterfalls as they spray down the steep promontories. You'll see otherwise inaccessible jungles, completely isolated from modern civilization.

The captains and crew members of most of the tour boats are well versed in local legends and the distinctive wildlife of the area. They are able to identify birds and marine life as they guide you through the Pacific wilderness. Plan on seeing dolphins, sea turtles, and, in season, humpback whales.

The tamest rides are in large catamarans, sailboats, or Boston Whalers and usually include a picnic lunch. Zodiacs, which are large, sturdy motorized rubber rafts, offer a slightly rougher ride but can fit into the various seaside caves for more in-depth exploration. About six or eight passengers can fit in a Zodiac boat. In the calm summer months, there are even escorted kayak trips to this picturesque coastline. Tours vary in price and length.

Dozens of companies are eager to share the beauty of Na Pali; the following list is merely a sampling.

- **Holoholo Charters** (808-335-0815 or 800-848-6130; www.holoholocharters. com) offers snorkeling tours to the Na Pali Coast, as well as an afternoon sunset champagne tour. $$$$
- **Blue Dolphin Charters** (808-335-5553 or 877-511-1311; www.kauaiboats. com) takes visitors in a catamaran. They also offer seasonal whale-watching tours. $$$$
- **Kauai Sea Tours** (808-826-7254 or 800-733-7997; www.kauaiseatours.com) explores the Na Pali coast on either an adventure Zodiac-style raft tour or a deluxe catamaran. $$$$
- **Captain Andy's Sailing Adventures** (808-338-6833 or 800-535-0830; www. napali.com) also takes visitors on the Zodiac-raft-type tours, as well as the 55-foot Gold Coast Catamaran. Reservations recommended; this is among the most popular tours and spaces fill up quickly. $$$$
- **Catamaran Kahanu** (808- 645-6176 or 888-213-7711; www.catamarankahanu. com). The longtime family-run operation offers trips that include cultural demonstrations as well as the standard swimming and snorkeling. $$$$
- **Na Pali Explorer** (808-338-9999 or 877-335-9909; www.napali-explorer.com). Trips are run on the Zodiac rafts and the crew specializes in snorkeling tours. $$$$

standing on Kauai.) Czar Nicholas never agreed with Schaffer, and the fort eventually fell into disrepair.

The fort was designated a National Historic Landmark in 1966; in 1970 it was acquired by the state to be developed into a historic park, but there hasn't been much activity to restore the structure.

Lucy Wright Beach County Park (all ages)

On the coast, at Waimea's eastern tip off Highway 50. Open during daylight hours.

The five-acre Lucy Wright Beach County Park facilities include restrooms, showers, picnic tables, and a playground. It's a popular recreational spot for the local community.

Waimea Canyon (all ages)

Follow Waimea Canyon Road, which veers up the mountain from Highway 50 in Waimea. The headquarters are open daily 10:00 a.m. to 4:00 p.m.

The spectacular Waimea Canyon should definitely be included on the itinerary of any Kauai visitor. It's commonly referred to as the "Grand Canyon of the Pacific" after its similarity to Arizona's natural wonder. The canyon is only 1 mile wide, but it's a whopping 14 miles long. It features a wide variety of trails designed for all levels of hikers.

Officially, Waimea Canyon State Park begins about a mile inland from Waimea, on the Waimea Canyon Road. The park borders the road for the remainder of its winding path, which culminates at Kokee State Park. Outfitters Kauai (808-742-9667, www.outfitters kauai.com) offers informative, exciting Kokee mountain-bike trips, during which guides explain the native plants, special geographic features, and local legends. Children must be ten years old. Outfitters offices are in Poipu Shopping Village.

Although quite curvy, the road is well maintained as it leads up the mountain, where the landscape changes almost immediately and the temperature drops a few degrees. Along the way don't miss the chance to park at one of the many scenic points. The views are expansive and get even more glorious as you climb higher.

The Arrival of **Captain Cook**

Capt. James Cook, on his ocean voyage searching for the Northwest Passage, landed in Waimea in January 1778. This forever changed the remote island environment and the people who lived in the secluded society here. A small monument marks the spot where Cook landed. Hawaiian scholars are quick to point out that Cook did not "discover" the islands, since the Polynesians had migrated here centuries before Cook found them.

Cook remained in Waimea just a short time, trading iron and nails for food. When he returned a year later, he landed at Kealakekua Bay, on the Big Island.

The Legend of the *Menehune* Ditch

In Waimea look for Kiki a Ola, more commonly known as the *Menehune* Ditch, built by *Menehune* Chief Ola and his followers. This is among the most impressive structures linked to the famous little people. It's said that the ditch was built in one night, and its unique design and distinctive stonework differ from any other archaeological structures in Hawaii.

When you reach an altitude of 3,100 feet, the first stop is Waimea Canyon Lookout, where you have a fantastic view of the canyon. At Pu`ukapele Lookout, about 3,700 feet up, there's a small rest area with picnic tables. The best views of the canyon are from Pu`uhinahina Lookout. A short trail beginning behind the restrooms leads to an even better view, where, if cloud cover permits, you can see Niihau.

The road ends at the 4,345-acre Kokee State Park, where another slew of hiking trails can accommodate any skill level. It gets cold up here, so bring warm clothes. Be sure to follow the road all the way to its end, at Kalalau and Pu`u O Kila lookouts. From Kalalau you can see deep into Kalalau Valley, the largest and widest valley in the Na Pali cliffs, and

Beaches of the **West Side**

Kekaha Beach stretches for miles and offers good swimming, surfing, and snorkeling. It butts up against Barking Sands Military Base. Beyond here, the official road ends, but a smaller cane road leads to the absolute end of the line at **Polihale State Park.** This beautiful, secluded wide beach is nearly always sunny, but the swimming conditions aren't optimal because the currents cause a strong undertow. Facilities include restrooms, showers, and a picnic area. Be sure to bring some snacks and water because Polihale is far away from convenience stores. *NOTE:* At press time this road was undergoing improvements and was accessible only for four-wheel-drive vehicles. Please check with your rental car agency before venturing out here.

This was a sacred area to Hawaiians of old. There's an isolated heiau out here, and this is one of a few spots statewide where the Hawaiians believed the souls of the dead left Earth to journey to the spiritual world.

Looking northward, views include the razor-sharp crags of the Na Pali Coast. If you're here when the sun is setting behind Niihau Island, you're in for a special treat as the cliffs are transformed into a spectrum of color ranging from forest green to golden brown.

This is the southern end of the Na Pali Coast, the rest of it being inaccessible by car, but it's definitely worth exploring either on foot, by boat, or by air. (See the sidebar on Touring Na Pali By Sea in this chapter.)

you can see the ever-beautiful Na Pali Coast from a different angle, as opposed to viewing it from the ocean. From Pu`u O Kila you also can see into Kalalau Valley, as well as across the Alakai Swamp to Mount Waialeale, in the center of the island.

Staff at the park headquarters can answer questions about the particular plants and animals in this region and about the conditions of certain trails. Be sure to pick up a **free** map that details all the trails in the park.

Kokee Natural History Museum (all ages)

It's easily found, being one of the few structures in the small town of Kokee; (808) 335-9975; www.kokee.org. Open daily 10:00 a.m. to 4:00 p.m. **free.**

Be sure to visit for a larger selection of maps of the area's hiking trails. There are also exhibits that explain the distinctive characteristics of the environment up here, as well as displays of native plants, birds, and animals living in the park.

Where to Eat

Waimea Brewing Company. At Waimea Plantation Cottages, 9400 Kaumualii Highway; (808) 338-9733; www.waimeabrewing.com. Hearty club sandwiches, salads, and pizza. Open daily for lunch and dinner, 11:00 a.m. to 9:00 p.m. $$

Wrangler's. 9852 Kaumualii Highway; (808) 338-1218. Features western-style grub: sizzling steaks, seafood, and salad. $$–$$$

Kokee State Park—
Wonderful Family Hiking Trails

Children should be able to navigate the initial curves of the **Kukui Trail,** well identified between mile markers 8 and 9. The first part of the trail is known as **Iliau Nature Loop** and is a wonderful, short, self-guided path. Beyond the loop, the trail descends 2,000 feet into the canyon through a series of switchbacks. Figuring that you'll have to climb back up, this may be difficult for young children. Take note of the grade and use good judgment.

A series of other trails branch off Mohihi Camp 10 Road, near park headquarters. It's wise to ask for recommendations at the headquarters for the trails that best suit your family's abilities. Everyone should be able to handle the easy 1-mile **Berry Flat Trail** and the ½-mile **Puu Ka Ohelo Trail.** Both are loops that take hikers through a picturesque forest.

The **Alakai Swamp Trail** is the most famous trail here, but it should be attempted only by the most experienced hikers—not young children. It rains 450 inches a year here, and scientists say this is the most fragile ecosystem on Earth.

Where to Stay

Kokee Lodge. In Kokee State Park; (808) 335-6061; www.thelodgeatkokee.net. Believe it or not, for those who really want to get away from it all, there are overnight accommodations up here. The Kokee Lodge offers rustic cabins that were built in the 1930s by the Civilian Conservation Corps, or CCC. $–$$. Nonguests are welcome to eat at the restaurant, which is open 7:00 a.m. to 6:00 p.m. $$–$$$$

Waimea Plantation Cottages. 9400 Kaumualii Highway; (808) 338-1625; www .waimea-plantation.com. The Waimea Plantation Cottages feature authentically restored

homes that are relics from the sugar industry. Each of the forty-six cottages throughout the property is decorated with period furniture and named for the families that lived there. $$–$$$$

Wailua and Kapaa

Heading north from Lihue on the Kuhio Highway (Route 56), Ma`ala Road (Route 583) turns inland and follows the Wailua River.

You'll notice that the fertile landscape is lush with sugar cane as you head toward the green velvety mountains. After a few miles Route 583 ends at Wailua Falls, where the river drops 80 feet into a large pool. Hawaiians say that the *ali`i* (royalty) would jump from here as an exhibition of their power. A trail leads down to the pool, but it's fairly rugged and not recommended for children.

Historic Heiau (all ages)

Along Route 56, just before the Coco Palms Hotel, a tall stand of palms on the east side of the river marks the heiau. On-site are the Hau`ola O Honaunau and Hikina O Kala Heiau. The first was a place of refuge, where *kapu* (taboo) breakers or soldiers on the losing end of a battle could seek refuge and be forgiven for all wrongdoings. After a kahuna cleansed their souls, the individuals could return to society with a clean bill of spiritual health.

A few miles north of Hanamaulu, you'll pass Wailua River State Park and arrive at the oceanside town of Wailua, a place that abounds with historic sites and attractions. At one time there were at least seven heiau from the river to the top of Mt. Waialeale. Religious processions would make the trek to the top, stopping at each heiau along the way.

Just as Route 580 veers inland, look for the Holo Holo Ku Heiau, one of Kauai's oldest. Although some ancient heiau were places of refuge, this was not. Here those unfortunate criminals of war or kapu breakers were sacrificed to the gods. Look in the corner for the large flat rock that was the altar of the heiau.

Kauai Trivia

The Wailua River is the only navigable stream in all Hawaii. It flows from Mt. Waialeale, through the Fern Grotto to the ocean at Wailua Bay. It's also known as one of the best kayaking spots on the island, although even the best kayakers will be able to navigate only about a third of the river. Motorized barges cruise up the river, docking at the Fern Grotto, one of the frequently visited sites on Kauai.

A guardrail leads up the hill behind the heiau to a Japanese cemetery, and beyond that, the large rocks were known as royal birthing stones. Wives of ali`i came here when they were about to deliver their babies, thinking that this area possessed great mana, or spirit.

Legend says Poliahu Heiau, just a few minutes' drive on Route 580, is another structure built by the industrious menehune. Today all that's left is an overgrown enclosure surrounded by walls. Down the ridge from here are the Royal Bellstones, rung whenever an ali`i gave birth.

The Sleeping Giant Hike (ages 11 and up)
Two trailheads, east and west. See text for directions.

If you look very carefully at the mountains above Wailua with a bit of imagination and an open mind, you should see a reclining form, known as Nonou, the sleeping giant.

You can hike up to the sleeping giant on the Nonou Mountain Trail. The eastern side of the trail is a bit more difficult than the western side. The eastern trailhead is just north of the junctions of Routes 56 and 580, at Haleilio Road. Look for a space to park near a water pump about 1½ miles up Haleilio (at mile marker 38). The trail starts across from the drainage ditch and proceeds up the mountain for about 1½ miles. It's a steady climb that concludes at a picnic site, complete with a shade-providing shelter and tables.

From here you can walk across the giant's face by taking another trail just south of the picnic site. Though you're afforded expansive views, this section of the trail is difficult and dangerous—suited only for experienced, hardy hikers.

To get to the easier, western side of the trail, turn onto Route 580, then 581, and look for parking at mile marker 11. There's a little path here that joins the trail. After about 1½ miles this trail joins the eastern trail and heads up to the picnic site. Bring plenty of water for whichever trail you choose.

The Fern Grotto (all ages)
You can venture here only by boat. $$–$$$

The Fern Grotto is a naturally formed amphitheater, framed completely by hanging ferns that flourish in the misty, moist air. It's a romantic, beautiful spot, the kind of place that typifies a tropical island, and it's a frequent spot for weddings. And whether or not your visit coincides with romantic nuptials, the "Hawaiian Wedding Song" is played here several times a day by local musicians.

Since 1947 Smith's Motor Boat Service (808-821-6895; www.smithskauai.com) has ferried visitors to the Fern Grotto. On the way, passengers are entertained by musicians, singers, dancers, and master storytellers of local legends. Cruises depart daily from Wailua Marina at 9:30, 10:00, and 11:30 a.m., and 1:30, 2:00, and 3:30 p.m. Cruise is $20 for adults, $10 for children ages three to twelve, **free** for children younger than three. Smith's offers other adventures as well—please check the entry later in this chapter.

Kauai Water Ski and Surf (ages 4 and up)

In the Kinipopo Shopping Village, 4–356 Kuhio Highway; (808) 822-3574 or (800) 344-7915. (Appropriate for water-safe children only.) Open Monday through Friday 9:00 a.m. to 5:00 p.m. and Saturday 9:00 a.m. to noon.

This is a complete water-sports shop that rents snorkel gear, kayaks, surfboards, and boogieboards and offers waterskiing excursions, complete with boat, driver, equipment, and instruction. Lessons cost $150 an hour, and usually three or four people need only one hour to take turns and get in a couple of rides each. Beginners need more time. Four or five passengers are allowed in the boat at one time, but not everyone needs to be a skier. They also offer guided kayak tours and surf lessons.

Smith's Tropical Paradise (all ages)

Wailua Marina State Park; (808) 821-6892; www.smithskauai.com. Open daily 8:30 a.m. to 4:00 p.m. $

Right next to the Wailua Marina are twenty-three riverfront acres with unusual birds, rain forest, and gardens. Smith's Tropical Paradise is a well-maintained cultural and botanical feast for the senses. You can walk among a striking collection of exotic plants and feel as if you're in the midst of a jungle.

On the grounds are a luau house and a theater; evening entertainment includes dinner, Hawaiian music, and a variety of South Pacific dances. A series of ethnic villages represents different local groups, including Polynesian, Filipino, and Japanese.

Visitors also can ride through the facility on a minitram for an additional fee of $6 for adults, $3 for children. The evening luau and performance is held Monday, Wednesday, and Friday and costs $75 for adults, $30 for children ages seven to thirteen, and $19 for children ages three to six. For just the show admission costs $15 for adults, $7 for children three through twelve. Reservations are necessary.

Opaeka`a Falls and Kamokila Hawaiian Village (all ages)

Continuing inland on Route 580, look for a sign pointing to Opaeka`a Falls. $

Although you can see the falls from the road, it's definitely a place to park the car and walk around. An overlook offers views of Kamokila Hawaiian Village, Wailua River, and pristine Kauai country. Across the highway from the falls overlook is a series of descriptive signs that offers information about Poliahu Heiau and the archaeological sites below, along the Wailua River. Some scholars believe Wailua was home to the highest-ranking ali`i, who worshiped at a private heiau.

Kamokila Hawaiian Village is reconstructed to appear just as villages did in Old Hawaii. This attraction is about as low-key as they come—there's no fancy gift shop and no hard sell. In fact, it's never even advertised. Visitors may walk around the village's thatched huts, including the traditional separate structures for sleeping and eating, and view the taro patches. There are demonstrations of Hawaiian crafts, such as poi-pounding.

Keahua Arboretum (all ages)

To get to Keahua simply follow Route 580 from Highway 56 all the way to its end. Open during daylight hours.

The thirty-acre Keahua Arboretum is no doubt one of the best-kept secrets on the island—hardly anyone ventures up here. In the mountains above Wailua, the arboretum features pools that beg to be jumped into and bubbling streams perfect for wading and exploring. The surrounding forests are so green they almost look more like a painting than real life. There's even a rope swing where kids, and kids at heart, can grab hold, take a flying leap, give a Tarzan yell, and plop into the stream. There is a series of trails within the arboretum, or you can walk upstream and explore what will seem like uncharted territory.

Beyond Wailua, the Kuhio Highway leads north to Kapa`a.

You can see virtually the whole town of Kapa`a just by driving through it on Kuhio Highway. It is fun to stroll among the colorful shops and eateries; it's a quaint place, serving the needs of visitors and locals. A host of recreational shops here offers a variety of rentals and adventures.

Free Hula Shows at the Coconut Marketplace (all ages)

On the Kuhio Highway heading north. Free hula show every Wednesday at 5:00 p.m.

The Coconut Marketplace is home to a large concentration of shops and restaurants.

Kauai Coconut Beach Resort Luaus (all ages)

Held at the ResortQuest Kauai Beach at Makaiwa; (808) 822-3455 or (877) 997-6667. Daily except Monday from 5:30 to 8:30 p.m. $$$$; kids younger than 6 get in free.

For evening entertainment the Kauai Coconut Beach Resort luau offers a traditional visitor-oriented production, complete with an imu ceremony, buffet dinner, and hula show.

Kealia Beach (strong swimmers only)

Continuing on the Kuhio Highway, look for a sign after mile marker 10 directing you to turn onto a small cane road that leads to the ocean.

Your next stop should be Kealia Beach and the tiny town of Kealia. It's not an official park, so there are no facilities, and swimming isn't recommended for young, inexperienced chil-

Local **Beaches**

On the way from Wailua on the Kuhio Highway, **Waipouli Beach County Park** is on the ocean side of the highway, just north of the Coconut Plantation Marketplace. It's a nice place for swimming (only in calm weather, please) and is connected to **Kapa`a Beach County Park,** which encompasses about fifteen acres and features picnic tables, showers, restrooms, and a pavilion for shade.

From the Kuhio Highway turn toward the ocean on Hanamaulu Road and go right on Hehi Road, which leads to the wonderful **Hanamaulu Beach County Park.** It's a great place for swimming and picnicking, and it's rarely crowded. A sheltered lagoon area, complete with natural pools, is an ideal playground for small children.

Lydgate State Park is well marked off Kuhio Highway (look for a tall group of palm trees east of the Wailua River) and is perfect for children of all ages. There are two large, naturally formed lava pools that make for year-round safe swimming and snorkeling. If you bring some fish food, which should be available at any convenience store, you can try feeding the fish right from the shore. Be sure to warn your kids to stay within the protected waters and off the slippery lava barriers.

dren, but the wide sandy beach is quite scenic and a good place to check out the talents of local surfers. During the summer the north end of Kealia Beach is tremendously popular with boogieboarders. If your kids are good swimmers, it's safe to let them try their boogie boarding skills here.

Where to Eat

Voyager Grill. 650 Aleka Loop, Kapaa; (808) 822-3455. The restaurant for ResortQuest Kauai Beach at Makaiwa, the Voyager serves lunch and dinner daily. $$$

Beezers Old Fashioned Ice Cream. 1380 Kuhio Highway; (808) 822-4411. Modeled after the 1950s style of diners, Beezers serves great shakes and malts, in addition to the standard sloppy joes, sandwiches, and burgers. $

Mermaids Café. 1384 Kuhio Highway; (808) 821-2026. Healthy, island-style sidewalk take-out joint that serves *great* food. Breakfasts are so tasty, as are the huge variety of wraps offered for lunch and dinner. Most of the food is locally grown. $

Ono Family Restaurant. 4-1292 Kuhio Highway; (808) 822-1710. This is a traditional Hawaiian-style family restaurant, nothing fancy, just hearty portions for families on a budget. Great place to start your day with macadamia-nut pancakes (coconut and banana offered as well) or eggs cooked dozens of ways. Also open for lunch. $

Bubba Burgers. On Kuhio Highway in Kapa`a; (808) 823-0069. Possibly the best burger you'll ever eat. $

East Side–Based Ocean Tours and
Snorkeling Rentals

- **Dive Kauai Scuba Center.** 1038 Kuhio Highway; (808) 822-0452 or (800) 828-3483; www.divekauai.com. In addition to full-scale tours and rentals, they also offer an introductory dive for first-timers, as well as certification classes from Junior Open Water Diver to the new Scuba Diver rating through instructor.
- **Rainbow Kayak Tours.** (866) 826-2505; www.rainbowkayak.com. They offer four-and-a-half-hour excursions on the Wailua River that include ancient Hawaiian sites, hiking to Secret Falls, swimming, and a picnic.
- **Kayak Kauai.** In the south parking lot of the Coconut Marketplace Shopping Center on Route 56, just a half-mile north of the Wailua River; (808) 826-9844 or (800) 437-3507; www.kayakkauai.com. (A second shop is located in Hanalei.) Offers kayak and bicycle rentals and guided excursions. Open daily 8:00 a.m. to 5:00 p.m.

Where to Stay

ResortQuest Islander on the Beach. 484 Kuhio Highway; (808) 822-7417 or (866) 774-2924; www.resortquesthawaii.com. Condominium resort; full kitchens, three pools, air-conditioned, maid service. $$–$$$

ResortQuest Kauai Beach at Makaiwa. 650 Aleka Loop; (808) 822-3455 or (866) 774-2924; www.resortquesthawaii.com. Recently renovated, situated on eleven beachfront acres amid a coconut grove that dates back almost a century. $$–$$$

Outrigger Waipouli Beach Resort. 4-820 Kuhio Highway; (808) 822-6000 or (800) 688-7444; www.outrigger.com. Offers one- and two-bedroom accommodations, each with a fully equipped kitchen featuring modern appliances. The resort also has a heated salt-water pool that wafts its way over two acres with flumed water slides and three sand-bottom whirlpool spas. $$$$

Aloha Beach Hotel Kauai. 3-5920 Kuhio Highway; (808) 823-6000 or (888) 823-5111; www.alohabeachresortkauai.com. This property fronts Lydgate Beach, a protected swimming and snorkeling beach (see page 165). $$–$$$

Pono Kai Resort. 4-1250 Kuhio Highway; (808) 822-9831 or (800) 456-0009; www.ponokai.com. A low-key family-oriented beachfront resort featuring tennis, volleyball, shuffleboard, croquet, and putting greens. $$–$$$

Kauai Sands Hotel. 420 Papaloa Road; (808) 822-4951 or (800) 560-5553; www.kauaisandshotel.com. $–$$

Outrigger at Lae Nani. 410 Papaloa Road, Kapaa; (808) 822-4938 or (800) 688-7444; www.outrigger.com. Condominiums. $$–$$$

Wailua Bay View Condominiums. 320 Papaloa Road; (808) 245-4711 or (800) 767-4707; www.prosser-realty.com. $$

Anahola and Kilauea

The Kuhio Highway meanders along the picturesque coast to Anahola. The drive offers superb sights as each turn reveals a more stunning view of lava arms jutting out into the ocean, being pummeled by a never-ending succession of crashing waves. The grass is green, the sky is blue with puffy white clouds, and the ocean sparkles brightly. The whole drive, all the way to Haena, is a must-do, for it feels as if you've left ordinary civilization behind and entered a virtual-reality tropical paradise.

Look for the turnoff called Anahola Road, which leads to the ocean and Anahola Beach County Park, a few miles north of Kealia. The park features restrooms, picnic tables, showers, and grills. Swimming is best in a little protected cove at the south end.

The road soon curves around and travels the northern end of the island. To visit Moloa`a Bay, a secluded, beautiful site, turn right on Koolau Road, which leads to skinny Moloa`a Road. At road's end you can park and follow the signs to the beach, a wide, picturesque, crescent-shaped strip of sand. Swimming is best at the southern end and safe only during calm weather, but the beautiful beach is a delightful spot to relax in Kauai's splendor.

The Kuhio Highway continues to roll through northern Kauai, and the next town worth a stop is Kilauea, the northernmost point of the main Hawaiian islands. You'll know you're there when you see the tall white lighthouse standing incongruously, although picturesquely, on the coast.

In Kilauea, on the Kilauea Lighthouse Road, the Kong Lung Company is worth exploring. It's an old plantation store that's been in business longer than any store in all Hawaii. You'll find a variety of gourmet food and wine and a bunch of interesting artworks, clothing, toys, and general paraphernalia. The store is open every day from 10:00 a.m. to 6:00 p.m. For information call (808) 828-1822; www.konglung.com.

Kilauea Lighthouse (all ages)

Kilauea Point, on Kilauea Lighthouse Road. The visitor center is open daily 10:00 a.m. to 4:00 p.m., closed holidays. $, children younger than age 16 are admitted free.

The lighthouse was built in 1913 and played an important role when ships frequented this area traveling to and from Asia. Although its light was turned off permanently in 1976, the lighthouse is now preserved as a National Historic Landmark.

Kilauea is a favorite spot of naturalists and ornithologists because it's a stopover site for such migrating seabirds as the Laysan albatross and the red-footed booby. But even ordinary folks will appreciate the great spectacle as the seabirds flit in and out of their

Kauai Trivia

Kilauea is the northernmost point of the main Hawaiian islands. Kilauea Point also has the largest colony of seabirds in the state.

nests within the crevices of these cliffs. Kilauea Point has the largest colony of seabirds in the state. Be sure to stop at the visitor center for **free** information about the birds. The center even lets visitors borrow binoculars for closer inspection of the flying creatures.

Anini Beach and Sailboarding Lessons (only good swimmers)
About 2 miles north of Kilauea. To get there turn right on the second Kalihi Wai Road, then turn left at the fork. Anini is at road's end.

Anini Beach is another of those wholly picturesque North Shore beaches. Anini is known islandwide as the best place to learn how to sailboard because the winds are gentle but steady, and it's fairly shallow and protected. Additionally, the longest exposed reef on Kauai makes it a great place for snorkeling. The beach features restrooms, picnic tables, grills, and a pavilion.

For sailboarding lessons contact Windsurf Kauai, (808) 828-6838. Kids should be at least seven years old and sixty-five pounds, but as long as they're good swimmers, the restrictions aren't too rigid. A three-hour introductory lesson costs $85. Hours vary, but the company is located right on the beach.

Where to Eat

Duane's Ono Charburger. Route 56, Anahola, next to Whalers General Store; (808) 822-9181. This roadside stand has superb burgers if you don't mind the slow service. Order the crispy, spicy fries. $

Roadrunner Bakery and Cafe. 2430 Oka Street, Kilauea; (808) 828-8226. Features organic local vegetables, thirty types of chil-

ies, pork, fish, and free-range chicken. Try the lobster fajitas and tacos. $$

Where to Stay

There are no major hotel or condominium properties on this side of the island. The closest are a few miles north at Princeville, and a few miles south in Kapa`a.

North Shore: Princeville

Highway 56 leads north to Princeville.

Princeville is the largest town on the North Shore, and within its 11,000 acres there is a host of great attractions, restaurants, and accommodations, and even a small airport. This area used to be Kauai's oldest ranch, started in 1853 by R. C. Wyllie, a Scottish immigrant. It was renamed Princeville after King Kamehameha IV, Queen Emma, and their son Prince Albert visited in 1860. Wyllie was so taken with young Albert that he renamed the area Princeville in his honor.

Princeville Ranch Stables (ages 8 and up)
On Kuhio Highway, across from the Princeville Golf Course; (808) 826-6777; www.princeville ranch.com. $$$$

Princeville Ranch offers four horseback-riding adventures. The longest one is a four-hour ride to a remote waterfall, where riders may spend some time frolicking about in the natural pool ($135). There is also a three-hour waterfall picnic ride for $125 per person, an hour-and-a-half country ride on the bluffs overlooking Anini Beach for $80 per person, and an hour-and-a-half cattle drive ride for $135 per person.

Hanalei

Just around the corner from Princeville; cross the tiny one-lane country bridge over the Hanalei River.

About 920 acres of this lush valley is designated as the Hanalei National Wildlife Refuge. Although no visitors are generally permitted in this area, there is restricted access, which permits you to drive along the river to find great fishing, hiking, and scenery. Just after the bridge take Ohiki Road inland. You'll pass simple, quaint farms set among picturesque wildflowers and taro patches.

Just around the corner from Princeville sit idyllic Hanalei town and Hanalei Bay, so pretty it's hard to believe they're real. Inland, a patchwork quilt of green taro fields and groves of papaya and banana flourish, providing fruitful harvests to most of Hawaii.

When you get over the bridge and see Hanalei Bay on the left, you'll definitely want to stop and marvel at this priceless view. In fact, many visitors and residents, myself included, think this is the most beautiful spot in all Hawaii. To the north are the famous "Bali Hai" cliffs that served as the tropical backdrop for the movie *South Pacific*. The bay itself sparkles in a dozen hues of blue and is wide and calm, inviting all sorts of water-sport enthusiasts, including swimmers, sailors, snorkelers, surfers, boogieboarders, and sailboarders. (The bay can get rough with winter storms.) There are showers and restrooms on-site.

Surrounding the bay are the famous Na Pali Cliffs, where centuries of wind and rain have carved deep gulches. If it's rained lately, there will be dozens of waterfalls tumbling over the gulches, creating a magical mist.

Continuing through town, look to the left for the Waioli Hui`ia Church. On Sunday the church choir sings lilting hymns in Hawaiian. The adjacent Waioli Mission House Museum is the former home of missionaries Abner and Lucy Wilcox. There are wonderful artifacts dating from the early 1800s, including dishes and home furnishings. The museum (808-245-3202) is open Tuesday, Thursday, and Saturday from 9:00 a.m. to 3:00 p.m. **free.**

Hawaii Trivia

At the time of statehood, Hawaii's population was larger than any other U.S. territory's upon entering the Union.

Kauai Trivia

Like Captain Cook, Kauai's first missionaries also arrived in Waimea on the brig *Thaddeus*, though they didn't get here until 1820.

Lumahai Beach (strong swimmers only, ages 12 and up)

One way to get there is by parking just west of Hanalei Bay and walking down the trail to the east end of the beach. Or you can keep driving until just before the bridge that crosses the Lumahai River. Look for a grove of ironwood trees (they look like Mainland pines); the beach is a short walk from here.

For those who rank Hanalei Bay as Hawaii's all-time most beautiful spot, Lumahai Beach is likely a close second. It's just north of Hanalei Bay and offers an inviting stretch of soft white sand framed by the glorious, majestic Na Pali Cliffs. This is where Mitzi Gaynor "washed that man right out of her hair" in the musical *South Pacific*. *NOTE:* The ocean currents can be quite fierce in winter, so be cautious when entering the water. But even if the weather is rough, by all means stop here, if only to appreciate one of the most majestically beautiful treasures of Kauai.

Ke`e Beach A

At road's end, Highway 56, beyond Hanalei.

Ke`e Beach is great for swimming in the summer months. It's also known islandwide as one of the best snorkeling spots in all of Kauai. You'll see a variety of colorful marine life, and the offshore coral reef makes snorkeling safe here even when it's choppy in other places. Suitable for strong swimmers only.

Water-Sports Rentals

- **Hanalei Surf Company.** 5–5161 Kuhio Highway; (808) 826-9000; www.hanaleisurf.com. Provides rentals for surfing, boogieboarding, and snorkeling.
- **Pedal and Paddle.** In the Ching Young Village Shopping Center; (808) 826-9069; www.pedalnpaddle.com. Here you can rent bicycles, kayaks, and camping gear. During the summer the store is open daily from 9:00 a.m. to 6:00 p.m.; it closes at 5:00 p.m. in the winter.
- **Kayak Kauai.** Kuhio Highway; (808) 826-9844 or (800) 437–3507; www.kayakkauai.com. Leads guided kayak tours, the most popular of which is on the Kilauea River, where you kayak to an isolated waterfall and swim in the pool below. If you want to explore on your own, you can rent river and ocean kayaks here. The guides also offer bicycle tours through the historic, charming towns of Hanalei and Kapa`a.

The Kalalau Trail (ages 10 and up)

One of the most difficult trails in all Hawaii begins at Ke`e Beach; not recommended for young children.

The hiking trail through the Na Pali Coast to Kalalau Valley is one of the most famous trails in all Hawaii, offering enchanting views, pristine beaches, and total seclusion. It's also one of the most difficult trails, however. The round-trip trek to Kalalau Valley cannot be completed in one day and is recommended only for experienced hikers and campers.

You needn't travel all the way to Kalalau to get a sampling of inner Na Pali's beauty. It's 2½ miles to secluded Hanakapiai Beach. You can make this round-trip in one day; allow about four or five hours. But proceed with caution; parts of the trail are very narrow and slippery. This hike is not recommended for kids younger than ten and should probably be undertaken only in dry weather.

As an alternative to hiking into the interior of Na Pali, a slew of companies offer a different view—from the ocean or the air.

Where to Eat

Bali Hai Restaurant. 5380 Honoiki Road; (808) 826-6522. The views are sure to knock your socks off as you dine outdoors overlooking scenic Hanalei Bay. They serve breakfast, lunch, and dinner—menu is Pacific Rim with a focus on Kauai-grown produce. *NOTE:* At press time, the restaurant was closed temporarily for renovations, but is expected to reopen soon. $$$–$$$$

Cafe Hanalei. 5520 Kahaku Road; (808) 826-9644. Open for breakfast, lunch, or dinner. The dinner menu features local specialties such as yose nabe and sashimi. $$$–$$$$

La Cascata. 5520 Kahaku Road; (808) 826-9644. Offers Italian cuisine for dinner only at the Princeville Hotel. Try the garlic soup with onion and Parmesan cheese. $$$–$$$$

Postcards Cafe. 5–5075 Kuhio Highway; (808) 826-1191; www.postcardscafe.com. Fresh and healthy with lots of vegetarian selections. Open for dinner daily. $$

Princeville Restaurant & Bar. 5–3900 Kuhio Highway; (808) 826-5050. Part of the Princeville golf complex, the restaurant serves breakfast, lunch, and Sunday brunch. Menu items are named with golfers in mind. A "Bogey" is a beef burger with a choice of cheddar, grilled onions, and bacon, while a "Birdie" is a teriyaki chicken breast topped with grilled onions. $$

Kalypso Island Bar & Grill. 5–5156 Kuhio Highway; (808) 826-9700. Serves king-size sandwiches, wraps, burgers, and burritos. Great service and good value. $$$–$$$$

Where to Stay

Hanalei Bay Resort. 5380 Honoiki Road; (808) 826-6522 or (800) 827-4427. Idyllic tropical environment. $$–$$$$

Hanalei Colony Resort. At the end of the road in Haena, 5-7130 Kuhio Highway; (808) 826-6235 or (800) 628-3004; www.hcr.com. This is a true "getaway"—there are no telephones or televisions in units. $$–$$$

Hanalei North Shore Properties. (800) 488–3336; www.kauaivacationrentals.com. This agency lists 130 accommodations ranging from a $600-a-week, two-bedroom condo to a $6,000-a-week, seven-bedroom house that belongs to an entertainer. Beachfront houses book up a year or two in advance and are especially scarce over holidays and summer vacation.

Historic **North Shore Heiau**

After a short walk west from Ke`e Beach, look for the series of stone platforms marking Lohiau Heiau. It's said that Pele, the goddess of volcanoes, fell in love here with the young prince Lohiau. Who knows, perhaps her affections were spurned, and that's why she's still blowing smoke and lava from Kilauea on the Big Island.

Nearby, along the coastal trail, are two heiau, Ka Ulu a Paoa and Ka Ulu o Laka, and wonderful coastline views.

Princeville Resort. 5520 Ka Haku Road; (808) 826-9644 or (866) 716-8110; www .princevillehotelhawaii.com. Top rated among all Hawaii's hotels. Princeville Resort offers a Keiki Aloha program for children ages five to twelve. Activities include snorkeling, beach play, lei making, sand castle contests, Hawaiian crafts, shell collecting, and more. Keiki Aloha is available Monday through Friday, 9:00 a.m. to 3:00 p.m. with advance reservation required. $$$$

For More Information

Kauai Visitors Bureau. 4334 Rice Street, #101, Lihue 96766; (808) 245-3971; www .kauaidiscovery.com.

Explore the **Lava Caves**

Almost at the end of the road, **Haena** is a must-stop—it features an amazing variety of naturally formed lava caves. You can explore the **Maniniholo Dry Cave** and two wet caves, **Waikapalae** and **Waikanaloa**. The ocean here is good for swimming and snorkeling, but only during the calm summer months.

Look toward the mountain for the large Maniniholo Dry Cave. You can walk right inside and explore the mysterious hidden spaces. If you're really daring, you can continue exploring through the whole structure, which ends at a small opening at the top of a cliff. Beware, however—the high roof at the cave's entrance lowers considerably as you get farther in.

The name Maniniholo comes from one of the head fishermen of the menehune. According to legend, the menehune were planning to journey to the interior of the island and leave this coastal site. They were catching fish at Haena to sustain them on their journey. They couldn't carry all the fish at one time, so they left half at what is now Maniniholo Dry Cave. Upon returning for their catch, they found that an *akua*, or evil spirit, had stolen their stash. They formed two parties to capture the akua. Half the menehune began digging down from the clifftop and the other half dug from its base. The result is the great cave you see today.

Molokai

Molokai is the fifth-largest and the least developed of the main Hawaiian Islands. It's nicknamed the "Friendly Isle," and after one visit you'll understand why. The environment here is more rural than a typical small town in Anywhere, U.S.A. There are no high-rises and no fast-food chains, and there's not a single traffic light on the whole island. I tried to include street addresses whenever possible for the attractions listed in this chapter, but on this very small island everyone knows everyone else, so if you can't find something, simply ask for directions.

Molokai is a twenty-minute hop by air from Honolulu. Its tip is a mere 22 miles from Oahu. Come to Molokai with a sense of adventure. Children love swimming at the base of a shimmering waterfall and snorkeling off Hawaii's only barrier reef. Molokai Ranch has added a mountain-biking park you can tackle like a pro after a lesson from cycling experts. The beaches are expansive and unspoiled—oftentimes you'll be the only people there.

Julie's
TopPicks for Family Fun on Molokai

1. Taking a trip on the Molokai Wagon Ride

2. Visiting wildlife at Molokai Ranch

3. Sampling fresh, hot-from-the-oven Molokai sweetbread

4. Exploring the tide pools at Make'Horse Beach

5. Snorkeling at Murphy Beach Park

6. Exploring the mountain-bike park at Molokai Ranch

7. Flying a colorful kite from the Big Wind Kite Factory

8. Sunning, swimming, and snorkeling at beautiful Papohaku Beach

9. Driving down to Halawa Valley and swimming in the bay

10. Exploring the Molokai Museum and Cultural Center

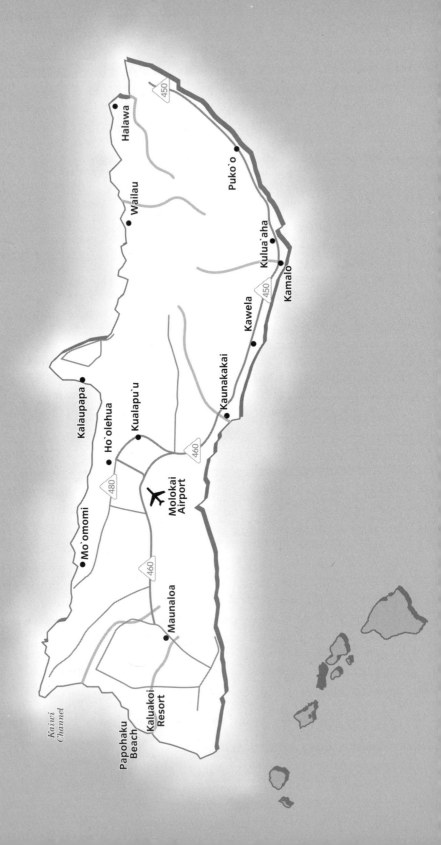

MOLOKAI

In ancient Hawaii, Molokai differed from the other islands, which were ruled by chiefs who controlled large armies of warriors. On Molokai the chiefs ruled through chants and religious power. The *mana* (spirit) here was considered to be the strongest and greatest in all Hawaii. It was a powerful spirit, handed down through generations, that lives on today in the depths of Halawa Valley or in the town of Maunaloa.

You can fly to Molokai from Oahu or Maui, on Hawaiian Air, Island Air, Air Molokai, Paragon, Pacific Wings, and Commercial Flyer. There is no public transportation on Molokai. The rental car companies are Budget (800-527-0700), Island Kine Auto Rentals (866-527-7368), Molokai Outdoors (808-553-5663 or 877-553-4477), and Molokai Rentals (808-553-8334).

The airport is in Ho`olehua, and most of the accommodations are on the western coast, except for Hotel Molokai in Kaunakakai. The island is long and narrow, and the main highway travels from the west end to the east end, with various smaller roads branching out on either side. This chapter begins in the west end, at Kaluakoi, and travels east to Halawa.

Western Molokai: Kaluakoi and Molokai Ranch

Before Western contact, when the civilization here was primarily Stone Age, Kaluakoi was regarded as one of the best adze quarries in all the islands. People traveled from the other islands to procure the strong stone of Kaluakoi.

Papohaku Beach (all ages; summer only)
Located 1 mile past Kaluakoi Resort.

Beautiful and spacious Papohaku Beach is among the largest in all the islands and considered by many to be one of the best. Its golden sands stretch for 3 miles along the coast; parking, restrooms, and showers are available at the park, in the middle of the beach. Swim with caution, as there are no lifeguards on duty here, but during the summer months the currents are mild. It is recommended to swim on the northernmost corner of the beach, where the water is somewhat protected from the wind and undertow. The snorkeling in this area is good as well. In the winter, however, the ocean churns up monstrous waves and the undertow is very dangerous. Swimming is definitely out of the question at this time of year.

A smaller beach called Kepuhi is located in front of the Kaluakoi Resort. Surfers flock here year-round to take advantage of the great surf breaks. Swimmers should use caution here; when the surf reaches higher than 8 feet, it is not safe to go in the water, as the currents and undertow are very hazardous.

Ka Hula Piko Festival

The slow-paced island lifestyle comes alive on the third Saturday of every May with the annual Ka Hula Piko Festival. The hula festival celebrates Molokai as the birthplace of hula, the ancient art form that has perpetuated the history and lifestyles of native Hawaiians through dances and chants passed down for centuries.

Hawaiian legend says that Laka, the first goddess to dance the hula, first danced at Ka`ana, in Maunaloa on the western part of the island. Laka then traveled from island to island, teaching the words and movements and helping to preserve what today is one of the few intact aspects of Hawaiian culture.

Laka's efforts and grace are celebrated at the festival, and visitors come from all over the world to join in the fun. The week prior to the festival includes a variety of lectures on Hawaiian history and hula, and excursions to the island's historic sites are sung about in many hula chants. The daylong hula festival is staged at picturesque **Papohaku Beach Park.**

Kawakiu Beach (strong swimmers)

Kawakiu Bay is about a twenty-minute walk from the Kaluakoi Resort. It is the northern-most beach on the west end of the island. Plan on a dry, hot hike along a four-wheel-drive road; during the summer months you can walk along the coastline. You can drive the rugged dirt road to the bay, but do so with caution; there are many areas that have washed out over the years making it difficult for even the most experienced four-wheel-drive experts to get around. The road ends at the bay. In calm weather (summer months) the beach is great for snorkeling and swimming, but be aware that there are no facilities here, and it's pretty isolated.

Make`Horse Beach (strong swimmers)

Located just north of the tenth tee at the Kaluakoi Resort, this is a great beach for kids in the summer. You can usually find the locals here on the weekends as there are many tidal pools for the kids to explore. This beach is not safe in the winter months (October through March).

Where to Stay

Kaluakoi Resort Complex. Kaluakoi is considered to be the largest resort area on the island in terms of available units. Many units at the resort are privately owned and operated. It is recommended that you contact the Molokai Visitors Association at (800-800-6367; www.molokai-hawaii.com) to get a full listing of the properties available. The properties listed below are handled by management companies:

- **Kaluakoi Villas.** (808-552-2721)
- **Ke Nani Kai Condos.** (808-552-0945 or 800-490-9042)
- **Paniolo Hale Resort Condos.** (808-552-2731 or 800-367-2984)

NOTE: You can also check out www.molokai resorts.com for more listings of vacation homes and condominiums.

Central Molokai:
Maunaloa to Kualapu`u

In ancient Hawaii, Maunaloa (not to be confused with Mauna Loa Mountain on the Big Island) was the cultural center of the island. It was here that the art of hula was born and soon spread to all the islands as an ancient form of communication. Today Maunaloa is a quaint, old-fashioned plantation town that's changed little since the large pineapple production companies pulled up stakes and headed for greener pastures in other countries.

Big Wind Kite Factory (all ages)

In Maunaloa; (808) 552-2364. Open Monday through Saturday 8:30 a.m. to 5:00 p.m.; Sunday 10:00 a.m. to 2:00 p.m. Staff members offer **free** flying lessons in the park adjacent to the store. Call ahead for lessons.

If you see a colorful kite flying in the wind, you'll know you've arrived at the Big Wind Kite Factory. You'll be amazed at the variety of kites available here, in such a remote small town. The inventory ranges from decorative wind socks to old-fashioned single-line kites and even flashy four-liners that carry enough pull to lift small children in the air! All are created by hand on the premises and are just like the slick sport kites sold in fancy sporting-goods stores.

Hawaii Trivia

Among the more than 450 species of fish endemic to Hawaiian waters, about 40 are sharks, which range from pygmy sharks, at about 8 inches long, to whale sharks, at 50 feet or more. (Shark attacks in Hawaiian waters are very rare, occurring on average two or three times a year.)

Molokai Trivia

The highest sea cliffs in the world are found just east of Kalaupapa; they surround isolated valleys that dot the northeastern coastline.

Also in town is the Maunaloa General Store, (808) 552-2346, where you can pick up general sundries, produce, and other food. The store is open Monday through Saturday 8:00 a.m. to 6:00 p.m.

Purdy Natural Macadamia Nut Farm (all ages)

In Ho`olehua; (808) 567-6601. Open for visitors weekdays 9:30 a.m. to 2:00 p.m. Tours on Saturday, Sunday, and holidays by appointment only.

In the tiny town of Ho`olehua are the airport, a small post office, and a few government offices. It's also home to Purdy's Natural Macadamia Nut Farm, where mac nuts have been harvested for more than seventy years. **free** tours are given of the farm, and there's a gift shop where you can buy, of course, macadamia nuts and other nut-related products.

Mo`omomi Beach (strong swimmers)

From Ho`olehua, continuing east on Maunaloa Highway (460), your next stop should be at Mo`omomi Beach. Turn left on Route 470, then left again on Farrington Avenue. Soon Farrington ends and the rough dirt road begins. You'll come to an intersection of sorts, at which you should bear right and continue to the road's end. (Swimming suitable only for older children in the summer.)

Although it's a bit of a struggle to get here because part of the road is severely pitted, it's well worth the drive. Car-rental agencies will warn against venturing here, but with careful driving, it's feasible. *NOTE:* Don't leave anything of value in your rental car. Mo`omomi is great for surfing, fishing, and swimming and is very popular with locals. Swimming is desirable and safe only during the summer months; winter storms often bring large rocks to the beach.

The Legend of Mo`omomi Beach

Look for a large black rock to the right of Mo`omomi Beach. Legend says that in Old Hawaii a woman became impregnated by the gods, which infuriated her jealous husband. He was angry that their child would be a spirit, and he sent his wife down to this rock while he contemplated their situation. She was so distraught with tears that she went into labor. One of her many tears was actually a tiny fish, which rolled off her cheek and into the ocean. This fish grew to become the powerful shark god that is featured in many Hawaiian chants and hulas.

From the beach a short walk west leads to a series of tiny coves and beaches that offer pristine beauty, isolation, and good snorkeling. Use caution while swimming if there's no one else around, and don't swim too far out, where the currents may be rough.

North Molokai: Kualapu`u to Kalaupapa

Route 460 continues east until it forks, and one direction veers south toward Kaunakakai, turning into Highway 450, while the other direction heads north to Kualapu`u as Highway 470.

When Del Monte was harvesting pineapples on Molokai, Kualapu`u was a booming town. Today it's a small stop on the way north. At the Kualapu`u Market, you can stock up on food and gas. It's open Monday through Saturday 8:30 a.m. to 6:00 p.m.; closed Sunday; (808) 567-6243.

Molokai Museum and Cultural Center (all ages)

In Kalae; (808) 567-6436. Open Monday through Saturday 10:00 a.m. to 2:00 p.m. $

A few minutes' drive north will land you in the tiny town of Kalae. Don't miss the Molokai Museum and Cultural Center, built around the old R. W. Meyer Sugar Mill, listed on the National Register of Historic Places. The mill was constructed in 1878 and has since been restored.

Visitors will be able to watch the various stages of processing sugar, from its natural cane form to the white powdery stuff you put on your cereal. The museum focuses on Hawaiian crafts, such as lei making, lauhala weaving, quilting, and woodcarving.

Palaau State Park (all ages)

At the end of Highway 470.

The facilities and the views make Palaau State Park the best place to camp on the island. Also near the entrance to Palaau is the Kalaupapa Overlook, where you can see the famous Kalaupapa Peninsula projecting out into the ocean 1,600 feet below.

Molokai Trivia

- The first Hawaiian fossils were discovered on Molokai, lodged in sandstone at Mo`omomi Dunes.
- You can't miss the huge water reservoir in Kualapu`u—it holds 1.4 billion gallons and is the largest of its kind in the world.

Father Damien—Hawaii's Beloved Priest

The story of Kalaupapa involves one of the most tragic, yet inspiring, periods of Hawaiian history. In the mid-1800s many of the Hawaiian people were afflicted with leprosy, which later became known as Hansen's disease. It was a highly contagious infection that affected the skin and central nervous system, creating grotesque ulcers that grew over time into hideous deformities.

To halt the spread of infection, the sick were banished to remote Kalaupapa, where the steep cliffs on one side and the rough ocean on the other formed a complete barrier to the rest of society. Paranoia rampaged through the island chain, and anyone, regardless of age and gender, with a suspicious-looking skin color or sore was banished forever to Kalaupapa. No one was sent to care for these terminally ill people—food and supplies were packaged in tight containers and thrown overboard from passing ships. The Kalaupapa residents were forced to swim out to the rough channel to collect the packages.

Then, in 1873, Father Damien de Veuster, a Belgian priest, arrived at Kalaupapa, intending to stay a few weeks and provide some spiritual relief and compassion to the residents. He ended up remaining on this isolated peninsula for the rest of his life, unceasingly and selflessly caring for the forgotten people for sixteen years. He eventually became ill with the disease himself and died in Kalaupapa. During his years here he built homes, a hospital, and St. Philomena Church, still standing today, and cared for the sick in what may be the greatest example ever of aloha and brotherly love.

Modern drugs have stopped the threat of Hansen's disease, allowing the longtime residents of Kalaupapa to leave if they wish. But most choose to remain here, acting as tour guides to the area, forever grateful to their benefactor, Father Damien.

Kalaupapa National Historical Park (ages 16 and older)

All visitors must procure advance permission, and children younger than age 16 are not allowed. Open Monday through Saturday, by invitation only. For more information contact Damien Tours, (808) 567-6171, or Molokai Mule Ride, (808) 567-6088 or (800) 567-7550; www.muleride.com.

You can explore this beautiful park by mule, by air, or by foot. The trail starts just past the mule barn on the right-hand side of Highway 470. You'll see cars parked there and it's best to not leave anything unattended while you're out and about. The curvaceous twenty-six-switchback trail descends 1,700 feet into Kalaupapa. The expansive vistas offer immense beauty. If you are planning to hike the trail, please make arrangements in advance. All mule and air transfers will be automatically booked on the ground tour.

Where to Eat

Coffees of Hawaii. Corner of Highway 470 and Farrington Avenue; (808) 567-9490; www.coffeesofhawaii.com. Five hundred acres of 100 percent pure Molokai coffee. Coffees of Hawaii offers walking tours of the plantation, mule-drawn wagon tours, and a beautiful gift and logo shop. The Espresso Bar, open Monday through Friday 7:00 a.m. to 5:00 p.m.; Saturday 8:00 a.m. to 4:00 p.m.; and Sunday 8:00 a.m. to 2:00 p.m., serves cappuccinos, lattes, and mochas, as well as sandwiches to eat in or take out. Their signature drink is the Mocha Mamma and it's definitely a must-do on Molokai. Coffees of Hawaii is a great place to order lunch and grab breakfast before heading down to Kalaupapa.

Kamuela's Cook House. Upcountry Molokai, 4 miles or so from Ho'olehua Airport on the way to Kalaupapa Overlook, just one block off State Highway 470; (808) 567-9655. The Cook House is a busy local standby, with good burgers of beef, chicken, or fish; plate lunches are offered too. They make tasty, fresh, old-fashioned pies for dessert. Open 7:00 a.m. to 2:00 p.m. Monday through Saturday, closed Sunday. $

Kaunakakai

This is the major town on the island, the site of the post office, the main place for shopping and banking, and it won't take you more than an hour to explore it completely. It's a quiet, quaint place. Businesses such as a health-food store, markets, a drug store, and a small selection of souvenir shops are situated along Ala Malama Street, the main drag.

Every Saturday is open market day in Kaunakakai. From 6:00 a.m. to noon, you can find the best handmade treasures, available for sale directly from the artists themselves, as well as fresh fruits and vegetables.

Molokai's Famous Rock

In the parking lot at Palaau State Park, a sign directs visitors to one of Molokai's most renowned landmarks, the Phallic Rock. Hawaiian legend says that Nanahoa, the male god of fertility, once stopped here to admire a beautiful young girl who was gazing at her own reflection in a pool. Nanahoa's wife, Kawahuna, became so enraged with jealousy that she pulled out all the young girl's hair. In retaliation Nanahoa struck his wife, sending her over a cliff, where she turned to stone. Nanahoa also turned to stone and today inhabits the Phallic Rock, which is shaped like what its name implies.

For centuries allegedly barren women have come to pray for fertility at this rock—and local townsfolk are full of their success stories.

About a 1½-mile walk west of Kaunakakai leads to the Royal Kapuaiwa Coconut Grove. These trees were planted during Kamehameha V's reign in the 1860s to furnish privacy and shade for the ali`i who bathed in the series of naturally formed pools here.

Where to Eat

Big Daddy's Cafe and Store. On Ala Malama Street; (808) 553-5841. Offers a selection of authentic Filipino dishes such as chicken papaya and pork adobo, as well as *bento* (Japanese lunch box), *poke* (raw fish in marinade), and shave ice (Hawaiian-style snow cones). $

Kanemitsu Bakery. 79 Ala Malama Street; (808) 553-5855. Open for breakfast, lunch, and dinner 5:30 a.m. to 6:30 p.m. Closed Tuesday. Fare is basic and inexpensive. Be sure to stop here, at the home of the world-famous Molokai Sweet Bread. Many bakeries throughout the state try to imitate this delectable treat, but none have a product as close to perfect as Kanemitsu's. The front half of the building is a bakery, the back half is a restaurant, and it has all been run by the same family for more than seventy years. The bakery makes nineteen kinds of bread each day. $

Molokai Pizza Cafe. On Wharf Road; (808) 553-3288. One of the most popular dining

Water-Sports Rentals and Ocean Tours

- **Molokai Fish and Dive.** 63 Ala Malama Street; (808) 553-5926; www .molokaifishanddive.com. This is a snorkel shop that not only rents equipment, but also provides directions to the island's most colorful underwater spots. Fish and Dive also offers Molokai's largest selection of original T-shirts, caps, and souvenirs. Their rentals include fins, masks, snorkels, boogieboards, rods, and reels. You can also find the famous Molokai books *A Portrait of Molokai* and *Lands of Father Damien* here and have them autographed by the author himself, Jim Brocker. The store is open Monday through Saturday 8:00 a.m. to 6:00 p.m. and Sunday 8:00 a.m. to 4:00 p.m.
- **Bill Kapuni's Snorkel and Dive Adventure.** (808) 553-9867. Feel the salty sea breeze from the deck of a Boston Whaler. From November to April you can watch humpback whales frolic in the channel.
- **Alyce C Sportfishing.** (808) 558-8377; www.alycecsportfishing.com. Capt. Joe Reich is one of Molokai's best fishing captains. With Joe you can say they're "catching charters" instead of "fishing charters." Joe offers catching for ahi, marlin, au, mahimahi, and ono. Whale watching is also available in season.
- **Fun Hogs Sportfishing.** (808) 567-6789; www.molokaifishing.com. Aboard the Ahi you can find Capt. Mike Holmes offering half-day and full-day fishing charters as well as whale watching in season and coastline and sunset tours.

places on Molokai, good for takeout or eat-in.
In addition to pizza, the menu offers chicken,
ribs, sandwiches, and pies. $

Where to Stay

There are a handful of vacation home rentals
on Molokai. Contact the **Molokai Visitors
Association** for a complete listing: (800)
800-6367; www.molokai-hawaii.com.

Southeast Coast: Kawela to Halawa

Continuing on Route 450, this beautiful country drive was once the most populated section of Molokai, and around almost every bend in the road is an important site, whether a
religious temple or an ancient battleground. You'll pass tropical deserted beaches, more
fishponds, ancient heiau, picturesque churches, and wonderful parks. Many important historic sites are unmarked, however, so it's a good idea to ask local residents for some hints.
Soon after One Ali`i, look toward the mountain for the Kawela Place of Refuge and, just
beyond, the Kakuhiwa Battleground, the site of a large battle between Molokai's Chief
Kakuhiwa and Kamehameha the Great. Then you'll pass Kakahaia Beach Park, a picturesque crescent of sandy beach that offers great swimming conditions.

You'll next arrive at Kamalo Harbor, where the wharf used to be the center of oceangoing activity before Kaunakakai's harbor assumed that role. Look around the next bend
for the small St. Joseph Church, built by Father Damien in 1876. A metal sculpture of
Father Damien sits outside the church.

At mile marker 13 sits the Wavecrest Resort Condominium, a good stop to pick up
food and drinks before continuing east. Next, look for the fortress-like Kalua`aha Church,
built in 1844 by Protestant missionaries Rev. and Mrs. Harvey Rexford Hitchcock. It was
the first Christian church constructed on Molokai. The last place to grab something to eat
and drink is at the Neighborhood Store-N-Counter located at mile marker 16. Open daily
except Monday 8:00 a.m. to 6:30 p.m.; (808) 558-8498.

Smith and Bronte Landing (all ages)
A few miles beyond Kamalo.

In 1927 aviators Ernest Smith and Emory Bronte were forced to make a crash landing here
after completing the first civilian flight in the Pacific region. They started at Kapiolani Park,
Oahu, and it took them more than twenty-five hours to reach the soggy banks of south
Molokai. Although they crashed, they instituted air travel to these remote islands that now
welcome more than six million airborne visitors annually.

Molokai Trivia

Molokai boasts the largest population of native Hawaiians—of the 6,000 residents, more than 2,500 have more than 50 percent Hawaiian ancestry.

Ili`ili`opae Heiau (all ages)

On Highway 460. Permission must be obtained to visit the heiau. For more information it's best to ask any of the staff at the island's hotels how to make the proper arrangements. To get there from Route 450, look for a bridge right after the Mapulehu Mango Grove on the right. On the left, there's a green gate. You have to park and walk around the gate; after a short trek inland, you'll see the trail heading into the woods where the heiau sits.

Next, look toward the mountain for Ili`ili`opae Heiau. Legend says this massive structure was built in one night by menehune who formed a body-to-body chain and passed the stones from Wailau Valley, on the northeast coast of the island. Ili`ili`opae was a *luakini*, a temple of human sacrifice. It's one of the largest heiau in all Hawaii, and, although on private land, it's designated a National Historic Landmark. The heiau is surrounded by vegetation, and the interior is as big as a football field.

Molokai Wagon Ride (all ages)

Near the Mapulehu Mango Grove. Tours by reservation only; (808) 558-8132. *NOTE:* **A minimum of eight guests is required for the ride. $$$$**

The Molokai Wagon Ride, a wonderful cultural experience that offers a great glimpse into Molokai's history, travels through the mango grove planted by the Hawaiian Sugar Company in the 1930s. It's one of the largest of its kind in the world. After the mango grove the trip goes to Ili`ili`opae Heiau, then returns to the beach, where guides demonstrate such local activities as net fishing, coconut husking, and hula. Throughout the trip the guides entertain guests with local lore, legends, and songs.

Local Beaches (all ages)

- **Puko`o Beach Park** fronts a small boat harbor and a sandy lagoon that offers wonderful swimming. A few minutes beyond Puko`o, you'll see a large stone that's been painted white, sitting at the side of the road. Locals refer to this as the octopus stone, and it's believed to hold magical powers, having once marked the site of a cave that was home to a mythical octopus.
- **Wailau Beach** is considered among the island's best for first-time surfers, snorkelers, and swimmers. It's tame and shallow. A short walk east will land you at another shallow beach where you can walk all the way to the reef.

Molokai Trivia

Meyer Sugar Mill, built in 1878, is the oldest mill still standing in Hawaii.

The **Famous Fishponds** of Molokai

Molokai is known for its abundance of fishponds. These were constructed in shallow waters with a wall, usually built of coral, that had a small opening. Young fish would swim inside the pond, fatten up, and then be unable to swim out, thus providing fishermen with large schools of easy-to-catch fish. The southeastern coast of the island is ideal for this form of aquaculture since it features miles of flat, shallow waters. In ancient times the area housed an extensive network of ponds, many of which remain today. Driving east from Kaunakakai on Route 450, the Kamehameha Highway, Kaloko`eli Pond is just a few miles away from town, easily seen from the road. A few more minutes' drive east, look for the large Ali`i Fishpond, right before **One Ali`i Beach County Park.** This is a great park for families: The swimming is safe virtually year-round and picnic facilities are available.

• Farther east, **Murphy's Beach Park** features another swimmable sandy beach with restroom facilities and expansive, breathtaking views. Another great beach is at mile marker 20, where there's a wide stretch of sand and a protected lagoon that makes for great snorkeling.

East Molokai: Halawa

Beyond Murphy's Beach on Route 450.

Prepare yourselves for a thrilling car ride to Halawa Valley. The road follows each little nuance of the curving coastline, and the views are spectacular. You'll see cozy deserted beaches, picturesque bays, and craggy cliffs. Eventually the road bends inward and heads to the Puu O Hoku Ranch and Kalanikaula, a kukui grove that's considered Molokai's most sacred spot. It was planted when Molokai's most powerful kahuna, Lanikaula, died.

The road ends at the dramatic Halawa Valley Lookout, truly one of the most majestic sites in all Hawaii. Looking hundreds of feet below, you'll see a series of sparkling waterfalls cascading down cliffs carpeted in velvety green vegetation. The turquoise ocean, full of foamy, frothy white water, drifts into and out of the bay.

Halawa Valley is Molokai's first permanent settlement; historians believe that Hawaiians lived here as early as the seventh century. People gravitated to this fertile valley for hundreds of years, farming taro and living off the land and sea. In 1946 a humongous tidal wave inundated the valley, leaving hefty ocean-salt deposits in its wake, thus rendering much of the land unusable.

The paved road leads right into the valley and stops at a beautiful freshwater stream, suitable for swimming. You can also swim in the ocean here, which is safe year-round, but

The Legend of **Mo`o**

Hawaiian legend tells the story of mo`o, a female lizard who lives in a pool at the bottom of the picturesque 250-foot Moalua Falls. Every so often, she gets lonely and will lure an unsuspecting swimmer to her underwater home. You can prejudge her disposition, which changes frequently, by throwing a ti leaf in the water. If it floats, the swimming is fine; feel free to jump in the cool pool. If it sinks, however, beware of the lonely mo`o and swim at your own risk.

don't venture beyond the bay, as the currents can be quite strong. Conditions for snorkeling, surfing, and fishing are optimum.

Moalua Falls Hike (ages 10 and up)
At the end of Highway 450, Halawa.

If your children are hardy hikers, and if the weather is cooperating, don't miss the chance to hike to Moalua Falls. From the parking lot at the end of the road, continue on foot along a small dirt road that turns into an even smaller footpath. A stone wall will be on your left. Ignore the signs and follow the water pipe situated at the left of Halawa Stream. Keep bearing left as the trail branches out in other directions, and listen for the falls. If it's rained recently, the stream, and consequently the falls, will be a rushing torrent. Rain also makes for a mosquito-laden, muddy trail—use repellent, good judgment, and caution. The trail can be difficult.

Beyond Moalua the trail is quite difficult and not recommended for children. Beyond Halawa, rounding the tip of the island, are the aforementioned tall sea cliffs, forming the valleys of Waikolu, Pelekunu, and Wailau.

For More Information

Molokai Visitors Association. P.O. Box 960, Kaunakakai 96748; 2 Kamoi Street, #200; (800) 800-6367 or (808) 553-3876; www.molokai-hawaii.com.

Molokai Trivia

- At one time, Molokai led the world in honey production before disease damaged the trees in which the bees built their hives.
- Ka Molokai Makahiki, held in January, celebrates the ancient Hawaiian "time of peace," when war ceased and games of skill took its place.

Lanai

Until the recent advent of tourism here, Lanai, nicknamed the Pineapple Island, always had been something of a silent, mysterious neighbor. The few visitors who ventured here came for hunting and stayed at the quaint, old-fashioned, ten-room Hotel Lanai. A few Maui resorts offered day trips here as part of their recreational programs.

While other islands were competing for the almighty visitor industry to grace their shores, Lanai quietly kept to itself—harvesting batch after batch of pineapple, formerly one of Hawaii's biggest agricultural products. Residents lived the epitome of a small-town existence. Everyone knew one another, and life moved slowly. The 41.2 square miles include one school and do not include any traffic lights.

In the late 1980s, as pineapple operations were phased out, construction began on two five-star megaresorts. Residents went from living plantation lifestyles to servicing tourists in a prime resort destination. From the mountain-high Munro Trail to the sparkling

Julie's
TopPicks for Family Fun on Lanai

1. Exploring Garden of the Gods

2. Visiting Luahiwa Petroglyphs

3. Snorkeling in Hulopo`e Bay

4. Riding on horseback around Koele

5. Beachcombing for treasures at Shipwreck Beach

6. Lawn bowling at the Lodge at Koele

7. Exploring the tide pools at Hulopo`e Bay

8. Taking a snorkeling excursion on the Trilogy catamaran

9. Watching sea turtles at Polihua Beach

10. Riding four-wheel-drive on Munro Trail

LANAI

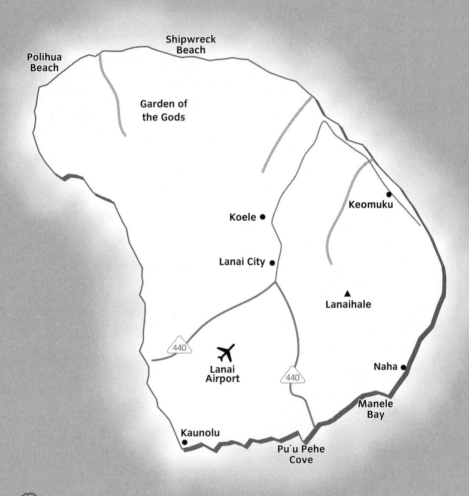

Polihua
Beach

Shipwreck
Beach

Garden of
the Gods

Koele •

Keomuku •

Lanai City •

▲
Lanaihale

440

✈
Lanai
Airport

440

Naha •

Manele
Bay

Kaunolu
•

Pu`u Pehe
Cove

waters of Manele Bay, Lanai's natural beauty sets the stage for an unsurpassed family vacation. The resorts on this quiet, culturally rich Hawaiian island are world renowned. Here, you can see a preview of the finest resorts in the world. The Lodge at Koele and the Four Seasons Resort Lanai at Manele Bay, overlooking the white-sand beach of Hulopo`e Bay, are rated among the top ten for tropical resorts worldwide. Both are pricey and ultradeluxe and beckon visitors with beautiful accommodations, recreational activities, and attractions. The notable activities are golf, diving, and sailing, said to be among the best in all Hawaii.

The transition from agriculture to tourism has been executed flawlessly, and Lanai is now a full-fledged attraction with plenty of family-oriented activities, from bountiful tide pools waiting to be explored to secluded bays beckoning to picnickers. The rare, endangered, giant Pacific green sea turtle (which can grow to 400 pounds) lives on and around Lanai. In Lanai City, the only "town" on the island, the Art Center (339 Seventh Street; 808-565-7503; www.lanaiart.org) is a combination school, gallery, cultural center, and studio. Programs throughout the year include seasonal exhibits, one-person shows, storytelling, visitor classes, and art services.

There's still much undiscovered terrain here, and six campsites 150 yards off Hulopo`e Bay are available. Permits must be obtained in advance from Lanai Company, P.O. Box 310, Lanai City 96763; (808) 565-3978.

Flights from Oahu are available on Island Air and Hawaiian Airlines. There is only one airport. If you're going to rent a car, reserve one early—only one place offers rentals: Lanai City Service (affiliated with Dollar), 1036 Lanai Avenue; (808) 565-7227 or (800) JEEP-808. With only 17 miles of paved road, it's a good idea to rent a four-wheel-drive vehicle; much of the good sightseeing requires one. Every visitor who rents a car is given a **free** map of the island. This map clearly identifies all the trails mentioned in this chapter.

Northern Lanai

Garden of the Gods (all ages)
Located along Polihua Road, 6 miles northwest of Lanai City. After the pavement ends (four-wheel-drives are recommended), stay on the road for ½ mile, then turn right. Keep going for 5½ miles. The "garden" is ½ mile beyond the sign for Lapaiki Road.

A definite must-see is the Garden of the Gods, at the northwestern tip of the island. This is an unusual, eerie-looking geological formation of rock piles set in red dirt. The whole place changes colors throughout the day. Depending on the cloud cover and the sun's position, the spectrum of colors ranges from red to gold to brown to pink to orange—it's especially vibrant at sunrise and sunset.

Hawaii Trivia

Common flowers for making leis include plumeria, puakinikini, ilima, pikake, orchids, ginger, and carnations. Leis made from maile, a green leaf found deep in Hawaii's forests, are worn for special occasions.

Awalua Trail (ages 10 and up)
Starts at the Garden of the Gods.

If your kids are up for a hearty hike, you may want to travel the 3-mile Awalua Trail from the Garden of the Gods to Shipwreck Beach. The trail is overgrown and therefore a bit difficult; don't forget to bring plenty of water.

Shipwreck Beach (water-safe children)
Take the Keomuku Road from Lanai City to the end of the road. The dirt road forks left (north) to Shipwreck Beach or straight ahead (south) to the abandoned town of Naha. You'll see the beached freighter to the left.

It's a beautiful drive to Shipwreck, and, unlike most other destinations on Lanai, it doesn't require a four-wheel-drive vehicle. Shipwreck Beach is so named because of the grounded

Ocean Tours

Lanai offers some of the state's best snorkeling, and **Trilogy Ocean Sports** (based on Maui but offering activities on Lanai as well) offers a variety of scuba and snorkel excursions. Best for kids is the snorkel, sail, and scuba trip offered weekdays. Crew members possess expert knowledge about the local marine life, and they will patiently teach snorkeling skills to those who have never seen a mask and snorkel before. The catamaran whisks passengers to the clear, unspoiled, and protected waters where snorkeling is first-rate. The cruise lasts from 11:15 a.m. to 4:00 p.m. and includes a hearty gourmet lunch prepared by the chefs at Four Seasons Resort Lanai at Manele Bay. It costs $189 for adults, $94.50 for children ages three through fifteen. Trilogy also offers whale-watching trips in season. For more information call (808) 661-4743 or (800) 874-5649.

Also on Lanai, **Spinning Dolphin Charters** provides half-day and full-day fishing trips from Manele Harbor, on the southern tip of the island. Children are welcome aboard, and Captain Jason always makes sure the kids have a great time. Weather permitting, you can fish, or customize your own sail and sightseeing trip. For more information contact Spinning Dolphin at (808) 565-7676; www.sportfishinglanai.com.

World War II ship that sits offshore. Of all the North Shore beaches, this is the easiest to get to, but you'll still find it very private. From this beach you can enjoy great, expansive views of Molokai and West Maui. Although the shallow reef makes the waters calm, it also makes swimming a little difficult because of sharp coral. It is safe, however, to swim in the shallow, sandy-bottom pools. There are no facilities here, so bring some snacks and water.

Along the drive you'll see several small stones piled atop larger boulders. These are called *uhu* and are a traditional Hawaiian offering for good luck while traveling. Feel free to make your own, but never under any circumstances should you disturb the ones already there.

Once at the beach, don't miss the opportunity to look for treasures in the sand. This is relatively untouched land here, and you never know what you may find. The most sought-after treasures are glass floats that have drifted over thousands of miles of open ocean from Japanese fishnets.

Polihua Beach (all ages)

Finding Polihua is tricky. The route involves several unmarked roads. It's best to ask someone at the service station for directions. (Recommended for sightseeing only, no swimming.)

Nature lovers shouldn't miss northern Polihua Beach, the longest, widest spot on the island. It's not great for swimming, even for adults, because the currents are strong and unpredictable. But if you don't mind the long, bumpy drive out here, the views are absolutely exquisite. Especially noteworthy here is the abundance of endangered green sea turtles. This is a popular breeding ground for them, and you can usually spot them swimming around. The translation of Polihua is poli (bosom) and hua (eggs).

Central Lanai

At 3,370 feet, Lanaihale Ridge is the highest point on the island. Be sure to take the road all the way to the top, where expansive views permit you to see all the other major islands in the Hawaiian chain. It's a good idea to bring along a guidebook detailing native plants, for you'll see a few interesting species here. Look for ohia, pili grass, and mountain naupaka. Be sure to bring some warm clothes, because it gets quite chilly here.

You'll also see quite an abundance of Norfolk pines, and you'll probably think they look out of place on a tropical island. You're right. They were planted by George Munro back in 1910. Munro was a New Zealander who was hired to manage the Lanai Ranch. He believed, correctly, that the pines would help cool the area and create moisture for other crops to flourish. Dole Park, located in the center of Lanai City, has more than one hundred Cook Island pines, each reaching more than 90 feet in height.

East of Lanaihale, on the coast in Keomuku, is the Kalanakilo o Ka Malamalama Church. This ancient roadside church has been renovated by the community. To get here, take the main road, Keomuku, which crosses Lanaihale heading northeast.

Horseback Rides (ages 9 and up)
Tours are arranged through the activities desk at the Lodge at Koele; (808) 565-7300 or (808) 565-4424. $$–$$$$

The Paniolo Ride costs $95 per person and lasts two hours. Children must be more than 4½ feet tall and nine years old to participate in the adult rides; otherwise they can go on pony rides for $10 for ten minutes.

Private trail rides cost $160 for two hours.

Southern Lanai

Hulopo`e Bay Beach Park (all ages)
On the south side of the island, Hulopo`e Bay Beach Park is one of the most beautiful, calm, and picturesque sites in all Hawaii. It fronts the Manele Bay Resort and offers perfect swimming conditions for kids.

Offshore, the waters are part of an underwater marine park, which means that fishing is illegal. This translates into great snorkeling.

Tide Pools (all ages)
Around the bend to the left of Hulopo`e Bay.

The large tide pools here are great discovery places for kids to see a variety of marine plants and animals.

Kaunolu Village (all ages)
To get to the ruins, take Manele Road toward the boat harbor. When the road hooks left and uphill (about 3½ miles from Kaumalapau Highway), go straight onto Kaupili Road. (It's a dirt road and may not be marked.) Follow this for 2½ miles and turn left at the intersec-

The Legend of **Sweetheart Cove**

A little farther beyond the tide pools is picturesque Sweetheart Rock, also known as **Pu`u Pehe Cove,** where legend says a man hid his sweetheart (Pehe), and later she was drowned. Pu`u Pehe Cove is much more secluded than Hulopo`e, so expect to do a little climbing on the way. Once there, however, the views are breathtaking, and there is excellent swimming and snorkeling. The beach is small, a tiny slice of sparkling sand bordered by 20-foot craggy cliffs. It's quite private here; you may have the beach all to yourselves.

tion. After ½ mile you'll come to another dirt road on the left. Turn here, and just up this road on the right is the trailhead. From the road to the ruins is 3³⁄₁₀ miles of flat terrain. Bring lots of water; it's very dry here, and the temperature will get quite warm.

Don't miss the National Historic Landmark of Kaunolu. In precontact Hawaii, before western civilization arrived, agrarian communities filled this area, purportedly growing yams in the nearby Palawai Basin. When pineapple harvesting was going full force, the area was filled to the hilt with the prickly fields. Today the fields remain fallow, but Kaunolu Village itself is full of archaeological treasures.

You'll see a series of ancient stone terraces and house sites where villagers lived and worked. There are remnants of a *heiau* (an ancient place of worship) and several petroglyphs that offer a glimpse into forms of written communication used by the Hawaiians of old. Kamehameha the Great, the first king to unite all the Hawaiian Islands under one rule, is said to have erected a shrine in Kaunolu to his fishing god.

Luahiwa Petroglyphs (all ages)

Heading south 1 mile on Manele Road, look for the sign on the left for Hoike Road. This is the former main pineapple road, once paved but now turned to gravel. On Hoike you'll pass two irrigation ditches; turn left at the second one, making sure the ditch remains on the right of your car. After a while you'll see a no trespassing sign, where you should park. Follow the trail that leads off to the left up the hill (a strenuous climb), until you see the large brown boulders. Most of the petroglyphs are found on the south faces of the rocks.

These are considered some of the best-preserved ancient rock carvings in all the islands. Some are drawings of symbolic circles; others are pictorial images, complete with canoes gliding under unfurled sails, dogs snarling with their jaws agape, and horses galloping. The petroglyphs were drawn on the rock faces more than one hundred years ago.

Where to Eat

Blue Ginger Cafe. 409 Seventh Street; (808) 565-6363. Offers inexpensive pizza and hamburgers. Serves breakfast and lunch only. $

Café 565. 408 Eighth Street; (808) 565-6622. This is a fun, casual place offering pizza, sandwiches, salads, and local-style food. $$–$$$

Four Seasons Resort Lanai at Manele Bay and the **Lodge at Koele** (see Where to Stay) provide upscale resort dining. The restaurants are pricey, but the service, food quality, and views are outstanding. $$$

Lanai City Grille. In the Hotel Lanai, 828 Lanai Avenue; (808) 565-7211. The restaurant is open Wednesday through Sunday. The menu was designed by renowned Hawaii

Regional Cuisine chef Bev Gannon (see Haliimaile General Store on Maui, page 75). The menu is extraordinary, and a must-eat when on Lanai! $$$

Nani's Korner. 1036 Lanai Avenue; (808) 565-6915. Serves hearty soup, salads, and sandwiches. Open daily. $

Pele's Other Garden. 2811 Houston Street; (808) 565-9628. The menu offers all sorts of deli foods and pizzas—they'll even pack a picnic basket for you. $–$$$

Where to Stay

Hale Moe. 502 Akolu Place, P.O. Box 196, Lanai City 96763; (808) 565-9520 or (808)

565-6656; www.staylanai.com. This three-bedroom, three-bath plantation home in the quiet south end of Lanai City has a deck, TV, VCR, and CD player. Your host is a fourth-generation Lanaian and a former tour guide. Breakfast included. $

Hotel Lanai. Uphill from Lanai City; (808) 565-7211; www.hotellanai.com. A quaint, renovated ten-room structure that's been accommodating guests since 1925. $–$$

Lodge at Koele. (808) 565-4000 or (800) 819-5053.; www.fourseasons.com/koele. In upcountry Lanai, amid Cook Island pines, the lodge is designed to resemble an English country manor. It has a great hall with a stone fireplace. Recently renovated, the property has been rated the best resort in the United States by the Zagat guide. Activities include horseback riding, game room, hiking trails, four-wheel-drive adventures, mountain biking, and sporting clays.

Together the Lodge at Koele and the Four Seasons (below) offer the Pilialoha Children's Program, for kids ages five to twelve. There are full-day, half-day, and evening schedules available, and activities include building volcanoes, making Hawaiian lei, horseback riding, treks through lush gardens in search of creepy crawlers, or catching fish in the koi ponds and waterfalls. Kids can play croquet, hide and seek, and golf. Other activities include tidal pool exploration, a scavenger hunt, snorkeling, tennis, marine art, and more! Evening activities include an ice cream social and pizza pool party. $$$$

Four Seasons Resort Lanai at Manele Bay. (808) 565-2000 or (800) 819-5053; www.fourseasons.com/manelebay. An upscale beachfront resort with a Mediterranean ambience. Thirty-six holes of golf, tennis, swimming (pool and ocean), snorkeling, scuba diving, white-sand beach, gardens, waterfalls. $$$$

For More Information

Maui Visitors Bureau (representing Maui, Molokai, and Lanai). 1727 Wili Pa Loop, Wailuku 96793; (808) 244-3530; www.visitmaui.com.

Destination Lanai. 730 Lanai Avenue, #102, Lanai City 96763; (808) 565-7600 or www.visitlanai.net.

Lanai's **Hiking Trails**

The island's most famous hike is **Munro Trail,** which crosses 3,370-foot Lanaihale Ridge, accessible on foot, bike, and four-wheel-drive. The trek is a little difficult and therefore not recommended for small children. There is quite a gain in elevation, but you needn't attempt to traverse the whole thing. The views are outstanding from every turn. Depending on cloud cover and how far you make it on the trail, you'll be able to see at least three, sometimes five, of the other islands. If your kids tire easily, you'll still be treated to expansive views from early points on the trail. From town take Hoike Road inland and follow signs for the Munro Trail.

An easier alternative to the Munro Trail is the **Kaiholena Trail.** It's a four-hour loop that can be crossed with minimal difficulty. Be sure to pack some snacks and plenty of water. You'll see the trailhead on the way to the Munro Trail.

Appendix: Annual Events

Hawaii travelers have a variety of year-round festivals, ethnic fairs, and cultural exhibits from which to choose. Some are held statewide; others happen on only one island. Most of the following events occur annually, but the exact dates fluctuate depending on community support, funding, and weather. For detailed information check the calendar sections of the local newspapers, the *Honolulu Advertiser* (www.honoluluadvertiser.com), and the *Star-Bulletin* (www.starbulletin.com). For events without a telephone listing, contact the island's visitor bureau, listed at the end of each chapter. The Hawaii Visitors and Convention Bureau Web site is another great source for year-round events. Check out www.gohawaii.com.

January

Sony Open, Oahu, among the premier sporting events in the Pacific, is a weeklong celebration of golf, featuring more than 140 of the world's leading professional golfers in the only full-field PGA Tour golf tournament held in Hawaii. Spectators get up-front views of their favorite golf swingers in person and on the spectacular 400-inch Sony JumboTron near the 18th green. Tickets cost $15. All activities are held at the Waialae Golf Course, just a short complimentary Waikiki Trolley ride from Waikiki's hotels. Information: (212) 833-8209.

Honolulu's **Cherry Blossom Festival,** Oahu, late January through March, includes a Japanese tea ceremony, flower-arranging demonstrations, a queen and princess pageant and coronation ball, and a cultural show. Information: (808) 949-2255.

The **Chinese New Year** celebrations, including the **Narcissus Festival,** range from mid-January to early February. Honolulu's Chinatown comes alive with color, and there are fireworks, Chinese cultural entertainment, lion dances in the street, a beauty pageant, and a coronation ball, as well as booths at the Cultural Plaza selling food, arts and crafts, and souvenirs. Information: (808) 533-3181.

The **Morey Boogie World Bodyboard Championships** are held on Oahu's North Shore. Competition days are determined by the best wave action.

Molokai celebrates its **Makahiki Festival** with traditional Hawaiian games, food booths, and arts and crafts. Information: (808) 553-3214.

The **Annual Pacific Island Arts Festival** is held at Kapiolani Park, **free** admission. The festival features art and handcrafted products of more than one hundred Hawaii artists, including all types of jewelry, clothing, stained glass, ceramics, quilts and bags, wood products, soaps, and candles. Information: (808) 696-6717.

The best golfers in the world gather on Maui for the **Mercedes-Benz Championship.** The exclusive opening tournament features winners from PGA Tour events and is held on Kapalua's Plantation Course. Information: (808) 665-9160.

The **MasterCard Championship** annually kicks off the PGA Champion's Tour season and features the world's greatest golfers as they gather at the beautiful Hualalai Resort. Information: (800) 417-2770.

A unique Hawaiian cultural experience awaits you at the **Ala Wai Challenge.** This popular annual event includes outrigger canoe racing and ancient Hawaiian land sport games (called Makahiki). The event is **free** to visitors and is at the Ala Wai Neighborhood Park. There are also a variety of crafters, food booths, and family activities. Information: (808) 923-1802.

February

Don't be misled into thinking the **Punahou School Carnival** is just an ordinary high school fund-raiser. This is one of the longest-running events in Oahu. In addition to the traditional rides and games, you'll find rows of food booths selling local delicacies, a white elephant sale, and arts-and-crafts booths. Usually held in early February. Information: (808) 944-5711.

Find ways to encourage a healthy lifestyle and physical fitness, along with discovering new products and services. Enjoy demonstrations, a fun contest, and sponsored prize giveaways at the annual **Great Aloha Run Health & Fitness Expo** at the Neal Blaisdell Center Exhibition Hall, Oahu. Information: (808) 528-7388.

Hilo's annual **Hawaii Wood Guild Show** is a popular event that showcases exquisite furniture, musical instruments, sculpture, and other creations by the Big Island's talented woodworkers. They use a variety of native woods including milo, mango, koa, and kamani. Information: (808) 331-0813.

To celebrate the **Chinese New Year,** Maui's Front Street stores in Lahaina Town host traditional lion dancing throughout the evening. Check local newspaper listings because Chinese New Year falls at a different time each year.

The **Keiki Great Aloha Run** on Oahu, an approximately two-mile course with entertainment. Fun Run starts at 8:30 a.m., followed by fun inflatables, entertainment, snacks, and refreshments. Entry fee. Information: (808) 528-7388.

If your kids think they're "masters" at sandcastle building, be sure to check out the real pros at the **Annual AIAS Sandcastle Event.** Students from the University of Hawaii school of architecture challenge practicing members of the architectural community in a friendly competition of designing and building sand sculptures at Kailua Beach. Information: (808) 956-7725.

At the **Keiki Whale-A-Thon,** Maui, kids can experience the life of a migrating whale in a fun-filled, **free** one-hour obstacle course game conducted by Pacific Whale Foundation's award-winning marine education team. The first 150 kids to register receive a prize. Parents must accompany children who are registering. For grades K through five. At Kalama Park, Kihei. Information: (808) 249-8811; www.pacificwhale.org.

Maui's **Whale Day Celebration** is the largest annual celebration of whales. This **free,** all-day family celebration features some of Hawaii's most popular entertainers and dancers on two stages, a Hawaiian craft fair with seventy local crafters, great food by Maui restaurants, a silent auction, children's entertainment and carnival, plus informational displays about whales and the ocean. Whale Day is a benefit for marine education programs for Maui's schoolchildren. Sponsored by Pacific Whale Foundation. Information: (808) 249-8811; www.pacificwhale.org.

Kamehameha Schools' Ho`olaule`a is an old-fashioned Oahu festival featuring continuous hula, Hawaiian and contemporary entertainment, arts and crafts, Hawaiian children's games, and food. Information: (808) 842-8444.

The **Waimea Town Celebration,** Kauai, is complete with island entertainment, food, craft and game booths, a beer garden, and lots of sporting events. Main Stage, Old Waimea Sugar Mill. **free.** Information: (808) 338-1332.

Buffalo's Annual Big Board Surfing Classic at Makaha Beach, Oahu, involves top-rated longboard surfers in an annual two-day competition. Weather and waves permitting, the event is usually held the last weekend in February and the first weekend in March.

The Big Island's **Annual Waimea Cherry Blossom Heritage Festival** showcases the blooming of Waimea's historic cherry trees and the Japanese tradition of viewing them, *hanami.* Enjoy Japanese and multicultural performing arts, plus demonstrations of bonsai, origami, sumie, calligraphy, and tea ceremony. A giant craft fair and mochi-pounding samples are at Parker Ranch Center. Information: (808) 961-8706.

The **Annual Lappert's Ice Cream Eating Contest** on Kauai features different age groups competing for the title of the fastest ice cream eaters in the West. Information: (808) 338-1332.

Waimea Round-Up Rodeo offers a great glimpse into Kauai's cowboy culture. Events include traditional rodeo competitions with a local-style flair. Information: (808) 338-1332.

March

The **Kamehameha Schools Annual Song Contest** includes competition between the high school classes at Kamehameha Schools, where only students of Hawaiian ancestry may attend. It's held at the Blaisdell Center in downtown Honolulu, Oahu, and is a wonderful chance to see young local musical talent. Information: (808) 523-6200.

Prince Kuhio Day is a statewide holiday on March 26. It pays tribute to Prince Jonah Kuhio, a member of the royal family and Hawaii's first delegate to the U.S. Congress. Celebrations vary between the islands.

A full day of festivities encompasses the **Prince Kuhio Celebration Luau and Concert** on Kauai; celebrating the birthday of one of the most beloved members of the Hawaiian royalty. Sponsored by Koloa Hawaiian Outrigger Canoe Club, in addition to the concert, other events include Makawehi sand dune hike, demonstrations of native Hawaiian arts and practices, commemorative ceremonies by the Royal Order of Kamehameha, and a Hawaiian luau. At Grand Hyatt Kauai Resort & Spa. Information: (808) 482-0594 and (808) 240-6369.

The **Annual Honolulu Festival** is Hawaii's premier event promoting cultural understanding, economic cooperation, and ethnic harmony among the people of Hawaii and the Asia-Pacific region. The festival features a variety of events at different Oahu venues and concludes with a grand parade down Kalakaua Avenue. Information: (808) 926-2424

The **Annual Magic Spectacular,** held on the Big Island, is an annual fund-raiser for the American Cancer Society and is the longest-running magic show in Hawaii, featuring magicians from the Big Island Magic Club, Honolulu, and usually a special guest performer from the Mainland.

Join United Cerebral Palsy's favorite rubber duckies as they dive into the infamous waters of the Ala Wai Canal on Oahu for the annual **Hawaiian Rubber Duckie Race & Festival.** If your duckie is one of the top fifty finishers, you could win some great prizes. Information: (808) 532-6744.

The **Annual Kona Chocolate Festival** promises chocolate lovers an outrageous treat for the senses. In addition to chocolate, there is champagne, wine, and live music under the starry Hawaiian sky, as Big Island chefs, caterers, and ice cream– and candy-makers gather for a night filled with gourmet chocolate decadence. Information: (808) 937-7596.

April

An annual **Easter Sunday Sunrise Service** is held at the National Memorial Cemetery of the Pacific in Punchbowl Crater, Oahu. This is a longstanding island tradition for locals and visitors. Information: (808) 262-7979.

If there's snow, the **Paniolo Ski Meet** is held atop the Big Island's Mauna Kea. Information: (808) 885-4188.

At the weeklong **Merrie Monarch Festival** in Hilo, the Big Island, you'll see the best hula dancers in the state. The competition is by invitation only and includes both modern and ancient styles. You have to write ahead for tickets and make hotel, rental car, and airline reservations way ahead of time. This is the most popular hula competition of the year. Information: (808) 935-9168.

The **Annual Hawaii Invitational Music Festival,** Oahu, is an international music festival that features bands and dance teams from throughout the world. Free concerts at the bandstand at Kapiolani Park. Information: (800) 448-2374.

Celebration of the Arts, Maui, is an annual event that pays tribute to the people, arts, and culture of Hawaii through demonstrations of hula and chant, workshops in Hawaiian art, one-on-one interaction with local Village Gallery artists, a traditional Hawaiian luau, and a special celebration concert by renowned Hawaiian musicians. Held at the Ritz-Carlton, Kapalua. Information: (808) 669-6200.

The **Annual East Maui Taro Festival** is held in Hana and features cultural demonstrations like poi-pounding, food booths, arts and crafts, and continuous entertainment, music, and hula by local favorite performers. Information: (808) 264-1553.

The annual **Hawaiian Scottish Festival,** held at Oahu's Kapiolani Park, features cultural competitions of strength, opportunities to discover your Scottish heritage, clothing and jewelry vendors, and Scottish scones. There is free entertainment throughout the day with music, bagpiping, and dance. Information: (808) 381-7216; www.scotshawaii.org.

One of Hawaii's largest street festivals is the **Waikiki Spam Jam,** a tribute to Spam, the popular canned meat. The event takes place on Kalakaua Avenue (closed to street traffic during the festival) and admission is free. There are two stages with entertainment, Hawaii's top restaurants serving Spam dishes, Spam-themed merchandise, and a variety of Hawaii craft vendors. Information: (808) 545-4195.

May

May Day is **Lei Day** in Hawaii, and colorful, fragrant celebrations expand to all the islands. This is the best time of the year to see all the different designs of leis. Look for the most popular to be strung from plumeria, puakinikini, orchids, ginger, carnations, and maile, a fragrant green leaf found in local forests. There are lei-making contests, where prizes are given to the most unique and distinctive garlands, and a lei queen. Information (Oahu): (808) 692-5751.

The **Captain Cook Festival** at Kailua-Kona, on the Big Island, features Hawaiian games and music.

On Oahu's North Shore, the **Haleiwa Sea Spree** is a four-day festival that includes outrigger canoe races, ancient Hawaiian sports, and surfing contests.

In Honolulu's Ala Moana Park, Oahu, the **Pacific Handcrafters Guild Fair** involves local craftspeople and a slew of colorful objects for sale. Information: (808) 721-9619.

The annual **World Fire Knife Dancing Competition** is really something to see. It's held at the Polynesian Cultural Center, Oahu, and sometimes a junior division is added for dancers ages seven to sixteen. Information: (800) 367-7060.

The **Filipino Fiesta** is a monthlong celebration of Hawaii's Filipino population.

The outrigger canoe season runs from May through August, and the races, or regattas, are an awesome spectacle as teams race from one part of Oahu to the other. Check local papers for specific events.

For **Memorial Day,** services are held at Honolulu's National Memorial Cemetery of the Pacific at Punchbowl, Oahu.

At sunset on Memorial Day, more than 1,000 candlelit lanterns are cast afloat from the shores of Ala Moana Beach Park by members and friends of Shinnyo-en Hawaii for the annual **Floating Lantern Ceremony,** a time-honored Buddhist tradition that is practiced throughout Japan to express respect for ancestors and comfort the spirits of the deceased. Information: (808) 947-2814.

The **50th State Fair,** Oahu, begins in late May and lasts for four consecutive weekends. Events include entertainment, rides, games, agricultural exhibits, and plenty of local-style fare. At Aloha Stadium in Honolulu. Information: (808) 682-5767.

The third Saturday in May is the **Molokai Ka Hula Piko Festival,** a celebration of the birth of hula. Molokai is believed to be the traditional birthplace of the hula, and this cultural celebration traces its roots from ancient times to today. Information: (808) 553-3673.

The Big Island's **Honokaa Town Western Week** is a popular annual celebration featuring a *paniolo* (cowboy) parade, an agricultural festival, and kids' activities and contests. There is a giant block party with live country-western dance music, a live auction, and a rodeo. Information: (808) 933-9772.

The **Maui Classical Music Festival** (formerly Kapalua Music Festival) brings world-renowned classical musicians to perform in different venues throughout Maui. Information: (808) 879-4908.

The **Starbucks Molokai Challenge** solo race is the world championship of kayak and one-person canoe racing. An international contingent of men and women race solo for 32 miles across the Kaiwi Channel from Molokai to the east shore of Oahu, finishing at Koko Marina. The Kaiwi Channel, referred to as the "Molokai Channel," is considered one of the most challenging and treacherous in the world. Information: (808) 222-5020.

June

Enjoy an afternoon of great music with some of Hawaii's finest slack key artists at Maui's **Ki Ho`alu Slack Key Guitar Festival. free** admission. Fresh flower leis, local-style food, and Hawaiian crafts are sold throughout the day. Information: (808) 242-7469.

One of the summer's best festivals is the Big Island's **Annual Dolphin Days Summer Fest.** This annual event at Hilton Waikoloa Village benefits Shriners Hospital for Children and the Pacific Marine Life Foundation. Activities include a special Dolphin Quest program, charity golf tournament, silent auctions, "Aloha Friday Luau at the Hana Hou Bar," and the weekend's signature event, the Great Waikoloa Food, Wine, and Music Festival, featuring dozens of guest chefs and wine, beer, and spirit purveyors outdoors under the stars with exceptional entertainment. Information: (808) 886-1234.

King Kamehameha Day falls in mid-June and celebrates the reign of Kamehameha I, the first king to unite all the Hawaiian islands. Many of the islands feature a floral parade. Information: (808) 327-3037 for the Big Island parade in Kona and (808) 989-4844 for the festival in Hilo.

The **Annual King Kamehameha Hula Competition** on Oahu is an international cultural event that features dance schools from the Mainland United States, Hawaii, and Japan. Dancers compete in both traditional and contemporary hula styles.

The **Annual Upcountry Fun Fair** is held in Makawao, Maui, and includes cowboy-style competitions and craft and food booths.

The **Annual Orchid Society Show** in Hilo, the Big Island, offers a chance to see the vivid varieties of orchids that grow in the Orchid Capital of Hawaii. It's held at the Hilo Civic Auditorium and, depending on the recent crops, is sometimes postponed until mid-summer. Information: (808) 933-9772.

The **Annual Big Island Bonsai Show** in Hilo's Wailoa Center features the finest state-wide examples of these miniature plants.

The annual **Pan-Pacific Festival** in Waikiki is quite a party—under the stars on Waikiki's famous Kalakaua Avenue. The ho`olaule`a (block party) features entertainers from Japan, Hawaii, the Mainland, and other pan-Pacific regions performing on six stages, as well as street performers, ethnic food booths, and more. The festival concludes with a big parade.

July

The **Makawao Statewide Rodeo** at the Oskie Rice Arena on Maui is an old-fashioned rodeo that offers lots of knee-slappin' good times.

Lanai is the site of the annual **Pineapple Festival,** which features arts and crafts, displays, demonstrations, an on-shore fishing tournament, a tennis tournament, local and ethnic music, and dancing. Information: (808) 565-3240.

Celebrate Independence Day early with your whole family at Oahu's Aloha Tower Marketplace for the **Third of July Fireworks & Entertainment Extravaganza.** There is live entertainment on multiple stages as well as face painting, a balloon artist, strolling entertainers, restaurant specials, and a spectacular fireworks finale.

The Fourth of July is always **Turtle Independence Day** at Mauna Lani Bay Hotel on the Big Island. Adult sea turtles raised in protected seawater ponds at the resort are released into the ocean in cooperation with Sea Life Park. It's quite a sight to see all the turtles waddling freely from sand to ocean. Information: (808) 885-6677.

Kauai's **Annual Concert in the Sky** fund-raiser benefits Kauai Hospice. Residents and visitors of all ages celebrate the Fourth of July at Vidinha Stadium from 3:00 to 9:30 p.m. with family fun, great food from Kauai's top hotels and restaurants, continuous live music, and a spectacular aerial fireworks show. Information: (808) 245-7277.

A wide variety of family activities takes place all afternoon and evening at Maui's **Old-Fashioned Fourth of July.** The Kaanapali resort hosts live entertainment, with activities for kids and music for adults, oceanfront at Whalers Village. Along scenic Front Street Lahaina hosts a fabulous fireworks display over the ocean. Resort entertainment and the fireworks show are **free.** Information: (808) 667-9193.

The **Annual Parker Ranch Fourth of July Horse Races and Rodeo,** the Big Island, is an Independence Day tradition that includes action-packed rodeo events, horse racing, food, and more. Parker Ranch *paniolo* (Hawaiian cowboys) are joined by other Big Island paniolo for a day of traditional rodeo events, including relay horse races, team sorting, double mugging, dally team roping, and more. The rodeo provides visitors a rare glimpse at real-life paniolo in action. Spectators can enjoy festive food and shop for Parker Ranch logo items at the Parker Ranch Store booth. Information: (808) 885-5669.

A weeklong celebration, **Koloa Plantation Days,** Kauai, includes a rodeo, historical tours, ethnic cooking demonstrations, Hawaiian Olympics, and much more. A parade and full-day celebration with live music, crafts, food, and fun are held on the final day.

Since 1971 Roy Sakuma and his sponsors have been keeping the ukulele alive and well by presenting the **Annual Ukulele Festival** on Oahu. Held every July at the Kapiolani Park Bandstand in Waikiki, the Ukulele Festival attracts thousands of residents and visitors to a **free** two-hour concert that showcases many of the finest ukulele players in the world, along with Hawaii's top entertainers, national celebrities, and a ukulele orchestra of more than 700 children. Information: (808) 732-3739.

On Oahu, the **Haleiwa Arts Festival** features more than 130 juried artists from Hawaii, Mainland, and international locations. The performance stages showcases musicians, singers, dancers and storytellers. There are cultural history trolley tours, student art displays, art demonstrations and children's art activities. All **free!** Information: (808) 637-2277.

The **International Festival of the Pacific** in Hilo, the Big Island, is also referred to as the **Pageant of Nations.** It includes folk dances with authentic costumes from all of Asia and the Pacific Islands. Information: (808) 934-0177.

Prince Lot Hula Festival offers an ideal chance to witness expert hula troupes, and it's a lot more accessible than the springtime Merrie Monarch Festival. It's held on Oahu at Moanalua Gardens. Information: (808) 839-5334.

There's another **Pacific Handcrafters Fair** in July at Thomas Square, Oahu, a repeat of the May event. Information: (808) 254-6788.

The **Annual Kapalua Wine & Food Festival,** the longest-running and most prestigious food and wine festival in Hawaii, is a four-day culinary extravaganza bringing together celebrated winemakers, renowned chefs, national media, and more than 4,000 wine and food lovers at the world-renowned Kapalua Resort. Information: (808) 665-9160.

The **Hawaii State Farm Fair** on Oahu features family fun in the country. It's held at Kapolei Community Park with a country market, plant and orchid sale, livestock exhibition, sampling and demonstrations, keiki activities, Meadow Gold Petting Zoo, favorite island musicians, and E. K. Fernandez Shows. Information: (808) 682-5767.

The **Queen Liliuokalani Keiki Hula Competition,** Oahu, is held in Honolulu's Neal Blaisdell Center and is a thoroughly charming event to watch. The children of Hawaii compete in ancient and modern hula dance styles. Information: (808) 521-6905.

August

The **Whalers Village Maui Onion Festival** celebrates the "sweetie" Maui onion with a weekend of fun, food, and cooking demonstrations as well as an onion-eating contest, amateur and professional cooking competitions, farmers' market, and music. Outdoors, Whalers Village in the Kaanapali Resort. **free.** Information: (808) 661-4567.

The **Hawaiian International Billfish Tournament,** the Big Island, consists of five days of fishing off the beautiful Kona Coast and several social and cultural events throughout the week. In this prestigious tournament, teams compete for the coveted Governor's Award, Koa Bowl trophy, and bronze marlin trophy. Over fifty teams from more than a dozen countries are expected. The public is welcome to attend daily weigh-ins at Kailua Pier, the opening ceremonies, the Billfish Parade, and HIBA Auction. Information: (808) 836-3422 or visit www.hibtfishing.com.

First Hawaiian Bank's **Made in Hawaii Festival,** Oahu, is a three-day celebration highlighting the unique and varied products of Hawaii at the Neal Blaisdell Center. The wide array of products includes foods, fashions, jewelry, gifts, plants, flowers, produce, music, books, and works of art by more than 300 companies from throughout the state. The festival also features cooking demonstrations by Hawaii's top chefs and entertainment by Hawaii's Hoku Award–winning musicians. Information: (808) 533-1292 or visit www .madeinhawaiifestival.com.

Pu'ukohola Heaiu, in Kawaihae on the Big Island, hosts the **Annual Cultural Festival,** which celebrates the heritage of ancient Hawaii. Information: (808) 328-2326, ext. 32 or visit www.nps.gov/puho.

The first weekend in August is **Establishment Day.** It's celebrated at the Big Island's Pu'ukohola Heiau, with traditional lei and hula workshops. Information: (808) 882-7218 or visit www.nps.gov.puhe.

August 17 is **Admission Day,** a statewide holiday commemorating the day when Hawaii became the fiftieth state.

The **Annual Kauai County Fair** offers the Garden Island's gardeners and craftspeople the chance to showcase their finest products. It's held at the War Memorial Center in Lihue. Information: (808) 639-8432.

The **Maui Sugar Plantation Festival** celebrates the cultural diversity of Maui's sugar plantation heritage. An authentic event featuring local foods, entertainment, demonstrations, kids' activities, and special discounted admission to the Sugar Museum. Information: (808) 871-8058.

The **Annual Greek Festival** on Oahu features authentic Greek cuisine, beverages, baked goods, and lots of entertainment held at McCoy Pavilion, Ala Moana Beach Park. Information: (808) 521-7220.

The **Annual Parker Ranch Round-Up,** the Big Island, is a western-style event that includes a horse-race relay, bull riding, wild-cow milking, and calf roping. Information: (808) 885-5669.

September

In the **Annual Waikiki Rough Water Swim,** Oahu, swimmers glide through a 2-mile open ocean course, from Sans Souci Beach to the Hilton Hawaiian Village. The swim is open to all ages and ability levels. Information: (808) 891-7913.

The annual **Molokai Music Festival** in Kaunakakai, at Meyer Sugar Mill, features entertainment, hula performances, craft demonstrations, and lots of *ono* (delicious) food. Information: (808) 567-6436.

The **Kauai Mokihana Festival** encompasses a variety of cultural events, the main one being the Kauai Composers Contest and Concert. Here, attendees have the chance to listen to performers from throughout the island. Other activities include an arts-and-entertainment day, lei-making competitions, and a folk-arts workshop. Some events are **free;** others charge a small admission fee.

The **Aloha Festivals** began sixty years ago and started as a weeklong party designed to honor and preserve the island's heritage. Today the festivals have expanded into a two-month period, and they circulate among the six major islands: Oahu, Maui, Hawaii, Kauai, Lanai, and Molokai. The festival is partially funded through the sale of Aloha Festivals ribbons, which are available for less than $5 at retail stores throughout the state. The ribbons come with a program guide that details all the events. Ribbon wearers are admitted for **free** or for a discount at many of the functions. The activities range from a steel-guitar contest to floral parades and singing and dancing celebrations. Information: (808) 589-1771 or visit www.alohafestivals.com.

Often scheduled as part of Aloha Week, the **Made with Aloha Festival** in Waikiki,

Oahu, features Hawaii-made products, music and hula performances, and local food. Information: (808) 589-1771.

The **Molokai-to-Oahu Canoe Race** for women (men in October) is the finale of the competitive paddling season. Teams navigate outrigger canoes from Molokai to Hilton Hawaiian Village in Waikiki, where they're met with a whopping, fun celebration. Information: (808) 259-7112.

The **Big Island Farm Fair** has become a treasured tradition to the families of the Kona community. Fairgoers sample and shop for fresh Hawaii-grown products in the Country Market, enjoy agricultural displays, exhibits, and sales in the Agriculture and Livestock Tents, and hone their game skills and thrill to the carnival rides on the E. K. Fernandez Midway. Information: (808) 324-6011.

The **Annual Taste of Hawaii's Big Island** is a culinary event under the stars at Four Seasons Resort Hualalai featuring the many talented chefs from the Big Island and a highly anticipated silent auction. Information: (808) 325-8000.

Maui's largest culinary festival is the **Taste of Lahaina.** It features dishes from new and established Maui County restaurants, Hawaiian music, and, for kids, a Fun Zone with inflatable rides and games. Held at Lahaina Recreation Park II. Information: (808) 667-9193.

Celebrate Hawaii's "soul food" at the Big Island's signature event—the **Annual Aloha Festivals Poke Contest** at Hapuna Beach Prince Hotel. The public is invited to taste amateur and professional chefs' masterful creations of different varieties of Hawaiian poke (pronounced: poh-keh), a Hawaiian dish of marinated raw, seared, or cooked seafood. Information: (808) 880-3028 or visit www.pokecontest.com.

October

Maui County Fair at the Maui War Memorial Complex in Wailuku involves a parade, arts and crafts, ethnic foods, amusements, and a grand orchid exhibition. Information: (808) 242-2721.

The **Pacific Handcrafters Guild Fair** is held again at Ala Moana Beach Park, Oahu. Information: (808) 254-6788.

The men's version of the **Molokai-to-Oahu Canoe Race** is held on the same course as the September women's race. Information: (808) 259-7112.

The **Annual Honolulu Orchid Plant and Flower Show** is held at the Lanakila Elementary School, Oahu. Information: (808) 247-3345.

The **Ironman World Triathlon Championship** at Kailua-Kona, on the Big Island, is the granddaddy of all triathlons, sure to inspire anyone who's lucky enough to be a bystander as the athletes pass. The Ironman encompasses a 2⁴⁄₁₀-mile, open-ocean swim, followed by a 112-mile bike ride, and topped off by a full marathon. Information: (808) 329-0063.

Kauai's **Annual Taro Festival,** held every other year either in October, November or December, pays tribute to Hanalei's famous agricultural product. Taro was the staple of ancient Hawaiian diets, used as much as Americans use potatoes. Events include arts and crafts, a produce market, and entertainment. Information: (808) 826-6522.

Hilo's **Annual Macadamia Nut Festival,** on the Big Island, is always fun, with entertainment, food booths, games, crafts, a parade, a recipe contest, and cooking demonstrations. Information: (808) 982-6562.

The place to be on Halloween is definitely Lahaina, Maui, where the wackiest, zaniest, creepiest costumes are seen in the **Annual Halloween Parade.** Information: (808) 667-9193.

November

The **Kona Coffee Cultural Festival,** the Big Island, celebrates more than 180 years of coffee harvest and a variety of cultural traditions. It is Hawaii's oldest food festival that brings the local community together, while attracting hundreds of visitors to celebrate Kona's famous harvest. The festival offers a variety of events including art exhibits, tastings, cupping competition, farm tours, sporting events, contests, and a parade. Information: (808) 326-7820.

Commemorating one of Hawaii's richest traditions, hula students from throughout the state congregate at Kaanapali Beach Hotel for the annual **Hula O Na Keiki,** Maui's only children's solo hula competition. The competition includes three main categories, including the Na Keiki (twelve years and younger), the Na `Opio (thirteen years and older), and the Hula Palua (boys and girls) division in both age groups. Information: (808) 661-0011 or visit www.kbhmaui.com.

The **World Invitational Hula Festival** at the Waikiki Shell, Honolulu, Oahu, includes *halau* (dance troupes) from Canada, Europe, Japan, Mexico, and the Mainland. Information: (808) 486-3185 or visit www.worldhula.com.

The **Hui Noeau Christmas Craft Fair** is in Upcountry, Maui, and features unique crafts and gifts—an ideal place to jump-start your holiday shopping. Information: (808) 572-6560.

Vans Triple Crown of Surfing is the first contest in the annual triple crown of surfing. This is when the big waves really pound Oahu's North Shore beaches, and the best surfers from around the world come to test their skills. Competition is held on the best four or five days during the waiting period. Alii Beach Park, Haleiwa, Oahu. Information: www .triplecrownofsurfing.com.

The Big Island also hosts an **Annual Aloha Taro Festival** in Honoka`a that highlights the growing and production of taro and related products with entertainment, a farmers' market, arts and crafts, and food booths.

At the Annual **Molokai Ranch Professional Rodeo and Stew Cook-Off,** riders and ropers from across the state and the Mainland compete under the bright lights of Molokai Ranch's arena. Information: (808) 552-2741.

Annual Christmas in the Country Gala in Volcano, on the Big Island, features artworks by local artisans in a special holiday atmosphere. Volcano Art Center. Information: (808) 967-7565 or visit www.volcanoartcenter.org.

The **Annual Molokai Business Fair and Food Festival** features top-rated chefs from Maui, Molokai, and Lanai who dish up unique recipes using Molokai products. Information: (808) 553-3773 or visit www.molokaichamber.org.

December

Maui County students from kindergarten through twelfth grade sing their hearts out in traditional Hawaiian songs at the annual **Na Mele O Maui Student Song and Art Contests,** held at the Maui Marriott. The admission fee raises scholarship funds. High schoolers exhibit original artwork based on corresponding Hawaiian themes. Information: (808) 661-3271.

Shining brighter than ever, **Honolulu's City Lights Spectacular** features children's entertainment, an electric light parade, and lighting of the city Christmas tree, followed by a concert and Santa for family fun. Held at Honolulu Hale and on the Municipal Lawn, Oahu. Indoor Christmas tree and wreath exhibits open daily. All **free!** Information: (808) 527-5759.

The **Annual Honolulu Marathon**'s 26-mile scenic course includes spectacular views alongside world-famous Waikiki Beach and Diamond Head. Information: (808) 734-7200.

Kauai Museum's **Christmas Fair** is an annual Christmas event known for offering the island's best in handcrafted items and home-baked goodies. Information: (808) 245-6931.

Kamehameha Schools Christmas Concert is open to everyone and lifts the Christmas spirit at the Blaisdell Center Concert Hall, Honolulu, Oahu. Information: (808) 842-8211.

Pacific Handcrafters Guild Christmas Fair, Thomas Square, Honolulu, Oahu, is a great stop for holiday shopping. Information: (808) 254-6788.

Triple Crown of Surfing continues on Oahu's North Shore, at Ehukai Beach.

The **Rainbow Classic** is held in Honolulu, Oahu, usually during the last week of December. The tournament features men's college basketball teams. Information: (808) 956-6501.

The **First Night Honolulu,** Oahu, festivities are ideal for families on New Year's Eve. It's an alcohol-free community festival of arts and entertainment that encompasses more than 250 events—music, jugglers, dance, magic, and theater arts—at seventy-five downtown Honolulu locations.

Celebrate the New Year with the **Wailea Village Annual Mochi-Tsuki Celebration** and learn to make traditional rice cakes the old-fashioned way. The old-timers share their stories of plantation era times and everyone takes a turn at pounding the glutinous sticky rice for good luck. Held at Akiko's Buddhist Bed and Breakfast at mile marker 15, Highway 19, on the Hamakua Coast. Information: (808) 963-6422.

The **Quiksilver In Memory of Eddie Aikau** is a one-day, big-wave event held annually at Waimea Bay in memory of one of Hawaii's legendary big-wave riders and the first Waimea Bay lifeguard, Eddie Aikau. Waves must reach a minimum of 20 feet for this event to be held. A lengthy holding period (from December through February) is set aside for this competition, which requires just one day to run to completion. When the event does get under way, it is a magnificent sight, as waves as high as mountains storm through Waimea Bay. The winner receives $55,000. Information: www.quiksilver.com.

Index

About the Author

As former managing editor of *Hawaii* Magazine, Julie Applebaum-DeMello became well versed in the beauty, history, culture, and activities of the Hawaiian Islands. Her career gave her the opportunity to explore the nuances of Hawaii's small towns, many beaches, and fun-filled attractions. She has felt the pulsating heat from the erupting Kilauea on the Big Island, sailed Kauai's Na Pali Coast, hiked to the top of Diamond Head, ridden mules on Molokai, picked pineapple on Lanai, and watched the dawn of a new day from the top of Haleakala. Julie currently works as a full-time mom, always searching for the next great family adventure.